IMAGES
of America

ALGONAC AND CLAY TOWNSHIP

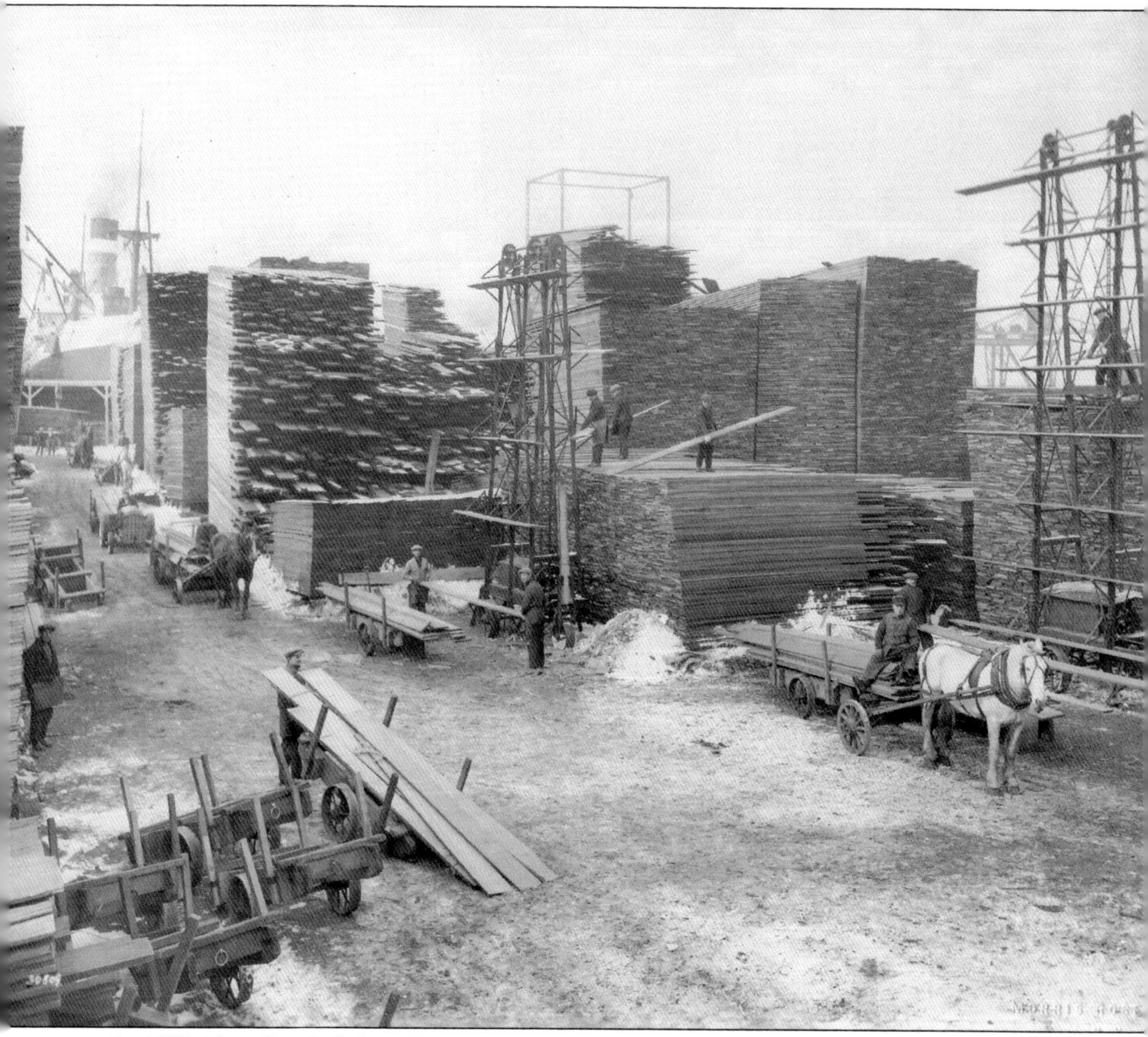

In 1927, Chris Smith & Sons Boat Company was contracting for one million feet of mahogany a year—more of this exotic wood than even the largest furniture makers in the world. This scene, taken in New York during the 1920s, shows a busy lumberyard much like those that supplied the Algonac runabout production lines. (Courtesy of the Algonac-Clay Historical Society.)

On the Cover: This photograph from the early 1930s shows workers laboring at the Chris-Craft boat factory. The Smiths were the first boatbuilders in the world to employ in-line production of standardized boats. (Courtesy of the Algonac-Clay Historical Society.)

IMAGES
of America

ALGONAC AND CLAY TOWNSHIP

Gary R. Mitchell and Forest Lee Chaney

ARCADIA
PUBLISHING

ISBN 978-1-4671-1523-0

Published by Arcadia Publishing
Charleston, South Carolina

Printed in the United States of America

Library of Congress Control Number: 2015944851

For all general information, please contact Arcadia Publishing:
Telephone 843-853-2070
Fax 843-853-0044
E-mail sales@arcadiapublishing.com
For customer service and orders:
Toll-Free 1-888-313-2665

Visit us on the Internet at www.arcadiapublishing.com

To my parents, John and Rosemary Mitchell; my brother Jay and his wife, Robin; my niece Sarah; and especially to my son Garrett, boatswain mate, third class, USS Bataan, *I am very proud of you.*

Contents

ACKNOWLEDGMENTS

I wish to thank Forest Lee Chaney for all his expert guidance and help, along with Joan Bulley, who provided me with unlimited access to the Algonac Clay Historical Museum so I could scan and perform my research. Special thanks to the Algonac-Clay Historical Society and their officers and board of directors, Terry Wallis, Martha Szymanski, Pete Beauregard, Sue Barker, Patty Allen, Ilene LaParl, George Burgess, Annie Cronce, Jean Bissett, Don LaCombe, Cora Fisher, and Cindy Hornbaker, for assisting me with all my questions. The staff members and volunteers who maintain these collections have earned my immeasurable gratitude and respect. Unless otherwise noted, all images appearing in this book were graciously and generously provided by the Algonac Clay Historical Museum.

I also wish to thank my editor at Arcadia Publishing, Liz Gurley, for her patience and guidance. Without her help and understanding, this book never would have been published.

Thanks to Dr. John Moore at Walsh College, who helped me edit. Also, many thanks to Selena Arredondo, Serena Arredondo, Jennifer Fishel-Santangelo, Jason Charrette, Pamela Williams, Prof. Sam Plaza, Marco and Debra Vitale, and Donna Montgomery.

INTRODUCTION

The following passage is an excerpt from the memoirs of Aura P. Stewart:

> For many years, I saw but little of Michigan, except that portion bordering on the shore Lake and River St. Clair. I came from an inland and thickly settled district, and had seen no flowing water save brooks and rivulets; I had seen no forests but in the distance, and though but a boy twelve years of age I could not but feel impressed with the wild beauty of my new home. The dense and almost impenetrable forests, the magnificent River St. Clair, the countless number of every variety of waterfowl flying over my head or resting and sporting on the bosom of the beautiful waters, the howling of the wolves at night, . . . and, last but not least, the merry songs of the French. Voyageurs toiling at the oar, propelling their boats swiftly over blue waters—these were new scenes to me, and called forth my wonder and delight . . . I have witnessed the improvements made in the county of St. Clair; flourishing towns have sprung up, and a large portion of our older settlers have become wealthy; all have shared in the conveniences of modern improvements and comforts, but yet, for my own part, I could enjoy no greater pleasure that for a short time to see Michigan as I saw it in 1815, wild and romantic as it then was; to traverse its dense forests, to paddle my canoe over its waters, surrounded by game of every description on river, lake and shore; and at night, while partaking of a supper of game taken through the day, hear the howling of the wolves, the hooting owls and other voices of the night. Fancy ofttimes [sic] leads me back to the dear old primitive days, and then I am a boy again. Alas, the vision lingers not! I am an old man with increasing infirmities, and nothing is left to me but the memories of the past.

Nearly 150 years before this little boy wrote of the primeval beauty of what is now known as Algonac and Clay Township, the first Europeans, two French priests by the name of François Dollier and René Bréhant de Galinée, had written of their voyage through the lake and river. Native Americans named the river Otsi-Keta-Sippi. When Dollier and Galinée traveled the river on May 25, 1670, they wrote of "the Streight."

Native Americans inhabited the Otsi-Keta-Sippi River long before Europeans had set foot in North America. Tribes such as the Hurons, Ottowas, Miamis, Illinois, Pottawatomies, Algonquins, Loups, Kickapoos, Santeurs, Ojibwas, Sacs, Menominees, Shawnees, Wyandottes, Chippewas, and Ottagamies lived along these beautiful waters. These tribes had their own emblems, such as the fish, owl, eagle, bear, beaver, and other symbols that distinguished them. Their canoes, made of strips of birch bark sewn with thongs and at times reaching over 20 feet in length, could travel 40 miles a day at a speed of eight miles per hour.

The second European explorer to travel the region was Robert Cavelier de La Salle, who piloted the historic *Griffon*, the first sailing ship to travel the Great Lakes, into the region on

August 12, 1679. Most historians agree that it was at the suggestion of La Salle's companion, Fr. Louis Hennepin, that the lake be named St. Clair in honor of Santa Clara, whose festal day was being honored.

Clay Township, whose name is derived from the deposits of clay that are found along the St. Clair River, encompasses an expanse of more than 30 miles. Even township officials cannot quote an exact figure because of the presence of so many islands. The township consists of 62 miles of lake and river frontage and a ratio of half mainland and half islands.

Early missionaries and explorers called this area of the St. Clair River "the Great Green Meadows." The land through which the river flows is so level that, over 100 years ago, a traveler wrote, "Another barrel of water would overflow the fields."

American occupation was slow in this area. Although a few French and English settled along the river in 1780, it was not until the end of the century that any recorded locations were found. At the time when Michigan became a territory in 1805, Angus MacDonald and John Martin, pioneers from Canada and New York State, were eager to find homes in the wilderness. Other pioneers such as Dr. Edward Purcell, who was stationed at Fort Gratiot as post surgeon for a time in 1816, purchased a large portion of what would become Algonac in 1818. It is here that the history of Algonac begins. In 1821, the year St. Clair County was organized by proclamation, the only taxpayers on the assessment roll living in what is now Algonac were Silas Miller, Ira Marks, and Angus MacDonald.

Four years later, in 1825, the opening of the Erie Canal allowed multitudes of immigrants from New York State and Canada to move into the region. Although the horse-drawn canal boats were slow and crowded, they were better than the impassable roads. Settlers pushed their way into Buffalo and then boarded steamboats to Detroit.

The wilderness made way for log homes and then more substantial homes. By 1836, a small community had been formed that was previously known as Manchester and Pointe Du Chene (Point of the Oaks). Henry R. Schoolcraft, an Indian agent, wrote in his personal memoirs that a friend had asked him to suggest an indigenous name for the new town. The name *Algonac* was derived from "Ac," meaning land or earth, and "Algon" from the word *Algonquin*. However, it was not until 1843 that the final name of Algonac was adopted.

Pioneers in this area spent most of their lives living in fear. It was not the fear of living among Native Americans, whom they found to be friendly, but the wolves that raided their livestock and the swarms of malaria-carrying mosquitoes. Malaria, which the pioneers called ague, caused the victim to have alternate spells of burning fever and shaking chills. The hapless victim would be too weak to work, and sometimes whole families were afflicted. When asked why his ancestors had settled on the unproductive sand ridge west of town, a resident of Algonac replied, "Malaria—the land near the river was too swampy."

One

Businesses

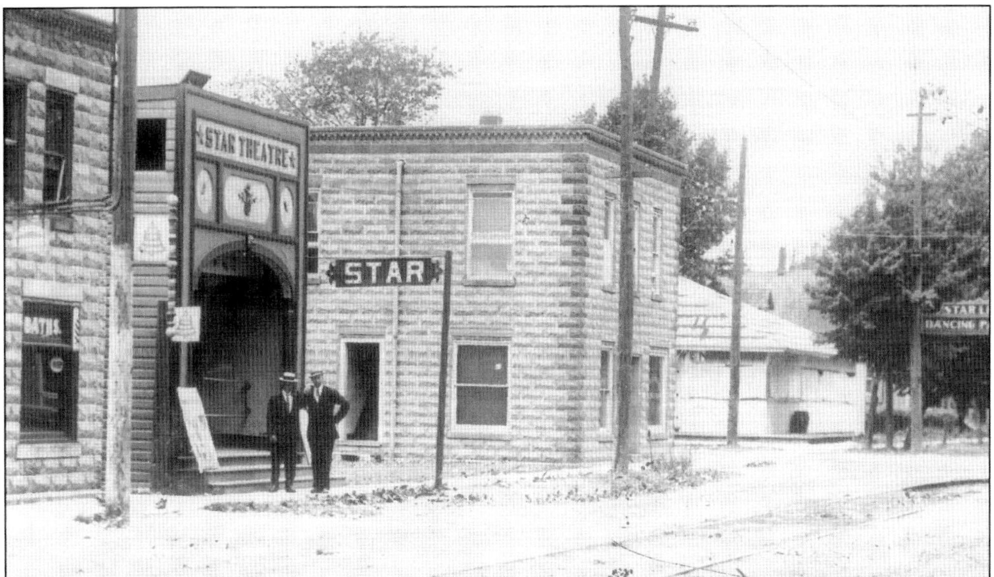

In 1908, the first theater came to Algonac. The Star Theatre was owned and operated by Mr. and Mrs. Foster, who lived in Pearl Beach. The frame building first stood on the south side of Pleasant Street, between Front and Michigan Streets. It was later moved to the east side of Front Street and bought or leased by James Harper, who used it for a vaudeville house.

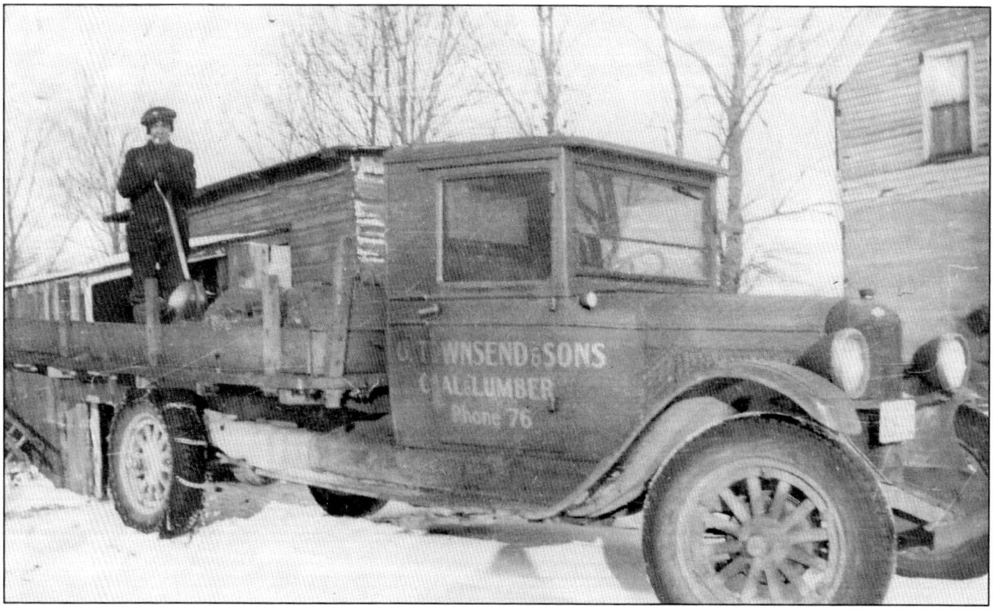

Bernard Townsend delivers coal for G. Townsend & Sons Coal & Lumber. In small communities, the telephone exchanges were usually privately owned. Townsend & Sons was customer No. 76.

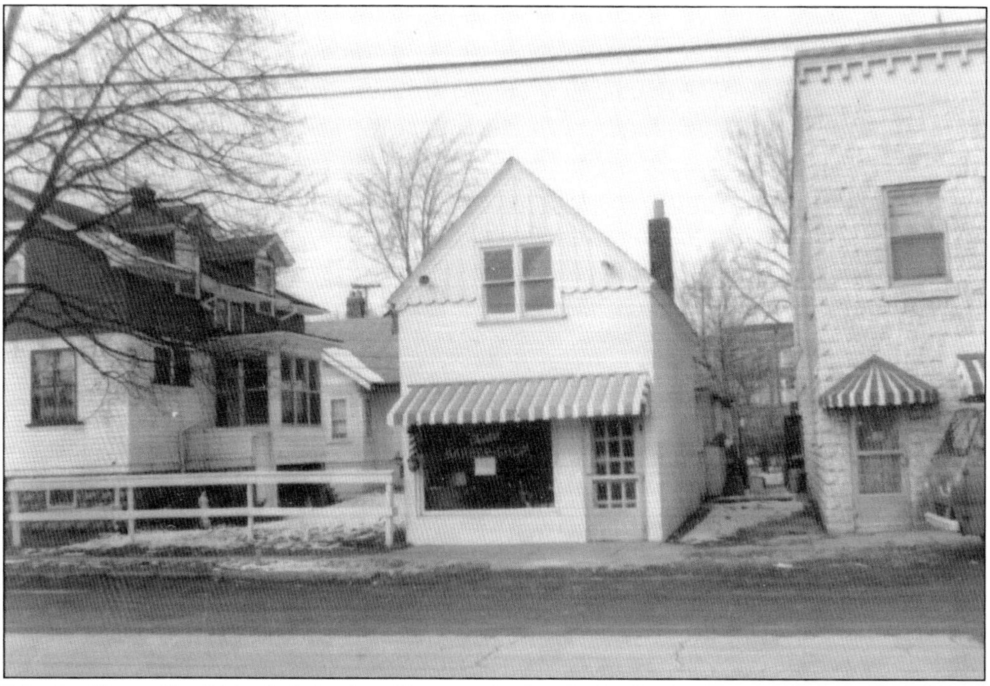

Charlie Wisswell of Charlie's Barber Shop worked with Andy Andino in the two-story block building next door until Andy's death in the late 1960s. He then moved to the small building at 1207 Michigan Street and converted what had been a flower shop into a two-chair barbershop, as seen here. Dr. Harland Richardson, DDS, continued to practice on the second floor next door.

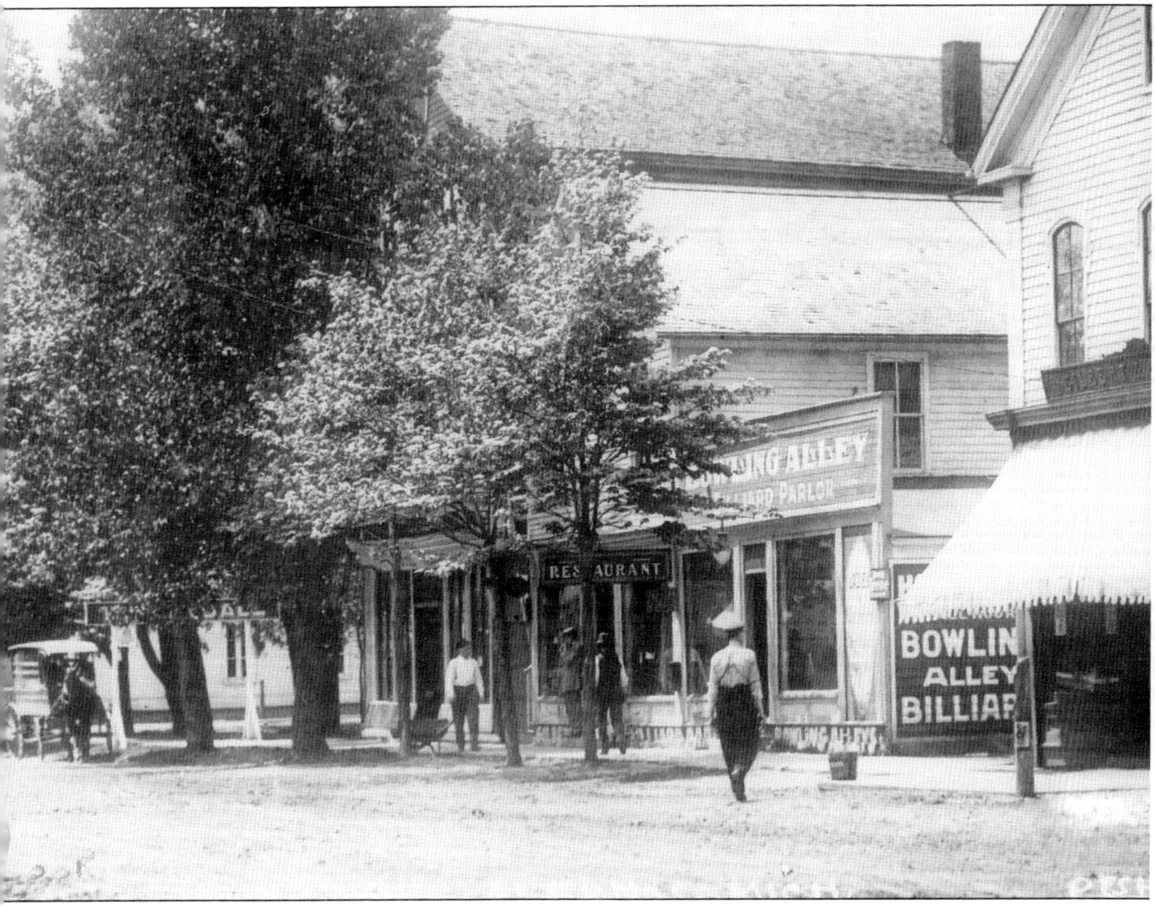

This photograph from 1902 shows the Kimball House and the E.R. Gilbert Bowling Alley. Before being moved to this location on the southwest corner of Water and Pleasant Streets, the Gilbert Hotel was originally built in 1869 as a residence at Water and Howard Streets by Capt. Danie Flood, a Great Lakes ship captain. Later, the hotel was turned into a livery stable, grocery, and furniture store.

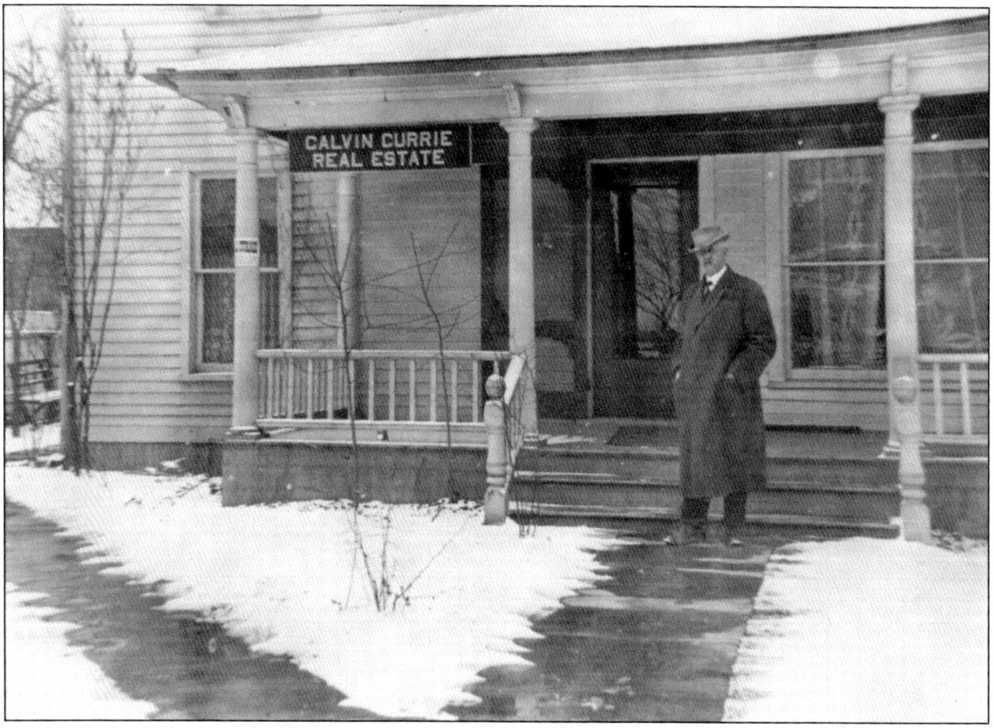

Calvin Currie is pictured here in front of his home and real estate office.

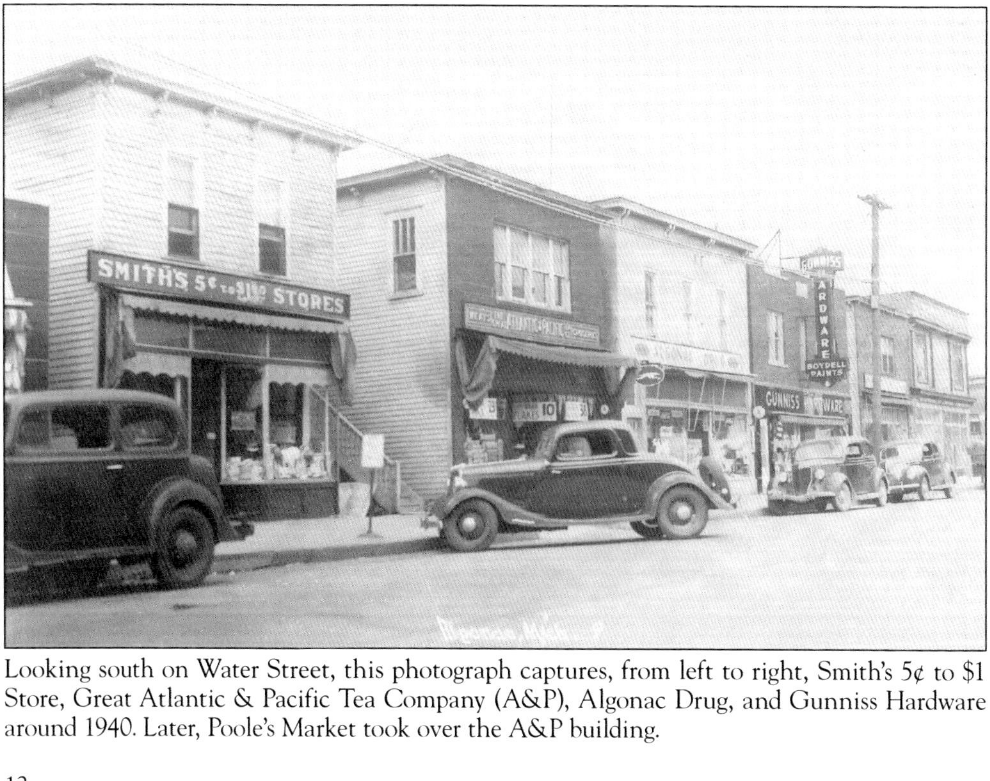

Looking south on Water Street, this photograph captures, from left to right, Smith's 5¢ to $1 Store, Great Atlantic & Pacific Tea Company (A&P), Algonac Drug, and Gunniss Hardware around 1940. Later, Poole's Market took over the A&P building.

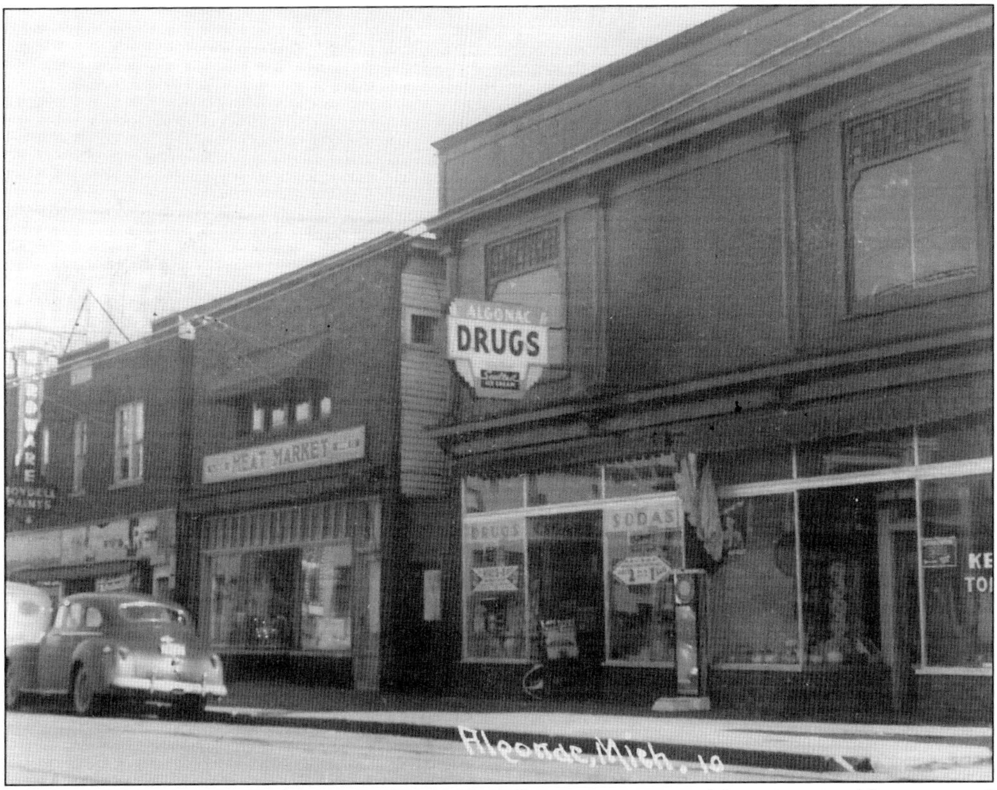

Algonac Drugs is pictured here in the 1940s. This was its second location in Algonac, and eventually the building was bought by Wallace Hardware.

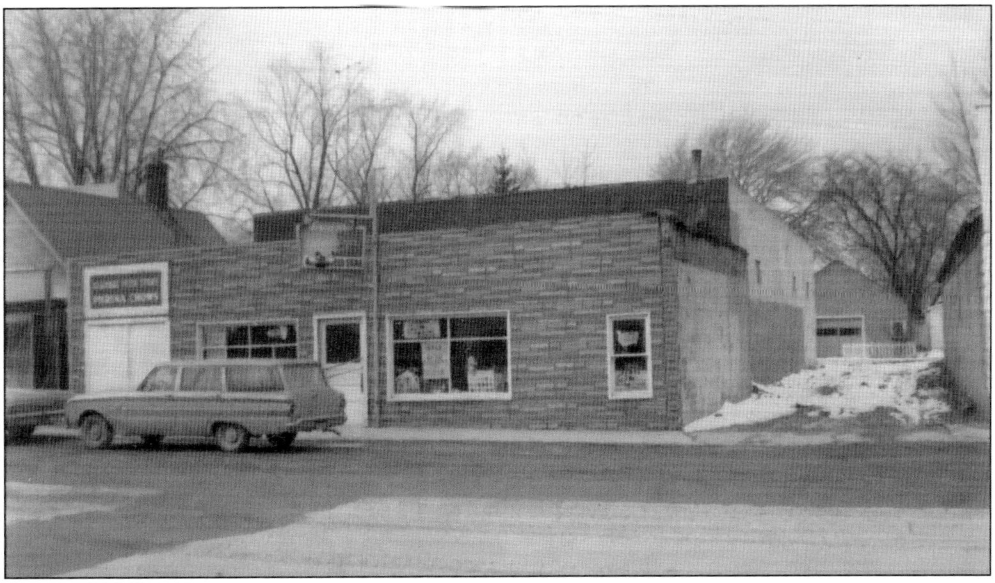
Operated by George Majors for many years, the Algonac Feed Store on Michigan Street supplied custom milling feed to local farmers and livestock breeders. Local women would stop by to check out the new prints on the spring seed and feed bags, while young children would sport the latest styles of clothing for summer wear.

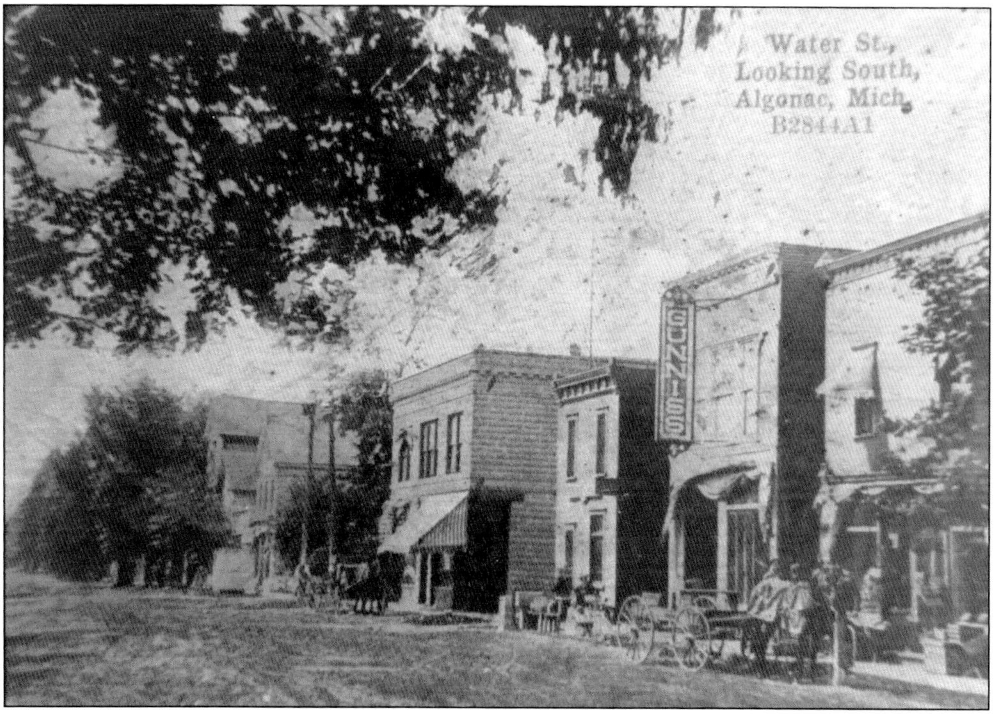

Gunniss Hardware is shown here during the 1890s. The horse and wagon are ready to make a delivery. The store was located on the west side of Water Street, between Clay and Fruit Streets.

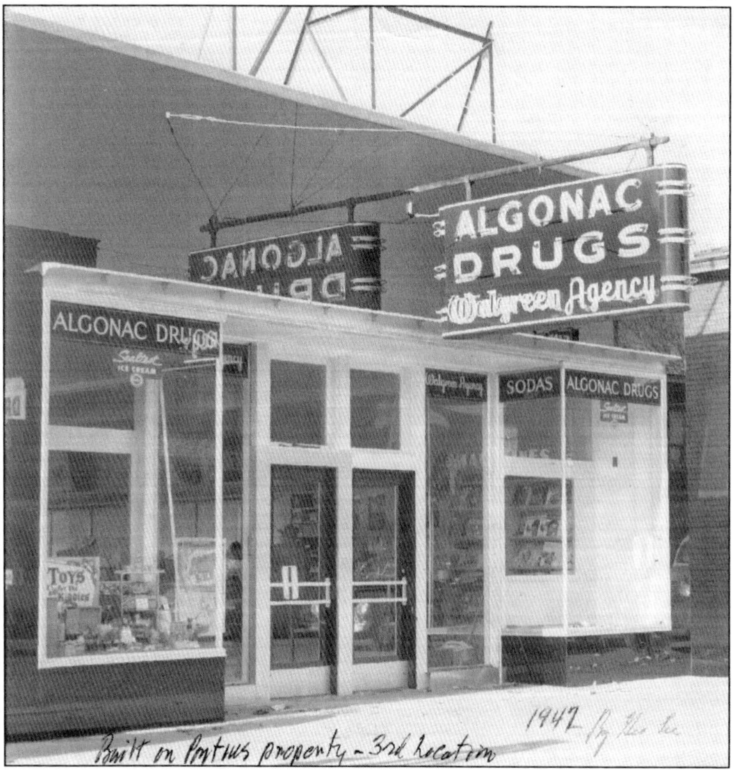

Algonac Drugs is seen in this 1942 photograph at its third and final location. This store was built on the Pontius property and operated by Marlie and Marjorie Pengery. Norm Foster bought the store in the late 1950s or early 1960s and operated it until it was replaced during urban renewal.

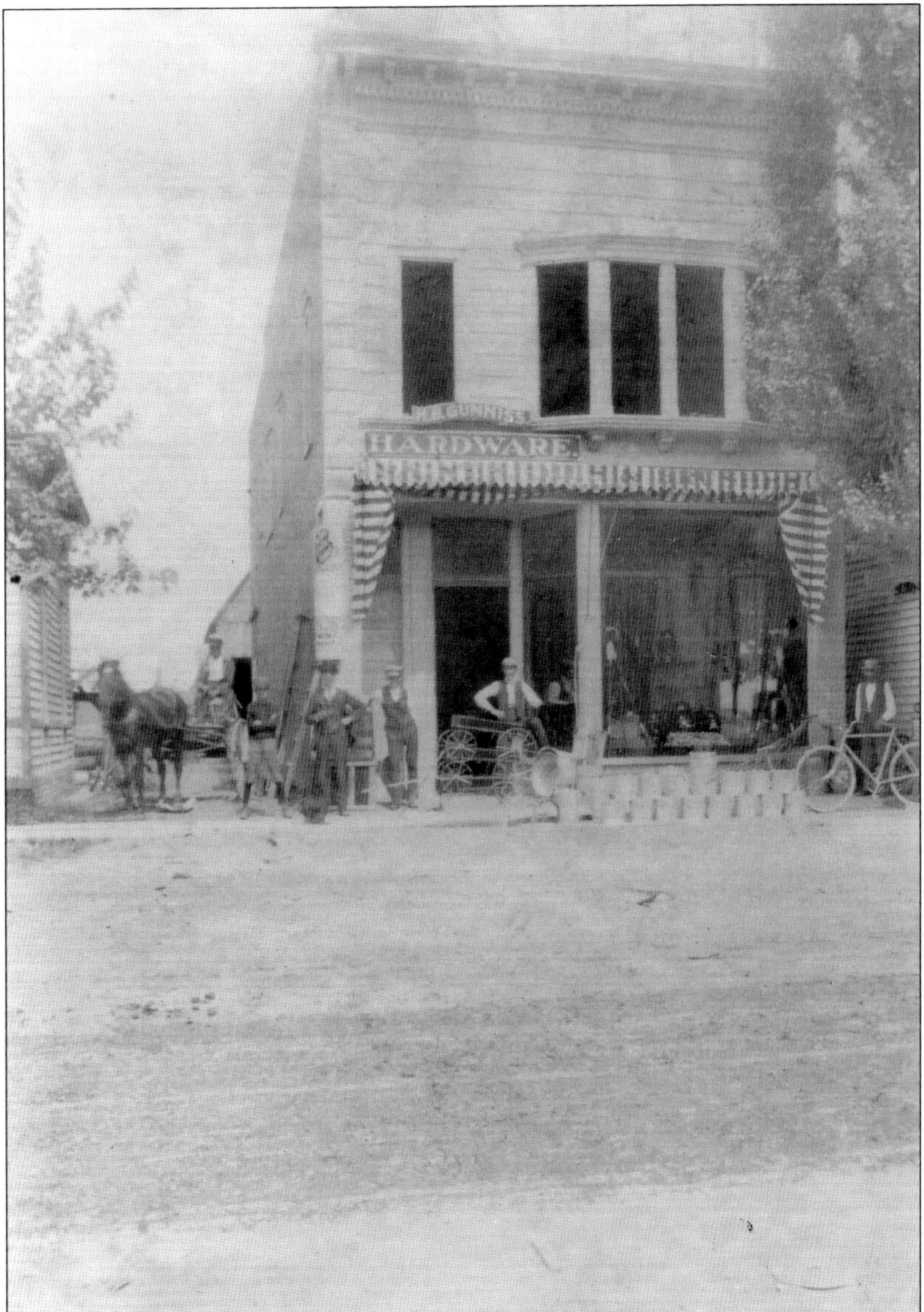

H.B. Gunniss's new hardware store opened on May 4, 1901, with a mandolin orchestra performance and flowers for the ladies. An advertisement for R.M. Lewis & Co. in the September 6, 1901, issue of the *Algonac Times Courier* included the following passage: "In bed we laugh, in bed we cry, in bed we're born, in bed we die; to sleep well, die well, buy good beds."

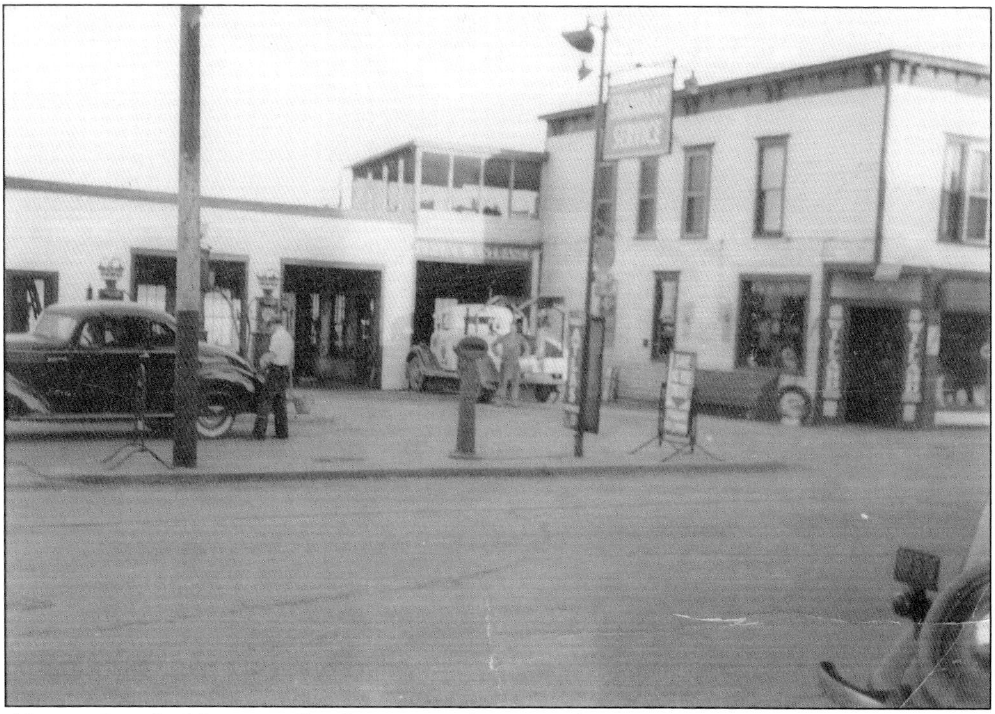

Algonac Standard Service offered customers free air at the curb, along with attendants to fill the tank, wash the windshield, and check under the hood. The shop also provided towing service and could handle major repairs. This location later became a Desoto dealership.

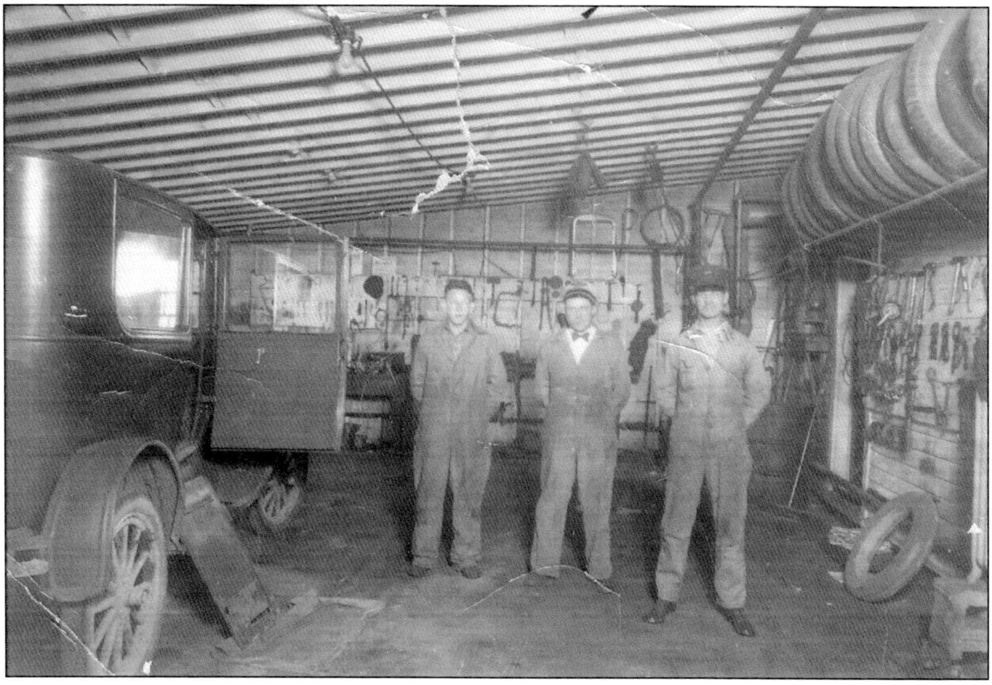

Here is a view inside an early automobile repair shop. Note the bow tie on the center mechanic, who is probably the owner.

The Barker Chevrolet and Oldsmobile Dealership provided a modern sales and service experience. The business was owned and operated by the Barker family for years before it was taken over by Jack Kilets. Freddy Alberts was salesman for at the dealership for many years.

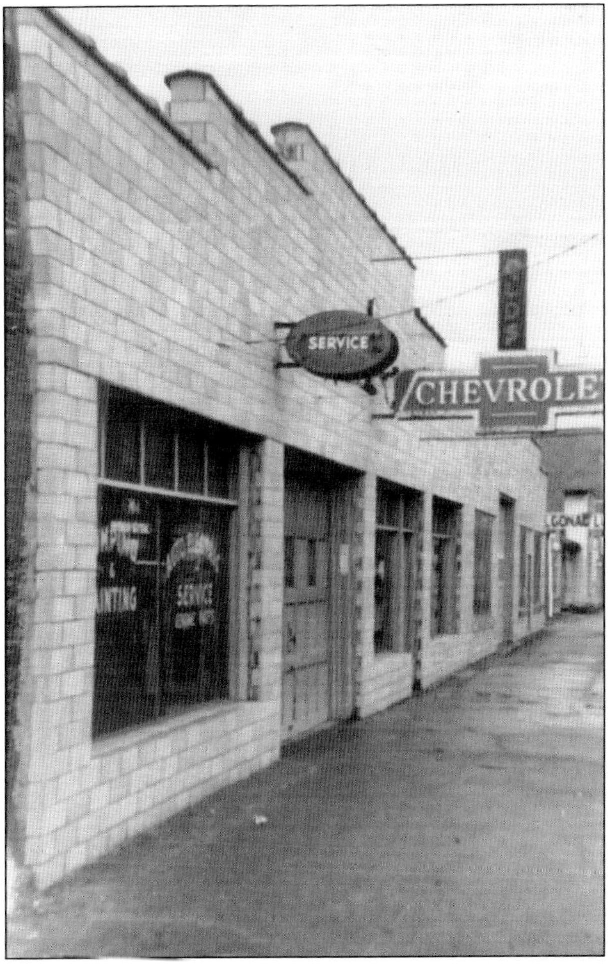

Two employees are standing in front of a Chevrolet parked at Hi-Speed Gas. A Shell station operated across from the Hi-Speed, and the two were always competing for business. Some days, the price war would bring the cost down to 10–15¢ per gallon.

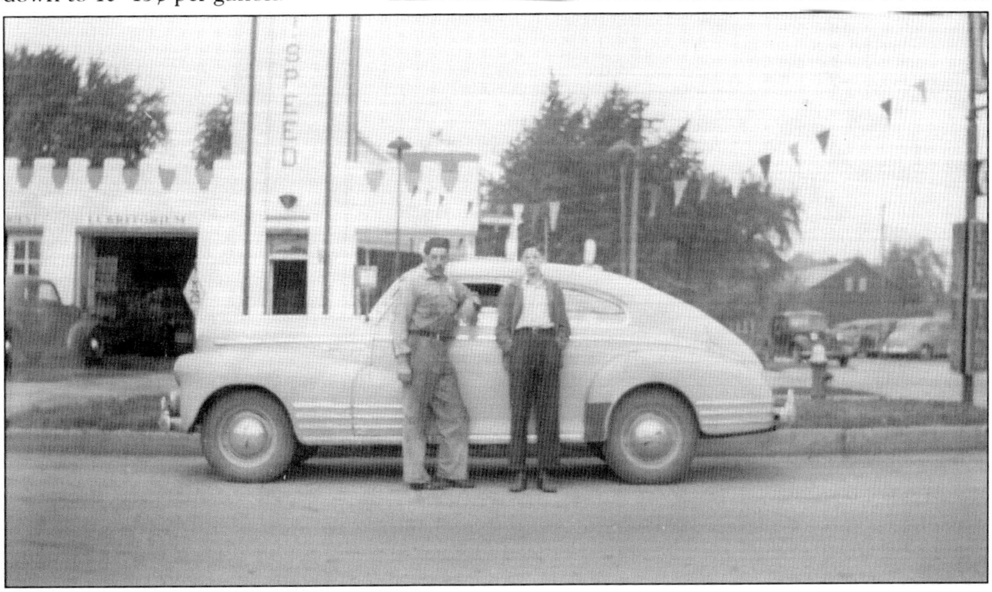

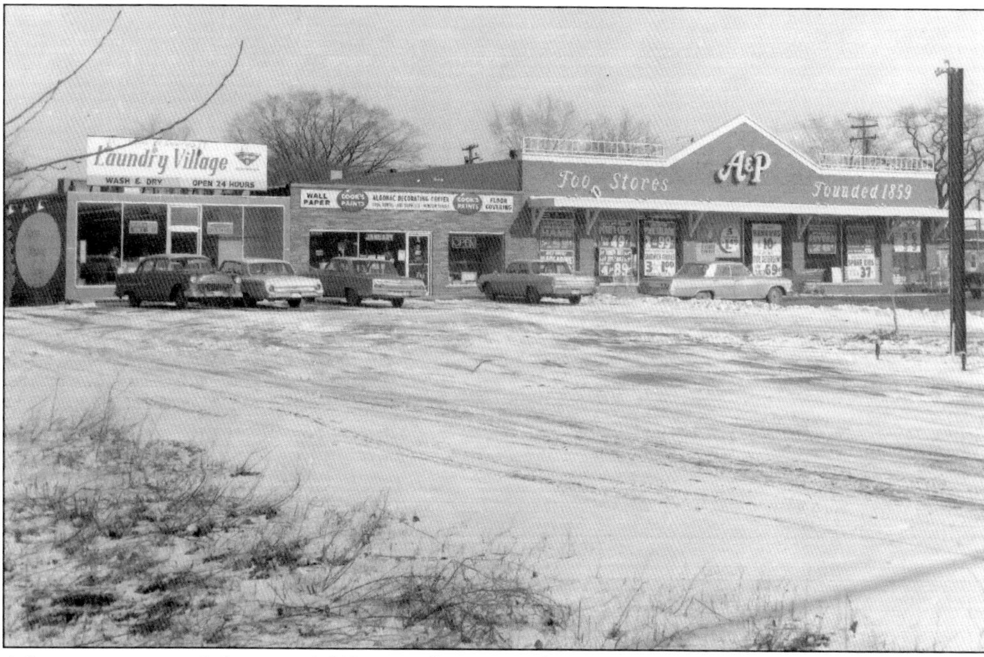

After many years of absence, A&P moved to a new location in a three-store shopping center at the curve of M-29 and St. Clair River Drive. The store would move again to a shopping center at M-29 and Nook Road.

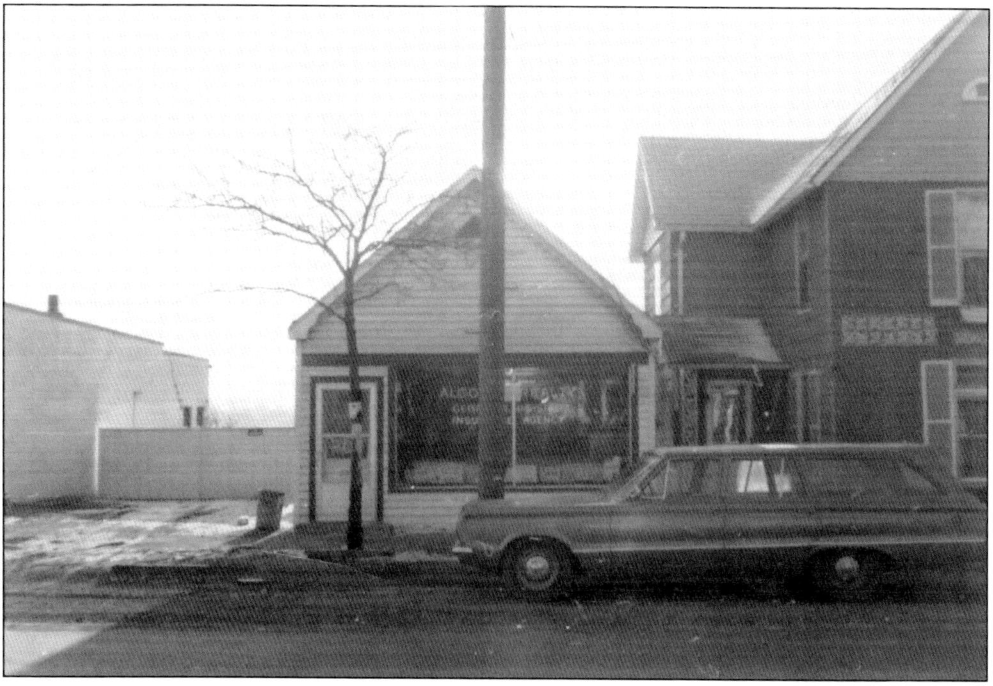

George Highstreet owned Algonac Reality, located on the south end of town. In the rear of the building was Ace's Barbershop. The building to the left was Charlie's Blue Water Grill, owned and operated by Charlie and Emma Busuttil. Emma and her daughter would take food across the street to the Maples Hotel.

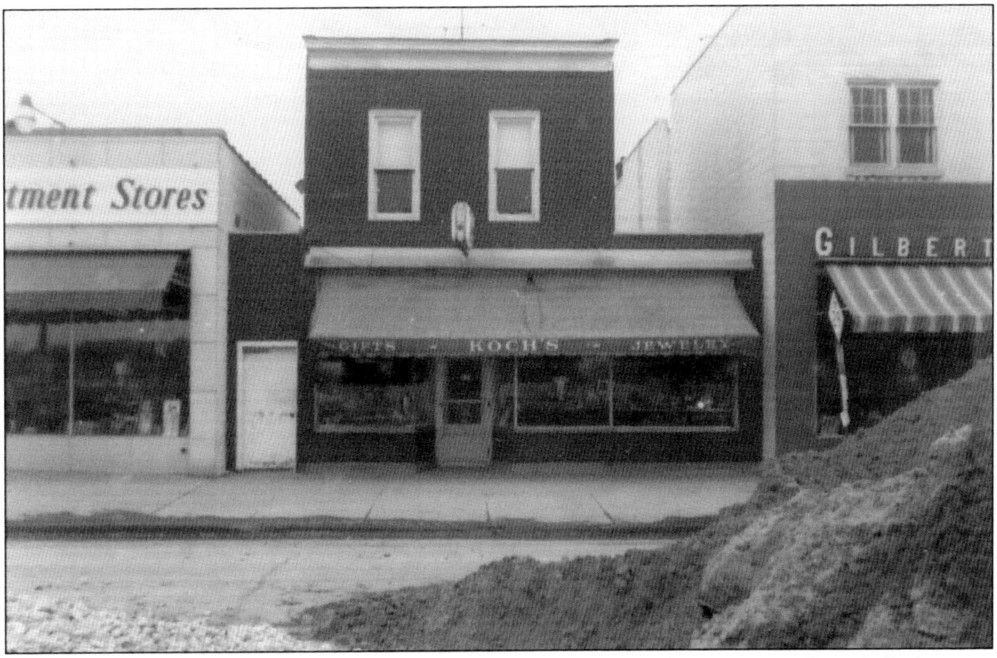

Koch's Jewelry was owned by Art and Thelma Koch. Jim Kane also ran a watch and clock repair store in this location. Formerly, it was also known as Pontius Jewelry. The building next door was torn down, and Gilbert's Furniture Store was built in its place.

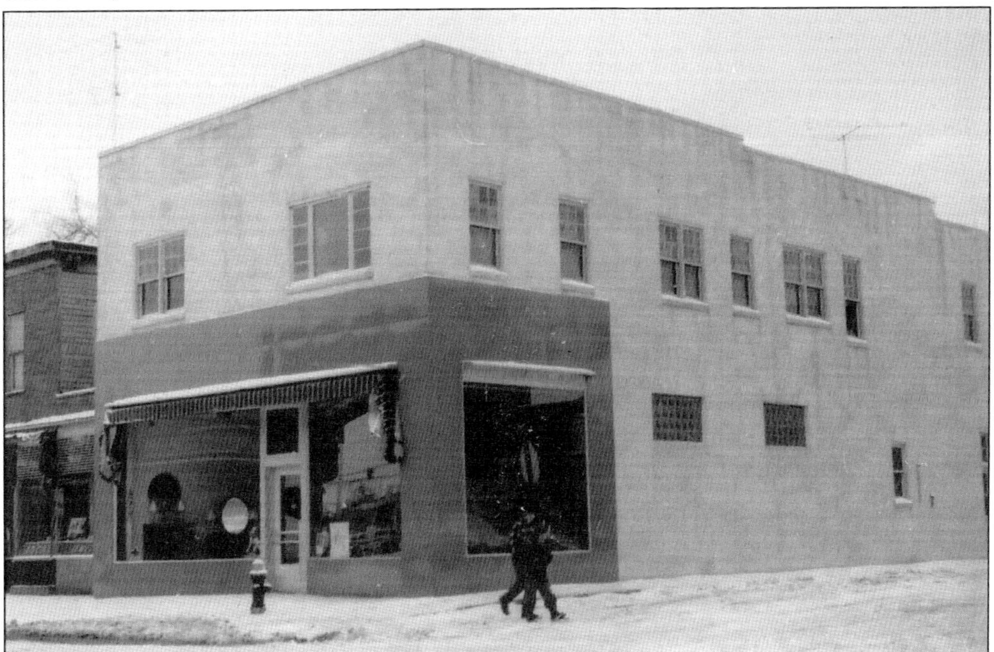

Gilbert's Furniture Store was owned by Judson "Jud" Gilbert, who also operated the Gilbert Funeral Home behind the furniture store. Members of the Gilbert family have been Algonac merchants since about 1890, when C.M. Gilbert purchased an old house built between 1844 and 1869. They added a large addition and a veranda, creating a fine hotel.

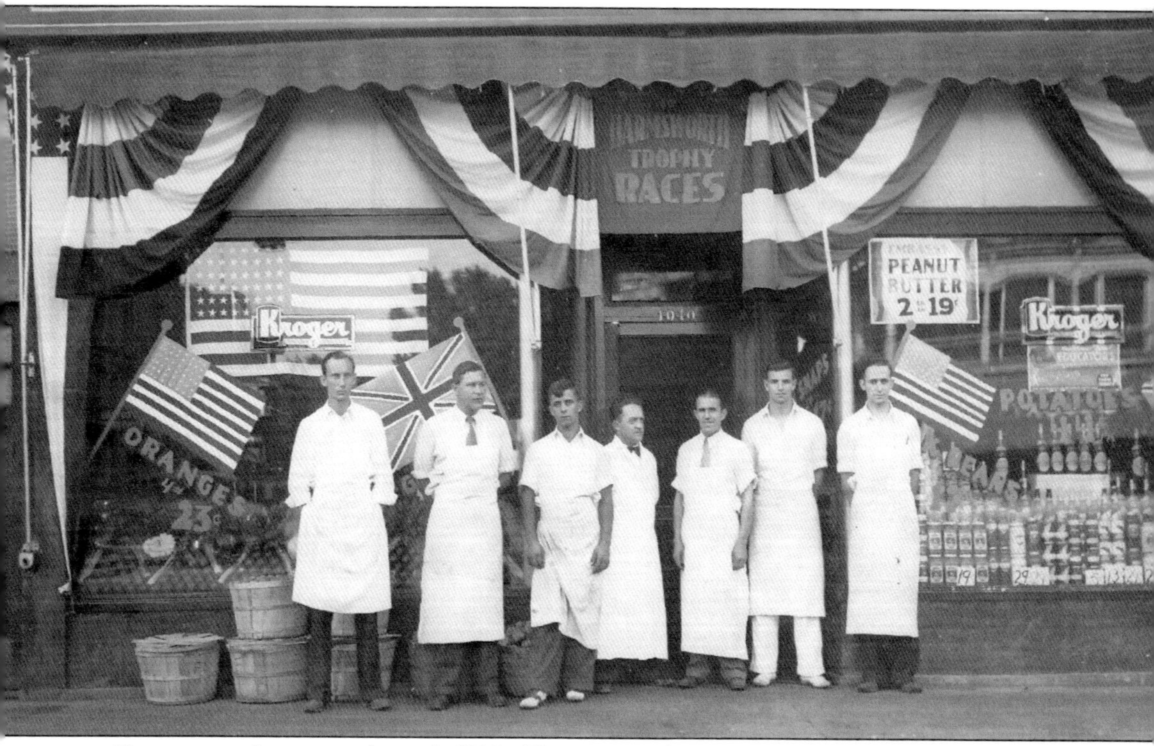

Kroger opened a store in the early 1930s. The supermarket was coming to life. People were helping themselves, putting items in a basket with wheels, and taking everything to a checkout counter. The gentleman at left is Ken Folkerts.

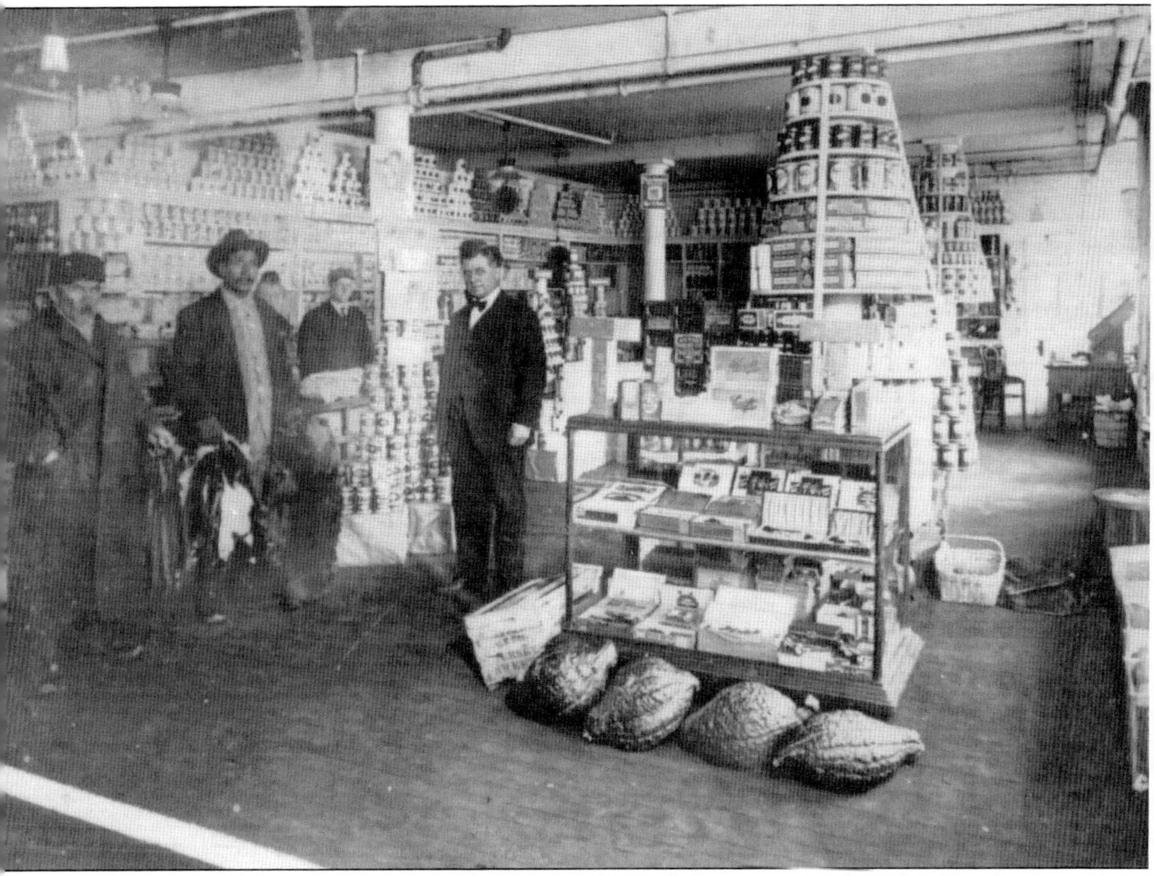

At J.W. Gilbert's Grocery Store, Leon Gilbert is seen behind the counter while J.W. Gilbert buys furs from natives of Walpole Island. The rear of the store had a dock where customers could come in, do their shopping, load the boat, and go home. Living upriver, it was easy getting to the store but hard going home. Living downriver, it was hard getting there but an easy trip home.

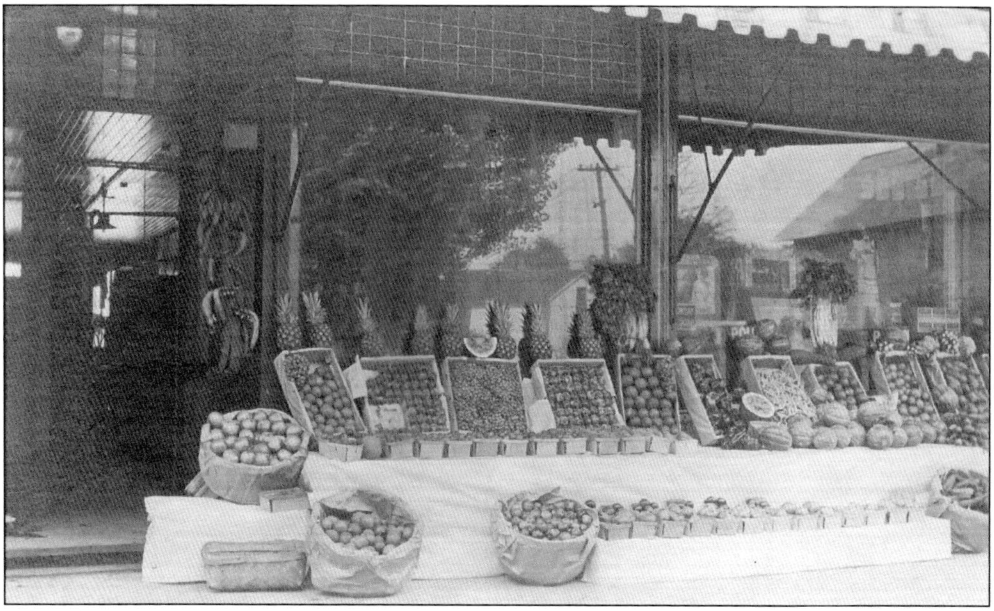

J.W. Gilbert's Grocery Store was stocked with fresh fruits and vegetables from around the world. Bananas and pineapples were ready to take home for that special treat.

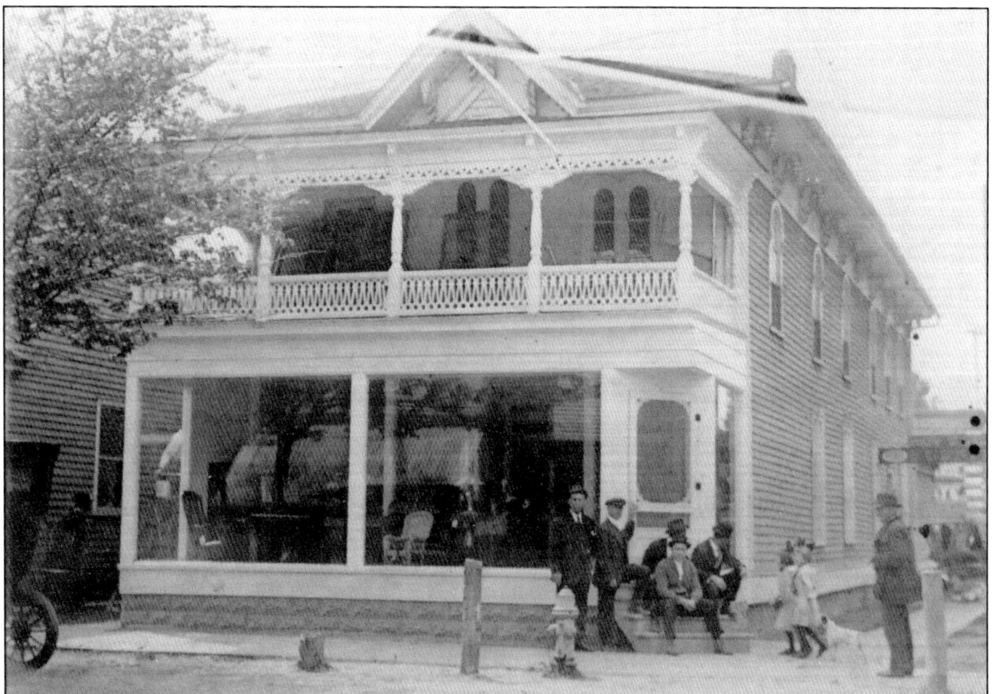

The Gilbert Hotel is now open for business in this photograph. Note that the veranda has been enclosed with glass for the comfort of guests. The fire hydrant and hitching post in front of the hotel show the progress of time.

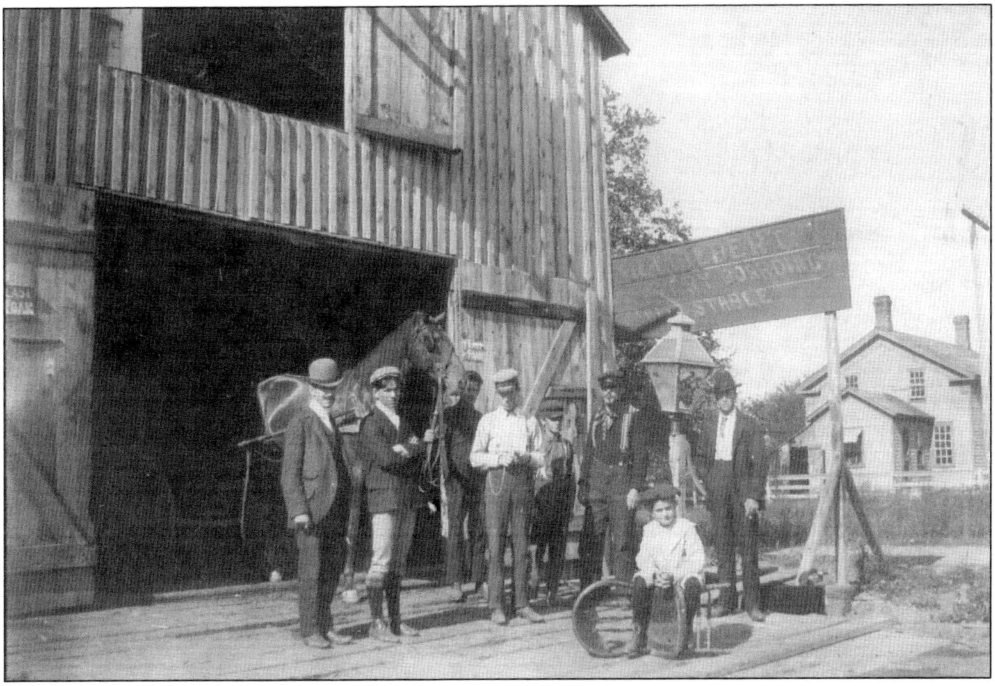

R.T. Gilbert Livery and Boarding Stable was located behind the hotel. A dapper young man and young fellow in nickers are going for a ride in a buggy. The stable was another place to catch up on the latest gossip and find out who was new in town.

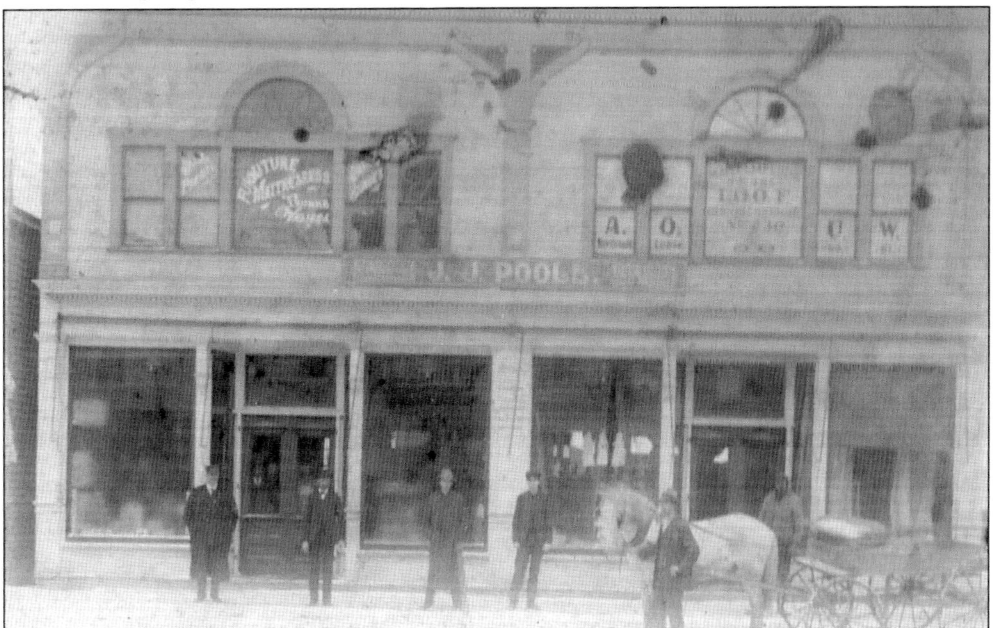

The J.J. Poole Grocery and Dry Goods store remained in the same building for close to 100 years. The Independent Order of Odd Fellows Hall (IOOF) was on the second floor, along with furniture and mattress displays. The Poole store moved several times over the years, ending up in North Algonac. It was recognized by the state as the oldest family-owned grocery store in Michigan.

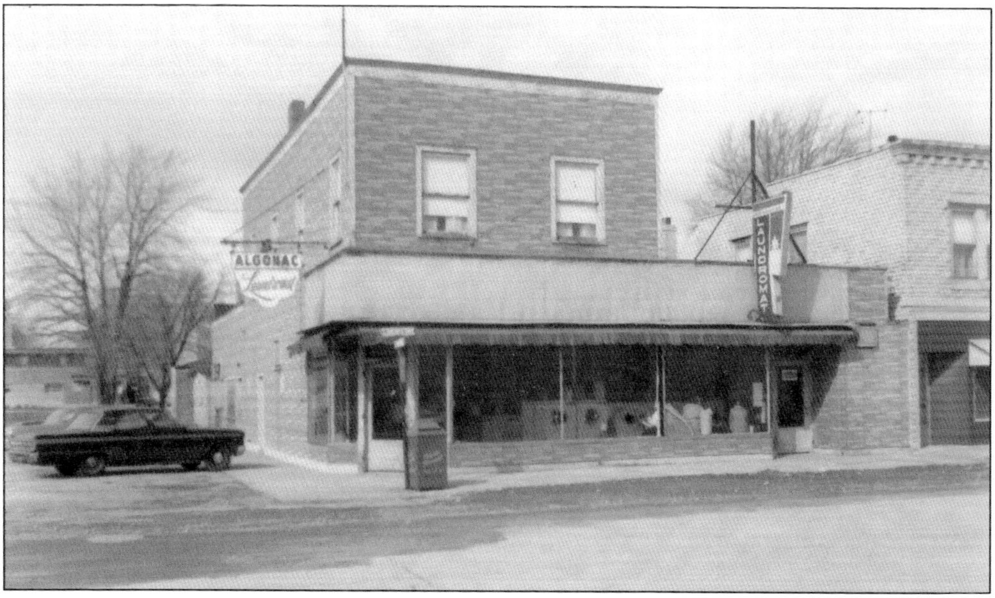

Algonac Laundromat moved to this Michigan Street location to expand its facilities, taking over the Babcock Dairy store. Babcock's was on the way to and from school, making it a good stopping place for teenagers. On Sunday mornings, the chief of police would buy a few dozen scrambled eggs and toast, stop by Don's IGA for some big bottles of ginger ale, and take it all to the men in the holding cell who had missed the last ferry, then send them on their way.

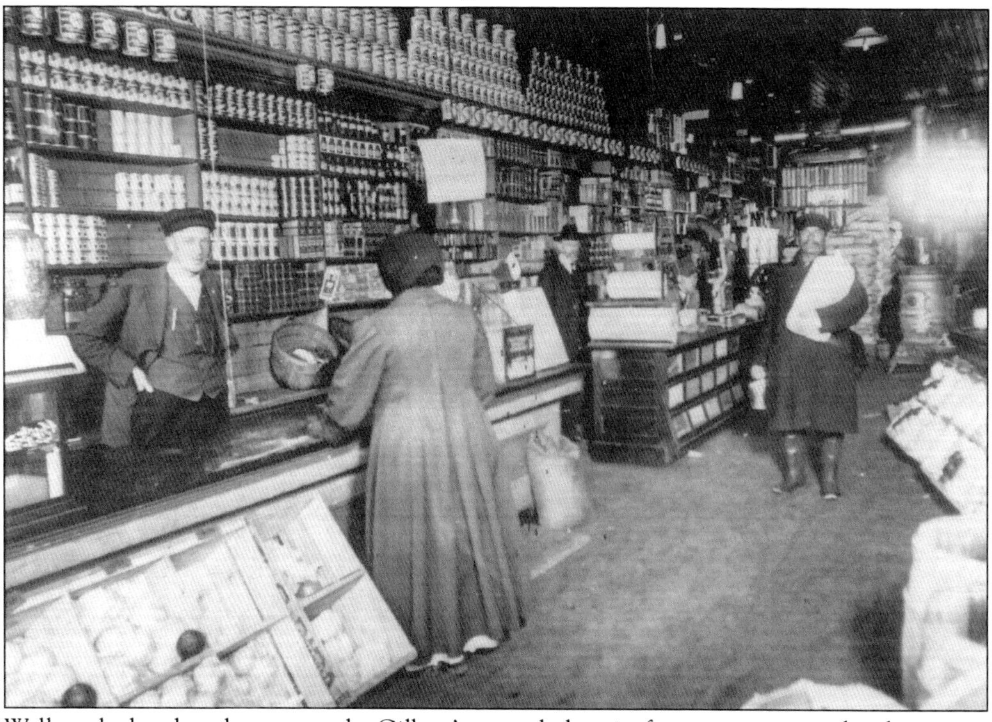

Well stocked and ready to serve, the Gilbert's store clerk waits for a customer to select her items. Gilbert's traded with the natives, exchanging animal pelts for groceries. In this image, the gentleman coming from the rear of the store might have finished his trade and is headed out.

Leo's Market in Pointe Tremble started as a one-pump gas station with a small building where odds and ends were sold. Leo and Sophie Szymanski worked long hours, building this small gas stop into a well-stocked market with beer, wine, and fresh meats. The gas pump is now gone, but the market is still serving the Pointe Tremble area.

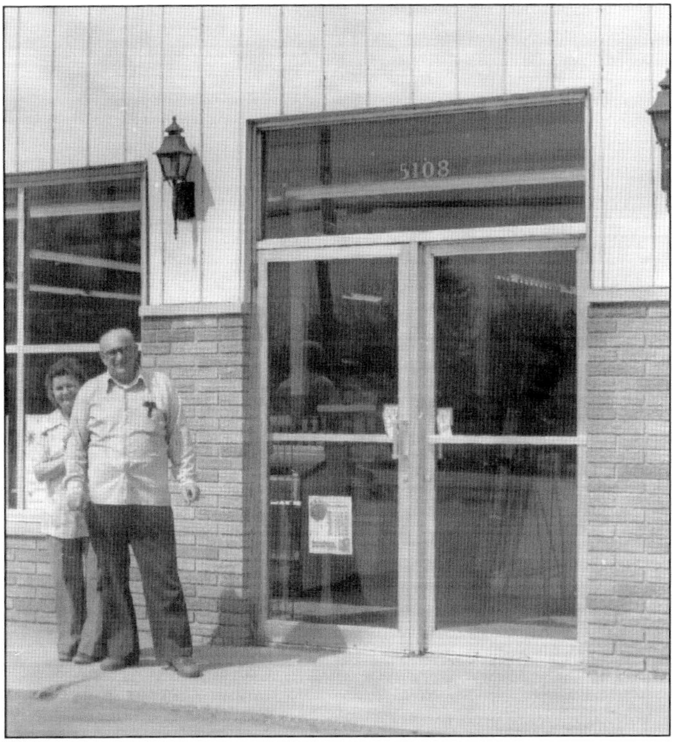

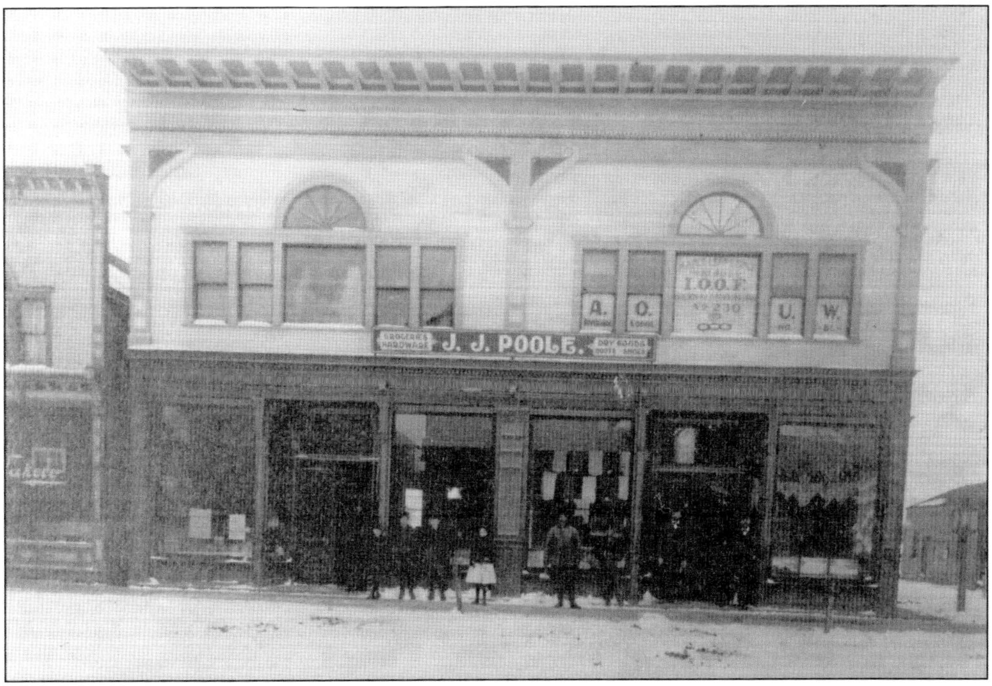

J.J. Poole operated this store for many years. Then his son R. Lee Poole took over and moved it a few buildings north, where he worked until his death. Poole dealt honestly with the Native Americans of Walpole Island, granting them credit when necessary, and always received payment. He was so well liked that the chief dubbed him honorary chief.

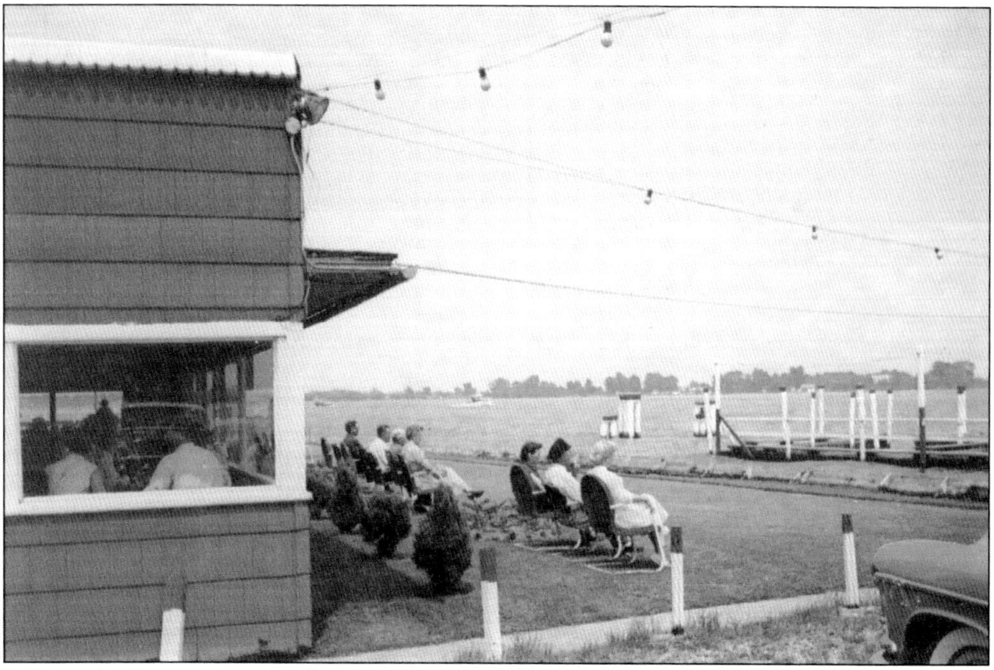

Sid's on the Seaway was one of the restaurants in the area that took advantage of the view of the St. Clair River and served delicious fish, chicken, and steak dinners. There was docking available for weekend boaters. If the dining rooms were full, there was a waiting area on the front lawn where patrons could have a drink and watch freighters and small boats pass by.

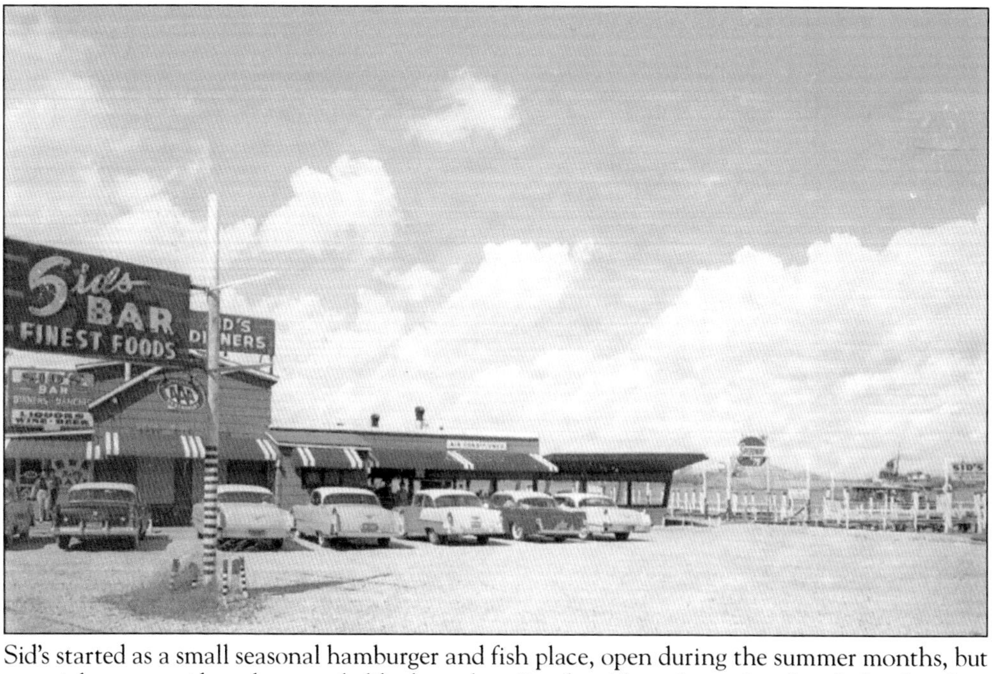

Sid's started as a small seasonal hamburger and fish place, open during the summer months, but soon it became evident that people liked to take a Sunday ride and stop for a bite before heading back to the city. The name changed over the years as new owners took over. Once the Black Angus Beef House and now Bobby Mac's, the location continues to attract guests.

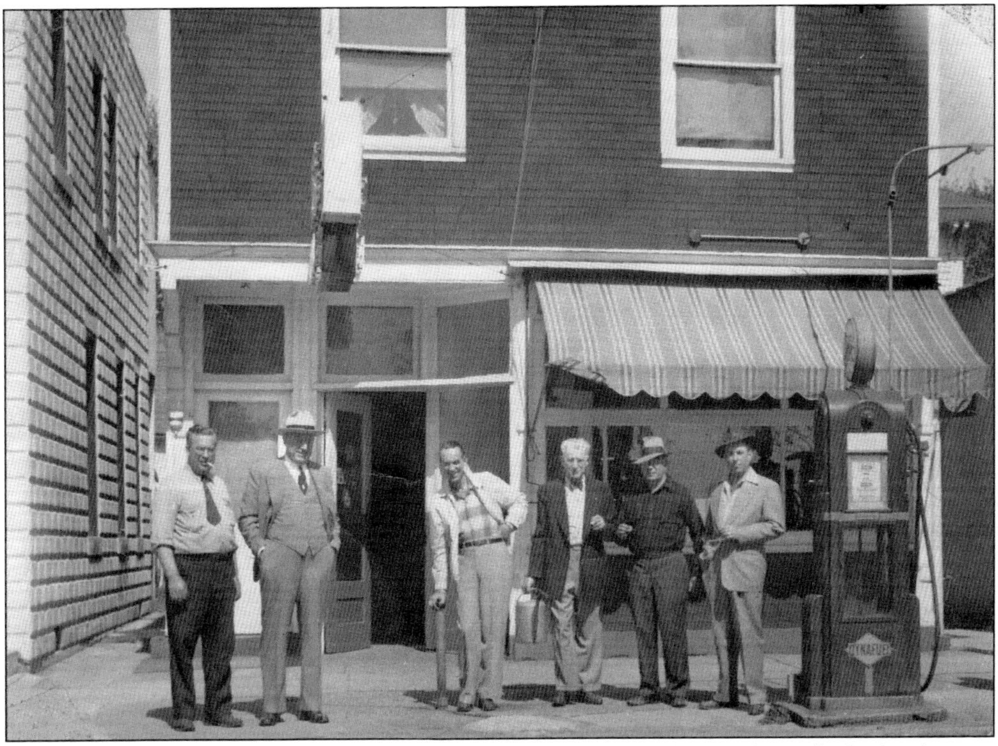

Jake Cole's Beer Store in downtown Algonac was flanked by John "Jack" Bell's barbershop on the left and Stringer's restaurant on the right. The gas pump remained at the curb until the early 1950s. Jake and his friends did not mind having a smoke by the pump. Jake's wife, Helen, was the school nurse for many years.

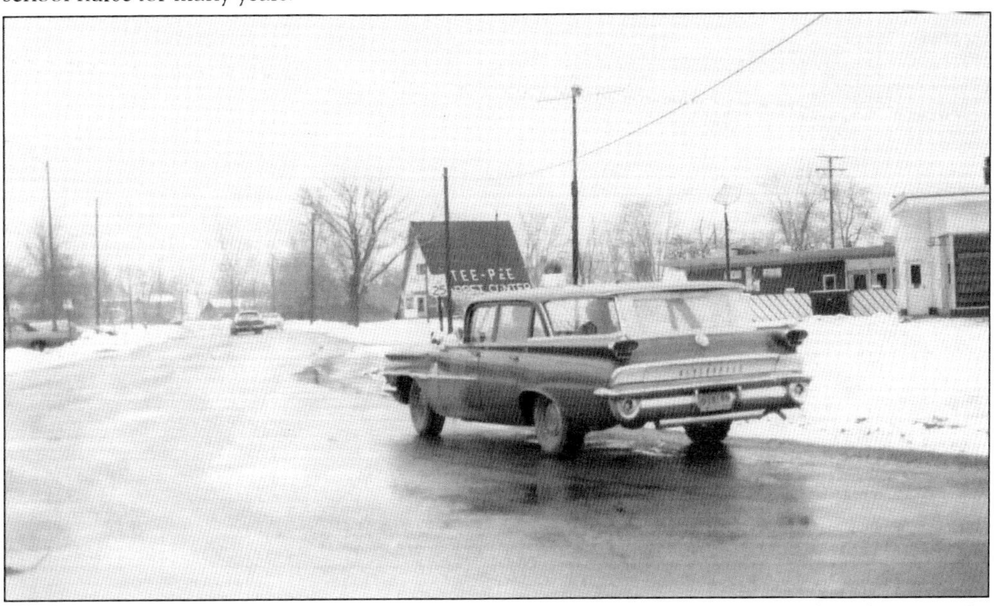

The owners of Hemery's Restaurant built the Tee-Pee in the 1960s to service the takeout trade. The Tee-Pee served most menu items from the restaurant on the river. When the restaurant closed, the building became a carpet showroom, as seen here.

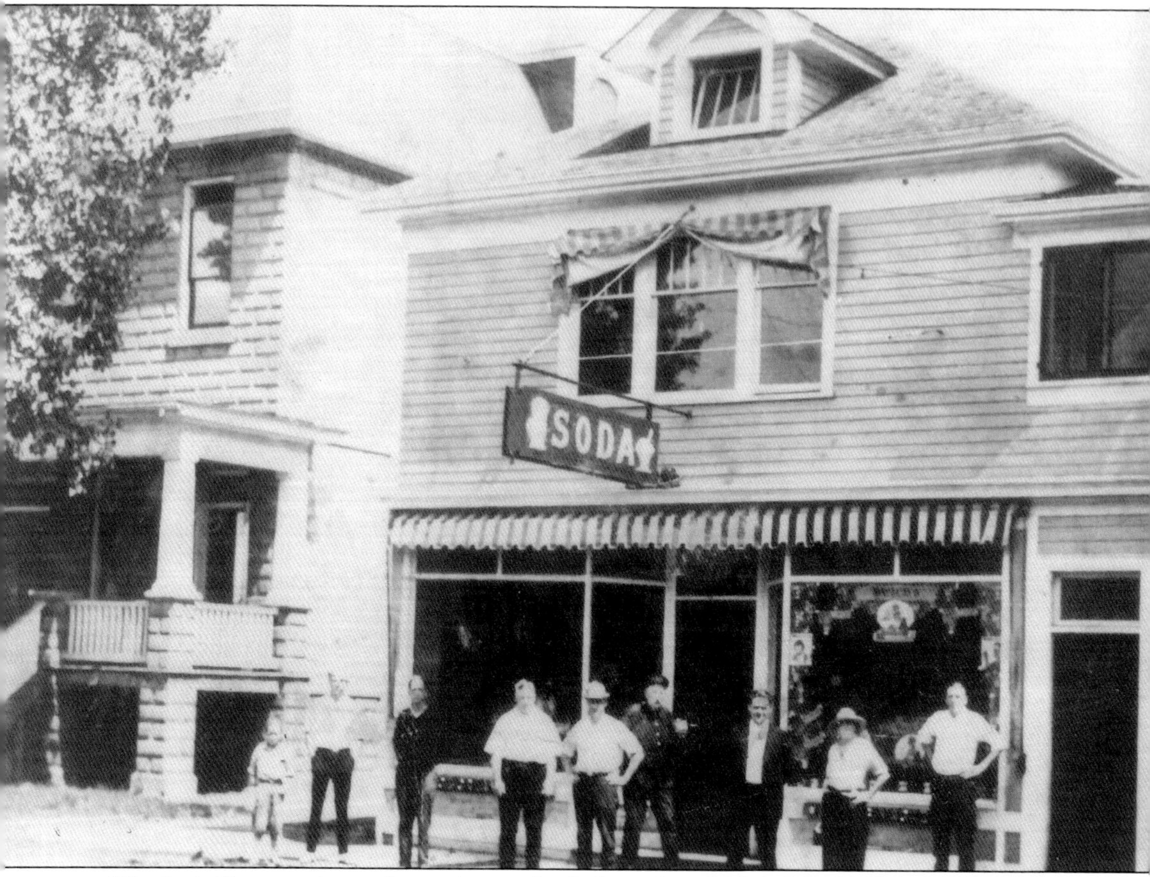

The Soda Shop was located next door to the Independent Order of Odd Fellows Hall, seen at left in this photograph. The hall later became the McKoan Building. Ice cream was big in the early years, so the Soda Shop was a popular destination for those with little or no air-conditioning. Later, the Soda Shop became a Laundromat.

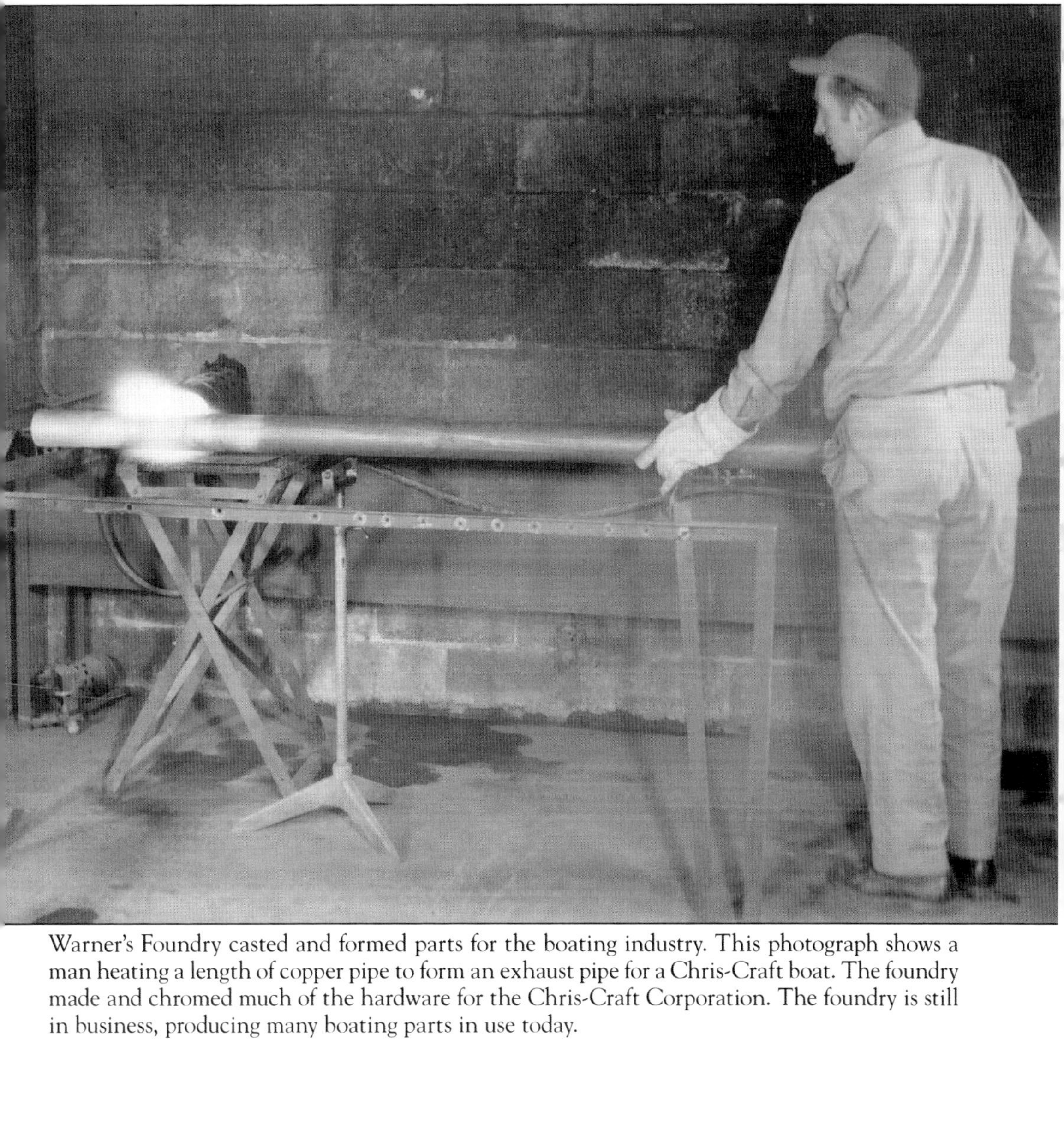

Warner's Foundry casted and formed parts for the boating industry. This photograph shows a man heating a length of copper pipe to form an exhaust pipe for a Chris-Craft boat. The foundry made and chromed much of the hardware for the Chris-Craft Corporation. The foundry is still in business, producing many boating parts in use today.

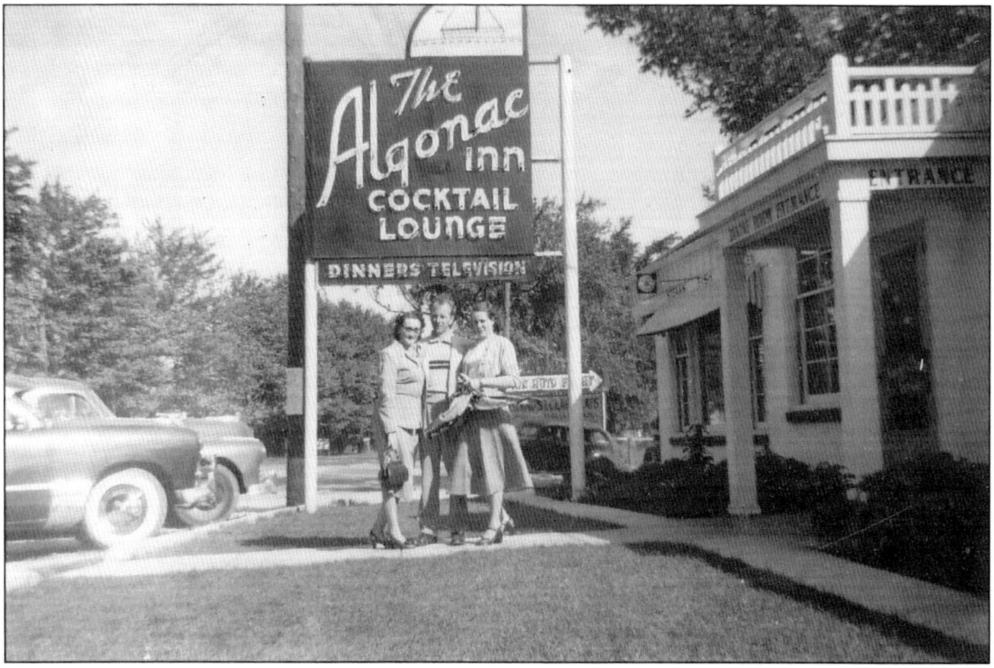

The Algonac Inn was owned and operated by Al and Thelma Tucker. The inn started out as a family home, but its location at the intersection of M-54 and M-59 seemed like a convenient place to have a restaurant. Those traveling to their cottages on Harsens Island had to wait for the ferry and often needed a place to eat. Expanded four times, it became one of the three biggest restaurants in the Algonac. The establishment was later named the Port-a-Call, and the building was replaced by a boat, which had a tendency to rock in rough weather and cause some discomfort while eating dinner.

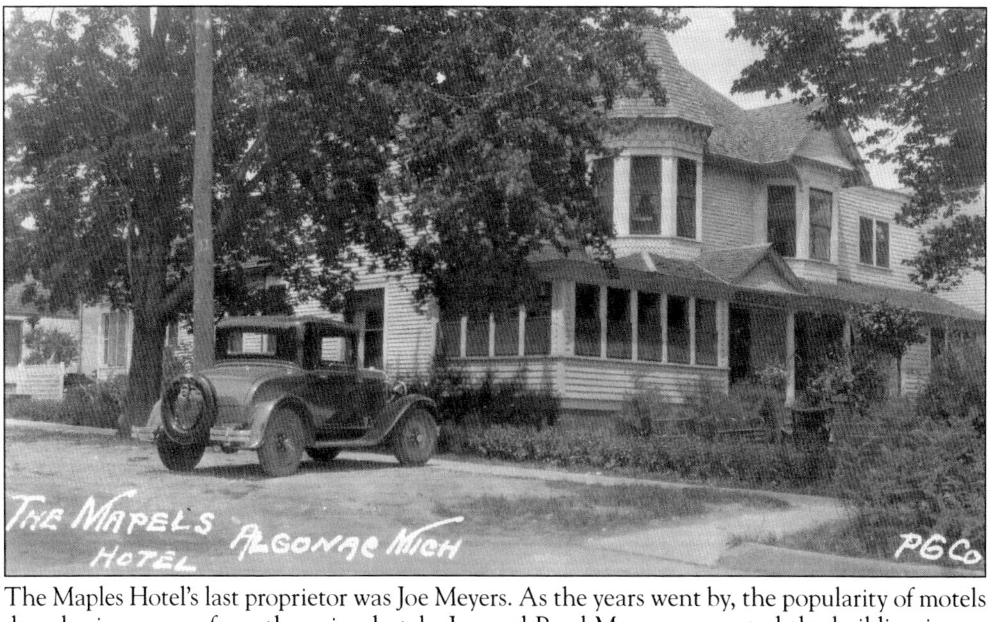

The Maples Hotel's last proprietor was Joe Meyers. As the years went by, the popularity of motels drew business away from the aging hotels. Joe and Pearl Meyers converted the building into a rooming house until The Maples was torn down.

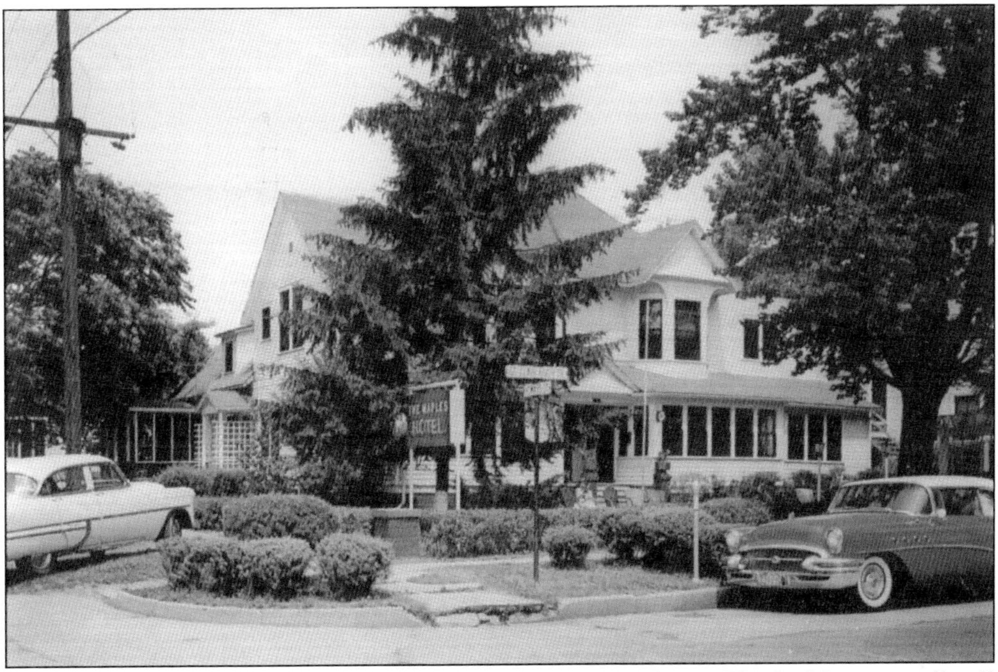

The Maples is shown here in 1964 during its stint as a rooming house. The building was still well kept and offered rooms to let for overnight travelers. Nearby, Charlie's Blue Water Grill, now a pizza parlor, offered carryout service to guests of The Maples.

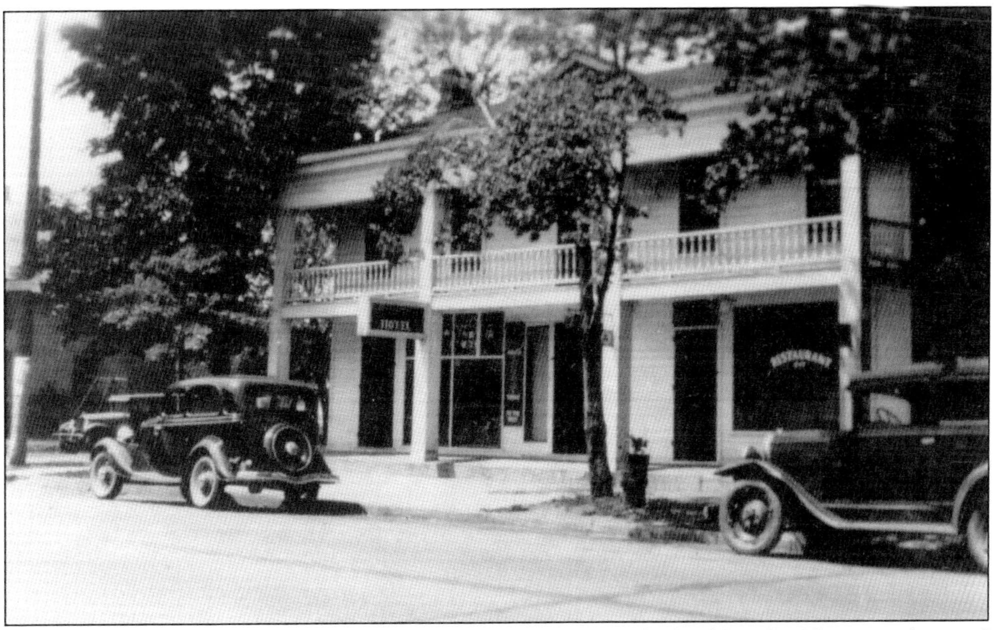

The Franklin House is pictured here during the mid-1930s. The building had been modernized but still maintained a reputation for serving the best meal in town.

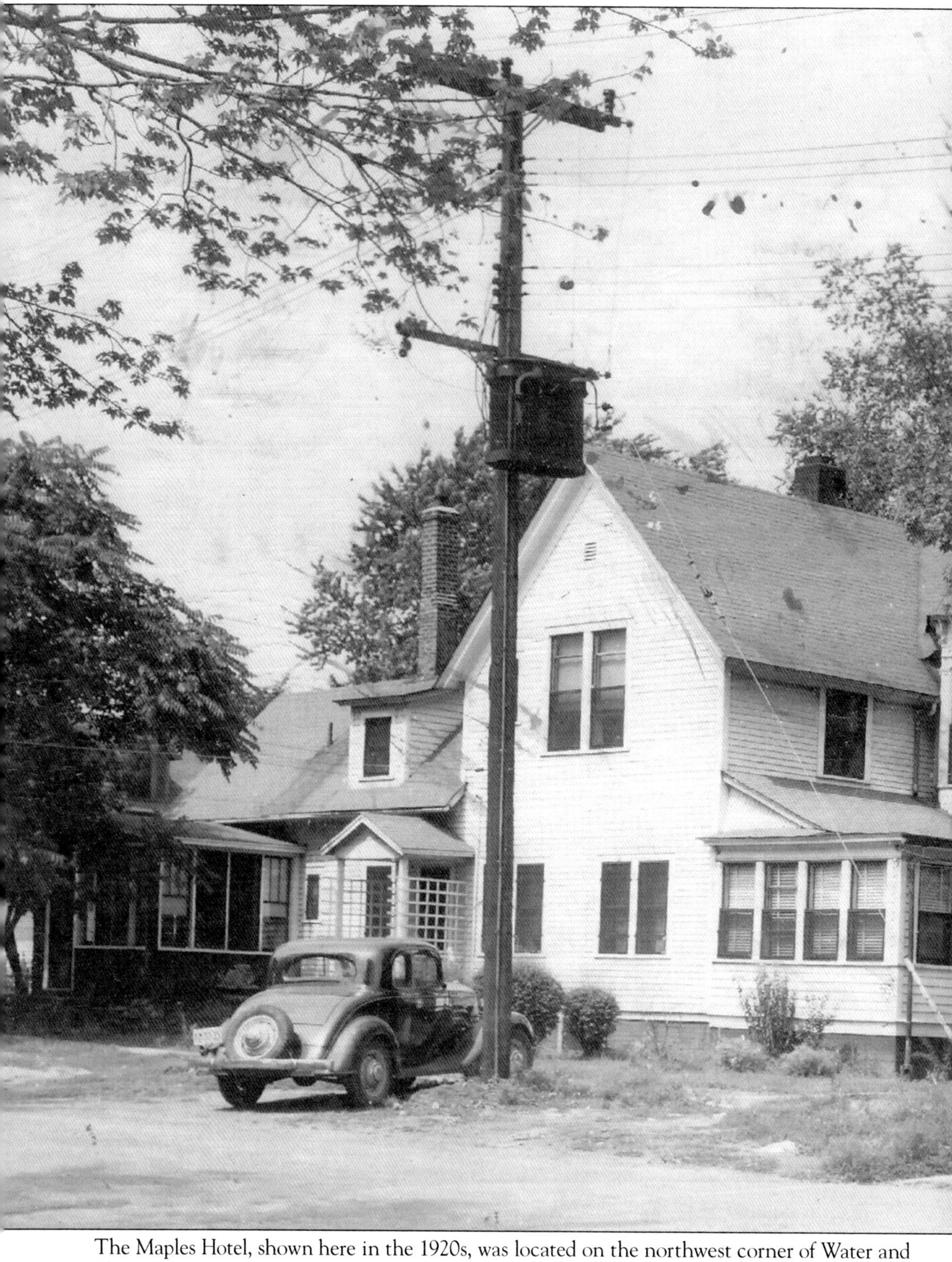

The Maples Hotel, shown here in the 1920s, was located on the northwest corner of Water and Pleasant Streets. Before the days of easy transportation, good roads, and motels, many people who

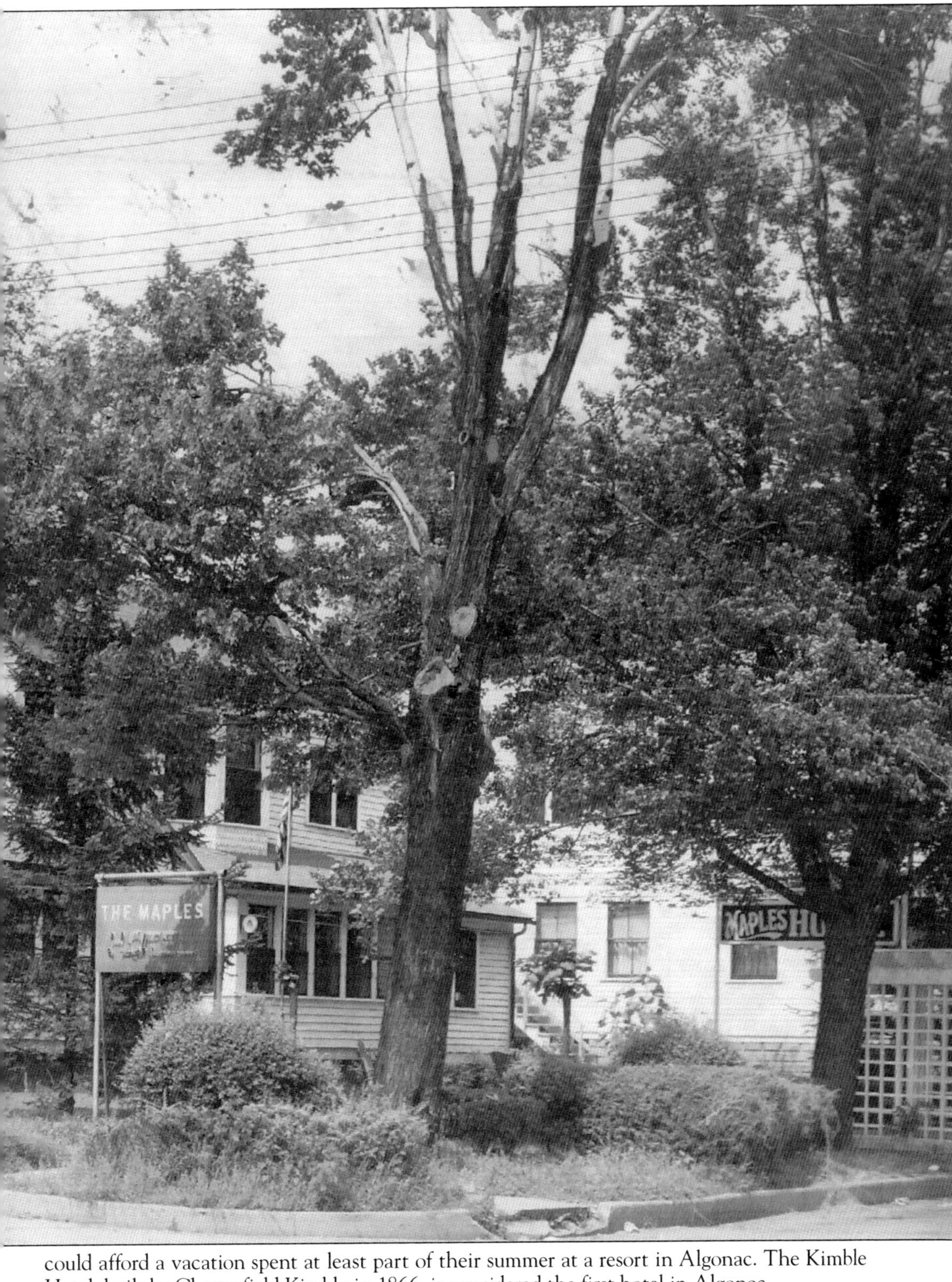

could afford a vacation spent at least part of their summer at a resort in Algonac. The Kimble Hotel, built by Chesterfield Kimble in 1866, is considered the first hotel in Algonac.

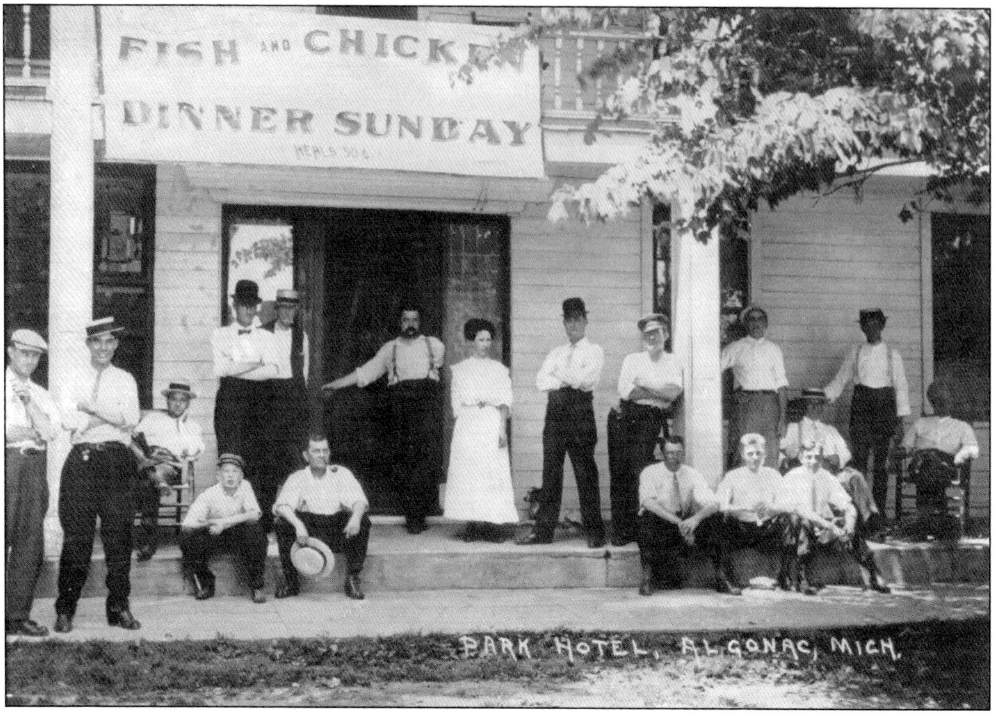

The Park Hotel served a Sunday special featuring either fish or chicken for 50¢. Satisfied customers would relax on the veranda on summer afternoons.

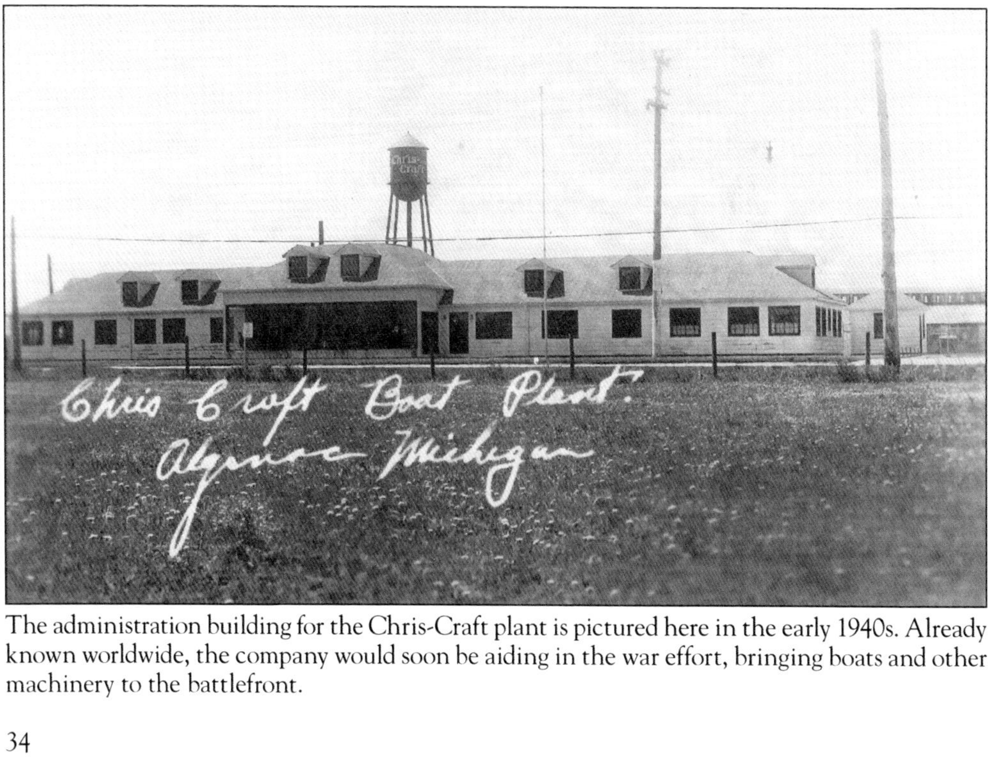

The administration building for the Chris-Craft plant is pictured here in the early 1940s. Already known worldwide, the company would soon be aiding in the war effort, bringing boats and other machinery to the battlefront.

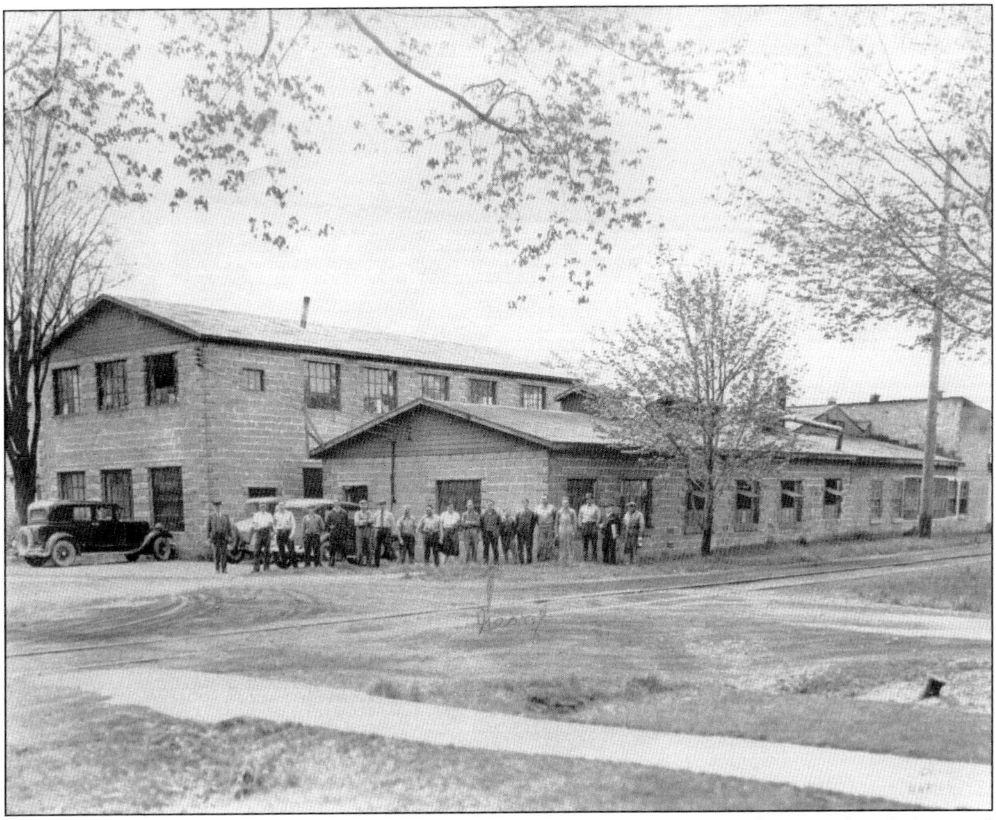

Located at the corner of Michigan and Columbia Streets, Warner's Foundry casted and chromed parts for Chris-Craft boats. Later occupied by the Ames Bicycle Shop, as well as a radiator and welding shop, this building was eventually modernized into a medical center.

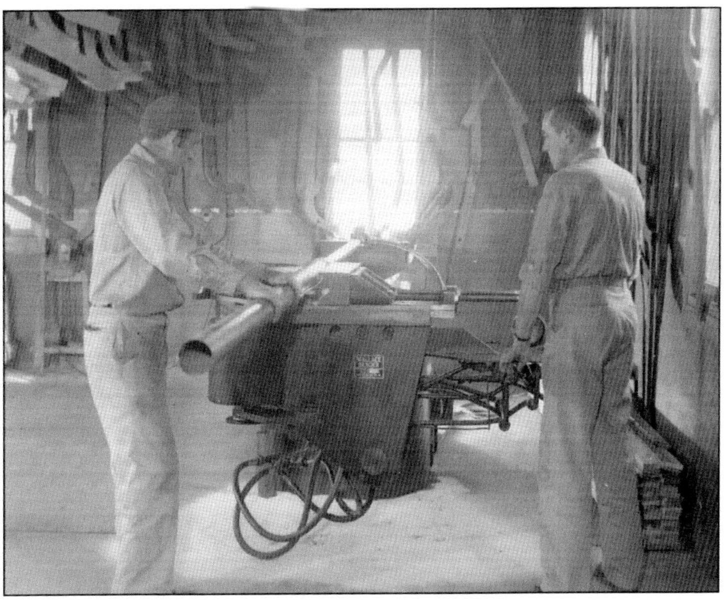

These Chris-Craft employees are bending a custom exhaust pipe, usually made from copper tube, then heated and bent with a hydraulic Wallace Bender. Warner's Foundry moved to Smith Street, where fittings for the marine industry are still casted today.

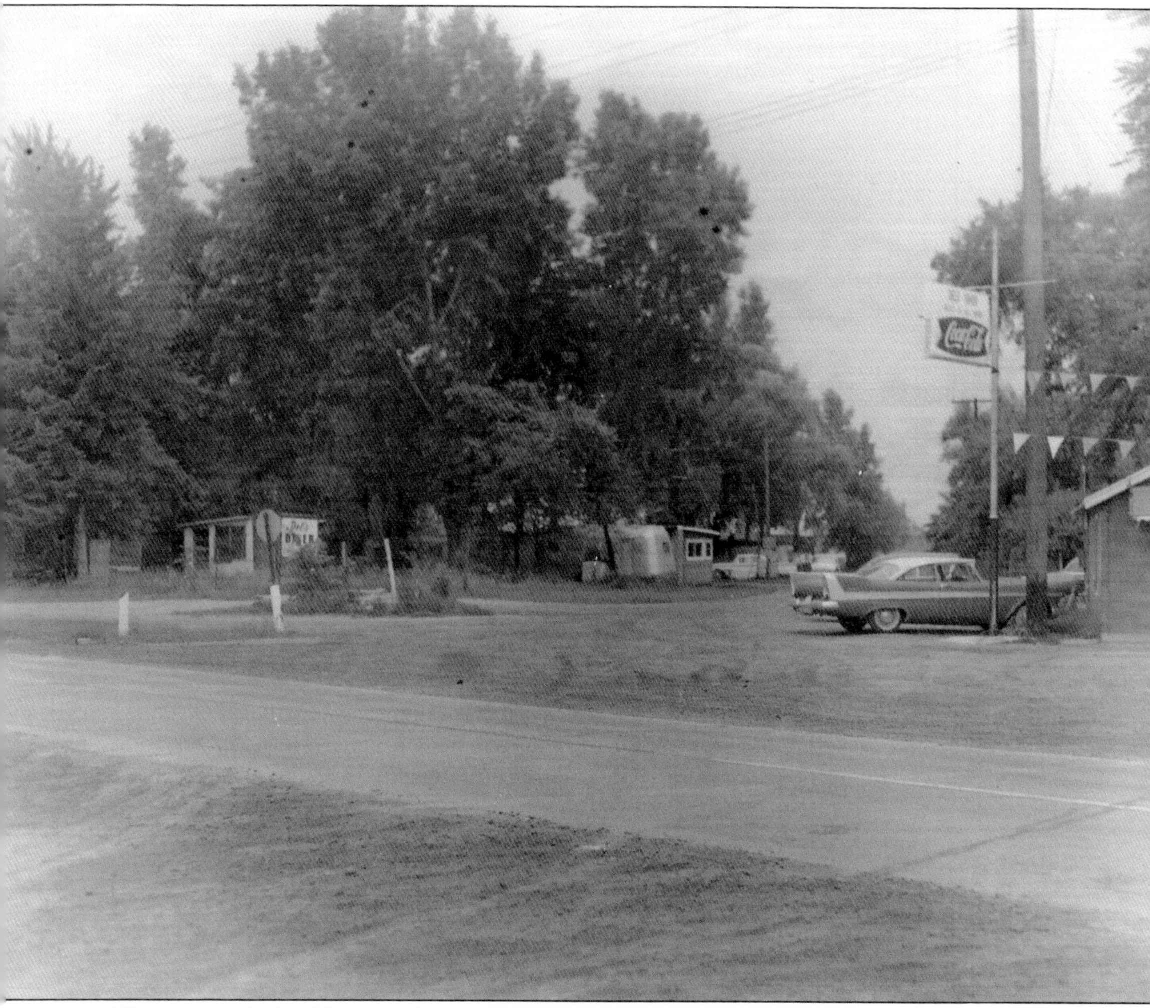

The corner of Island Drive and Pointe Tremble Road is captured in this photograph. The building on the right was the Pearl Beach Lion Club House. Later, it was repurposed as a bait store and coffee shop, then the bait shop was closed and Dell Fisher opened Dell's Dinner. Margret Jean Achatz later bought the property and operated Margret Jean's restaurant, serving home-cooked meals for many years. The area on the left is Gene Kirwin's boat rental. He also rented small house trailers so fishermen could stay the night and get an early start in the morning.

Two

STREET SCENES

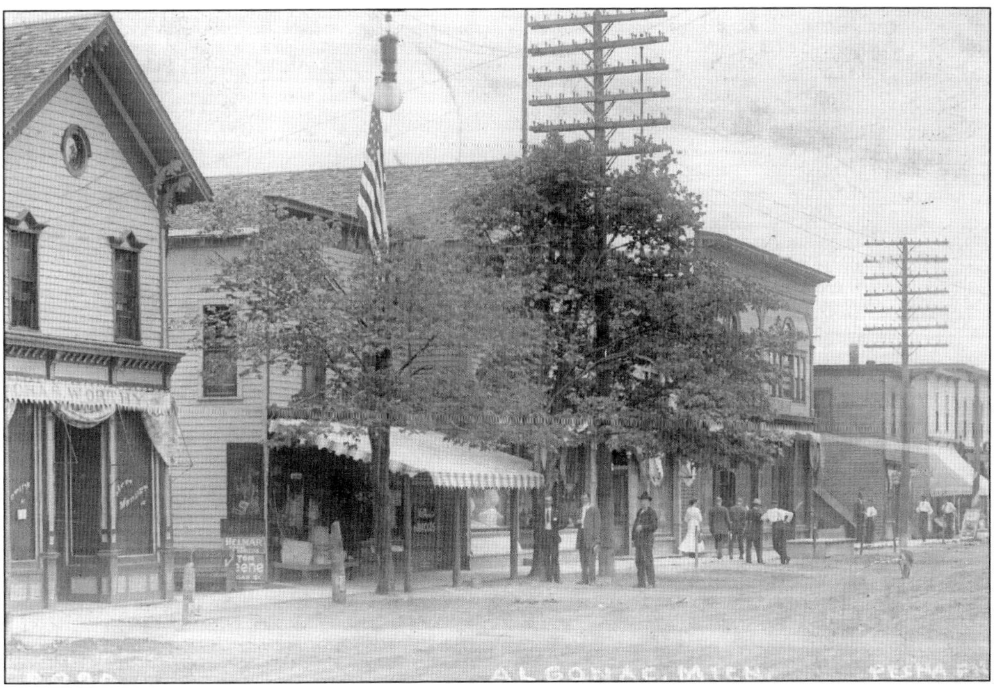

This section of downtown Algonac, pictured here in the 1900s, shows what the streets were like before automobiles became prevalent. In the late 1880s, an unusual practice was started in Algonac and other communities up the river in which many businesses closed at noon on Thursdays. This practice originated to allow residents the opportunity to attend the horse races on Thursday afternoons and stayed in effect until the 1920s.

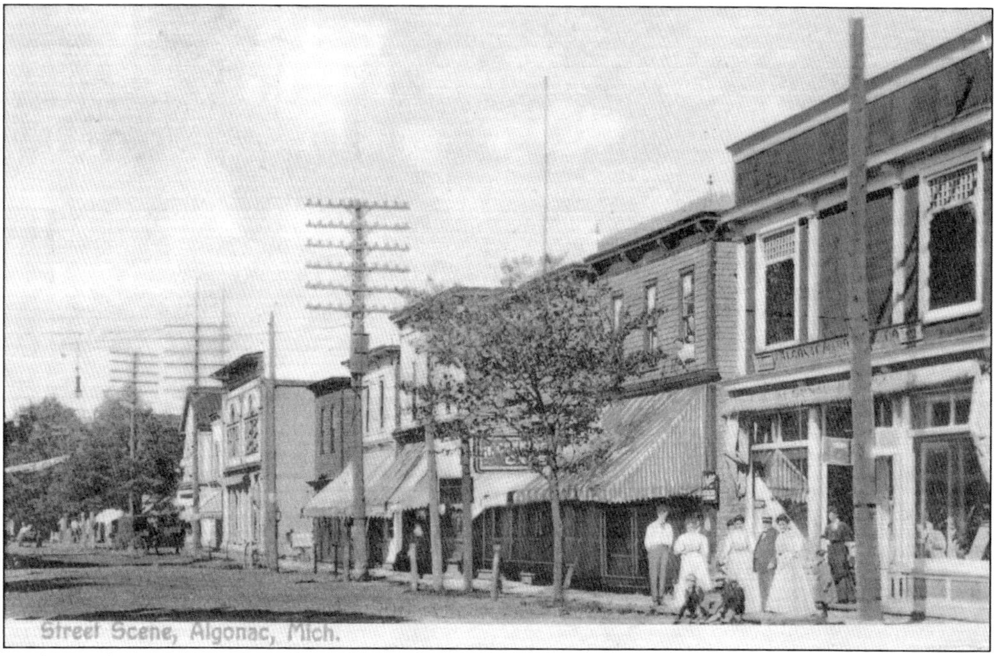

In this early scene of Water Street, it is apparent that electricity is becoming popular. Telephone lines and electric lines shared the same poles. Automobiles are still rare, however, as hitching posts are still being used.

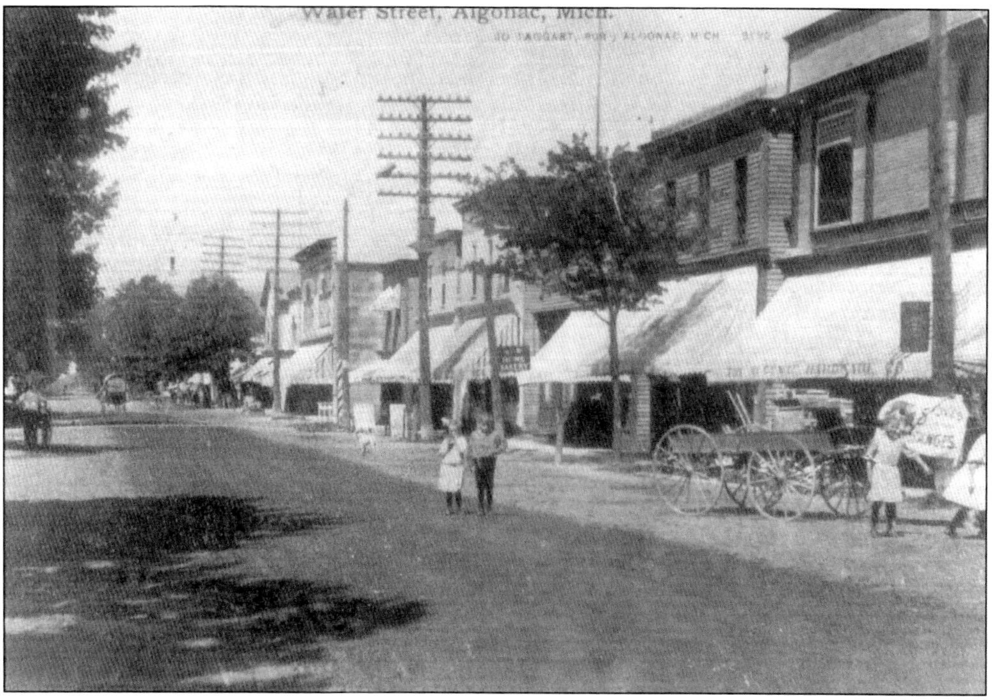

In this early-1890s scene of Water Street shows what life was like before automobiles. The Home Bakery and the Algonac Hardware Company were popular stops. Note the delivery wagon's horse with a blanket advertising stoves and ranges.

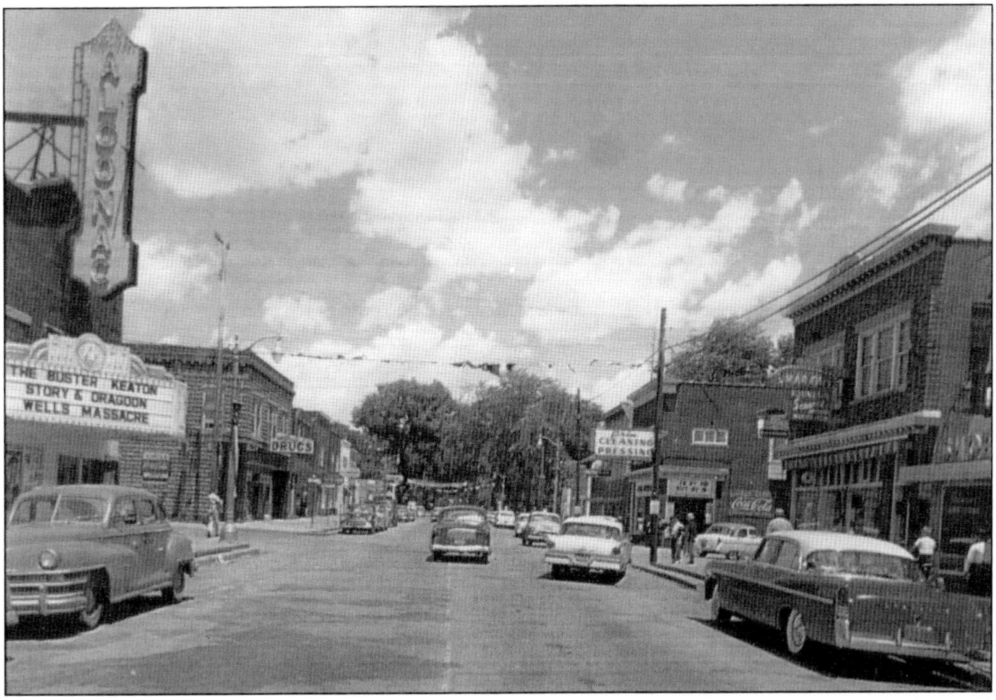

This street scene from around 1957 depicts St. Clair River Drive. The Classik Theater had turned into the Algonac Theater at left, and a right turn at Marion's Fountain Service and Prim Cleaners would lead to Walpole Island and the customs office.

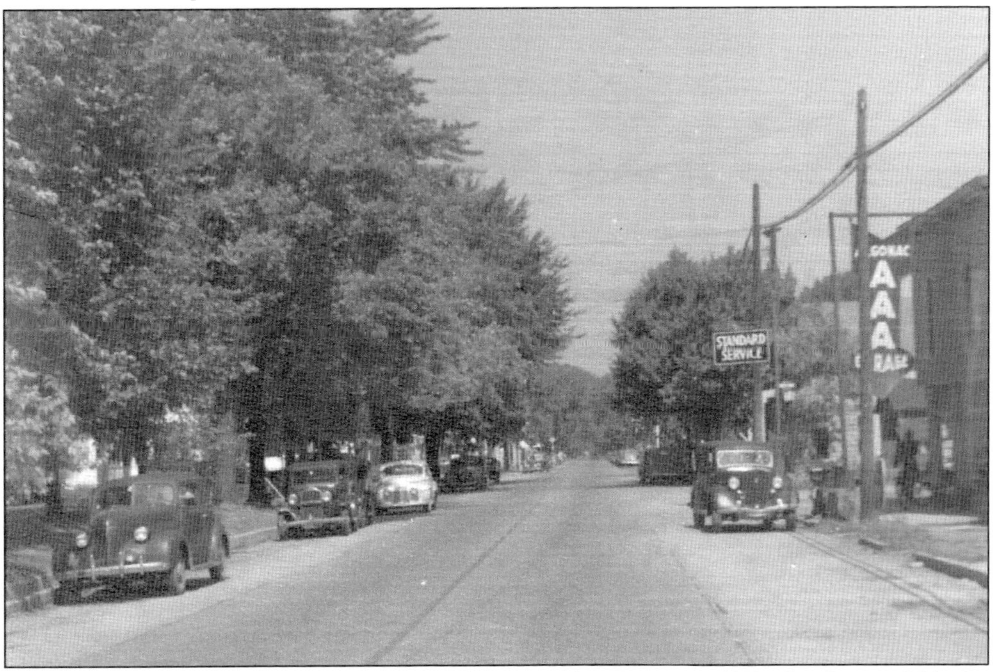

This image of the south end of town shows Stub Cartwright's Garage and Wrecker Service. Vehicles of this era were lower to the ground than previous models because of paved roads; however, they still required lots of maintenance.

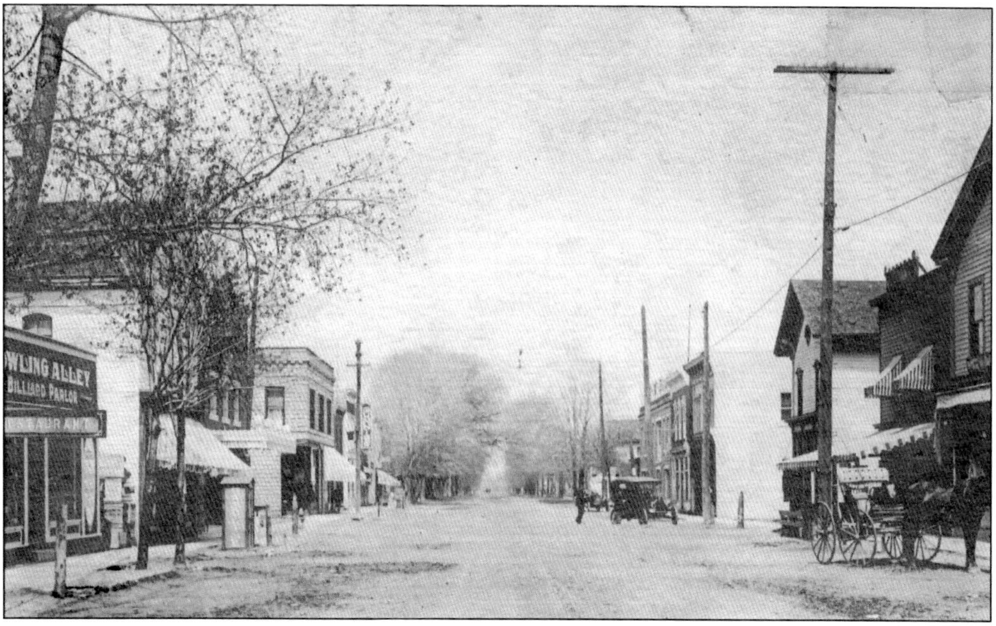

In this early 1920s image, looking north on Water Street, there are signs that automobiles are becoming more popular, as gas pumps appear next to the hitching posts.

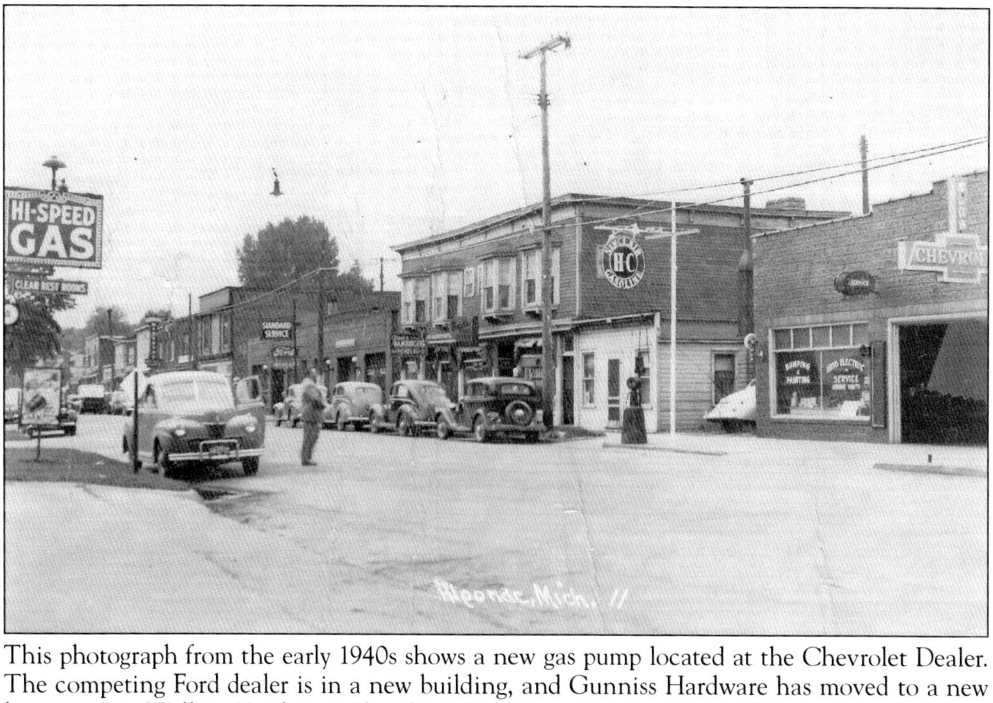

This photograph from the early 1940s shows a new gas pump located at the Chevrolet Dealer. The competing Ford dealer is in a new building, and Gunniss Hardware has moved to a new location near Wallace Hardware. The phone lines have been strung in cable on the poles below the electric because too many telephone repairmen were being electrocuted.

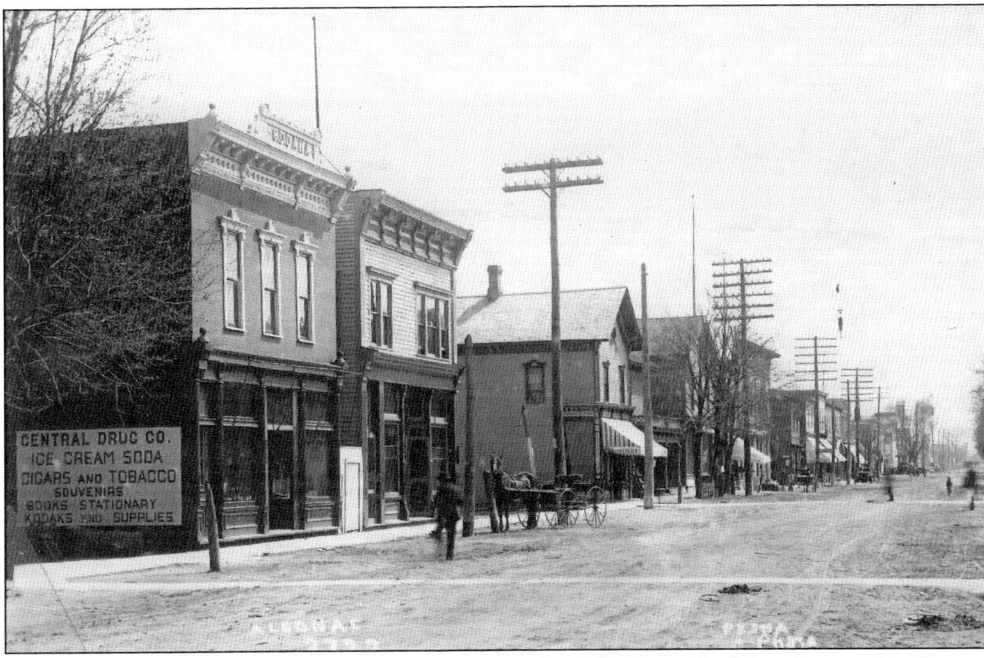

In another image looking south on Water Street, the G.D. Dana Building houses the Central Drug Company. Note the door between the stores, which leads to an exterior stairway for the tenants living in the flats above the stores.

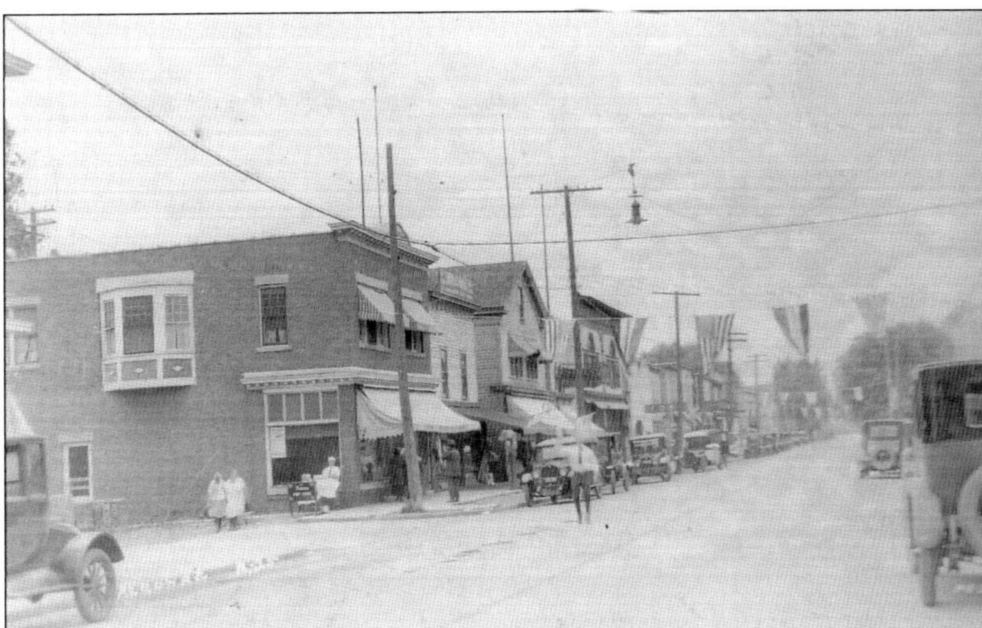

A vendor sells frozen treats at the entrance to the Walpole ferry dock on a busy summer day along Water Street.

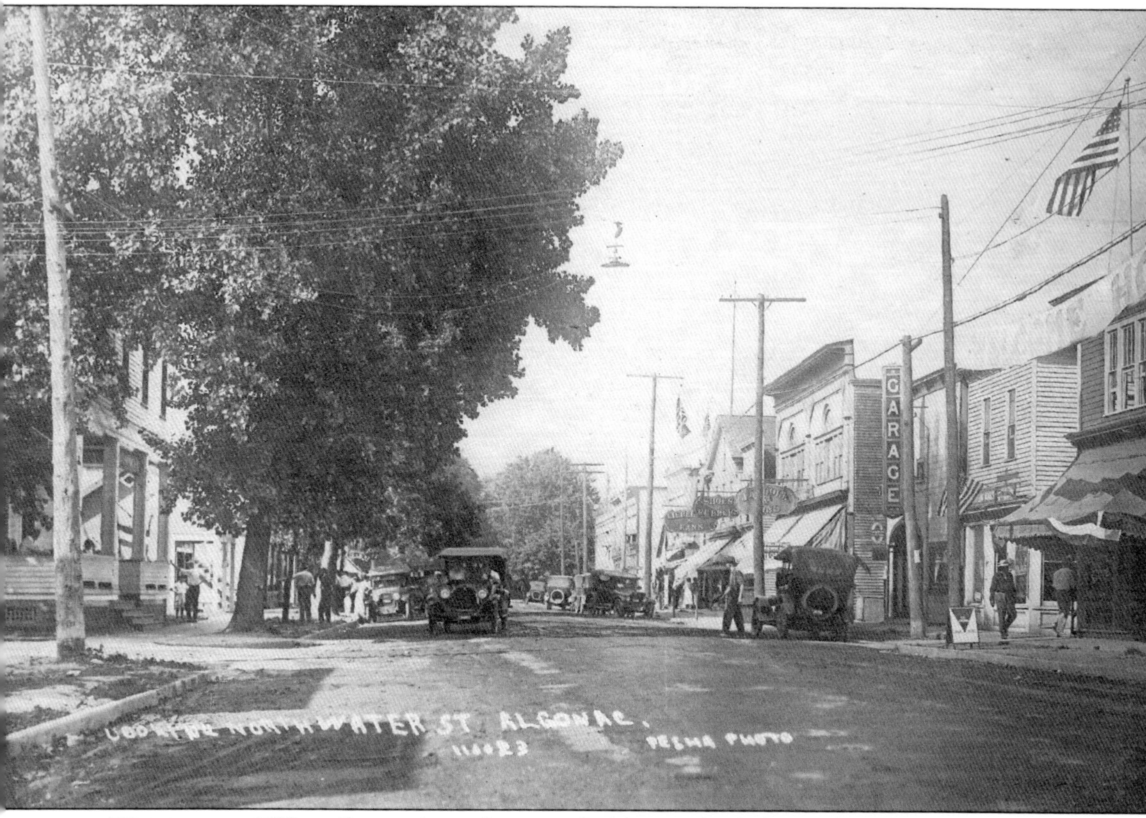

This image of Water Street shows how much Algonac had changed in the 1920s. With the abundance of automobiles, roads became a problem. Roads were dirt, and the bridges at the turn of the century were one lane, wooden, and slippery from clay. In April 1919, the Good Roads Amendment was added to the state constitution. The local rallying cry to help pass the amendment was "Help pull Clay Township out of the mud."

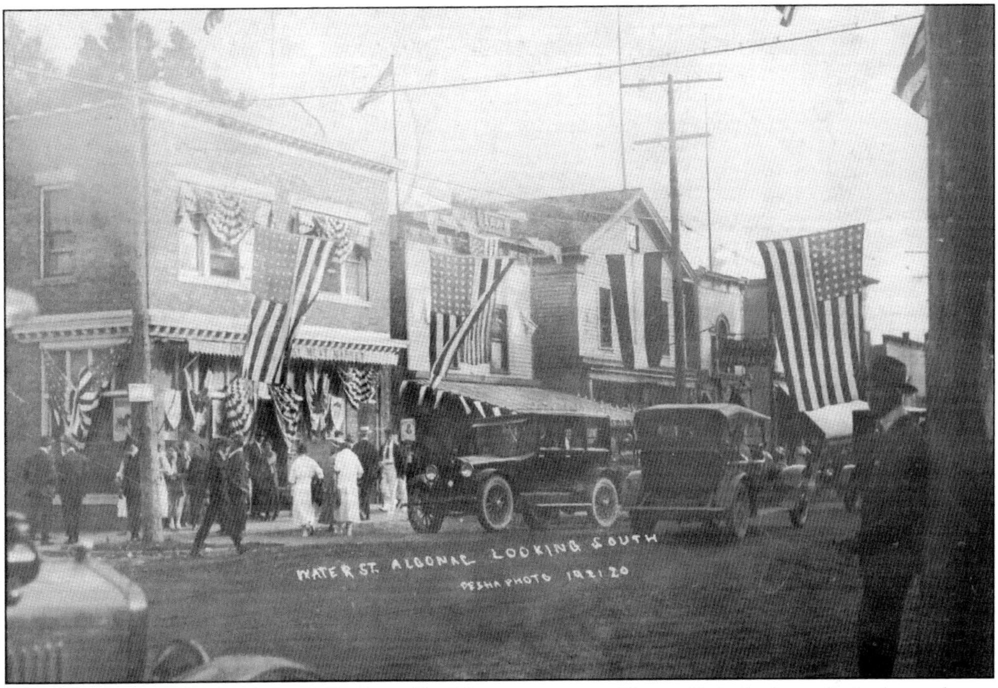

Worthy Meat Market and the G.D. Dana Building are pictured here all decked out for Independence Day festivities.

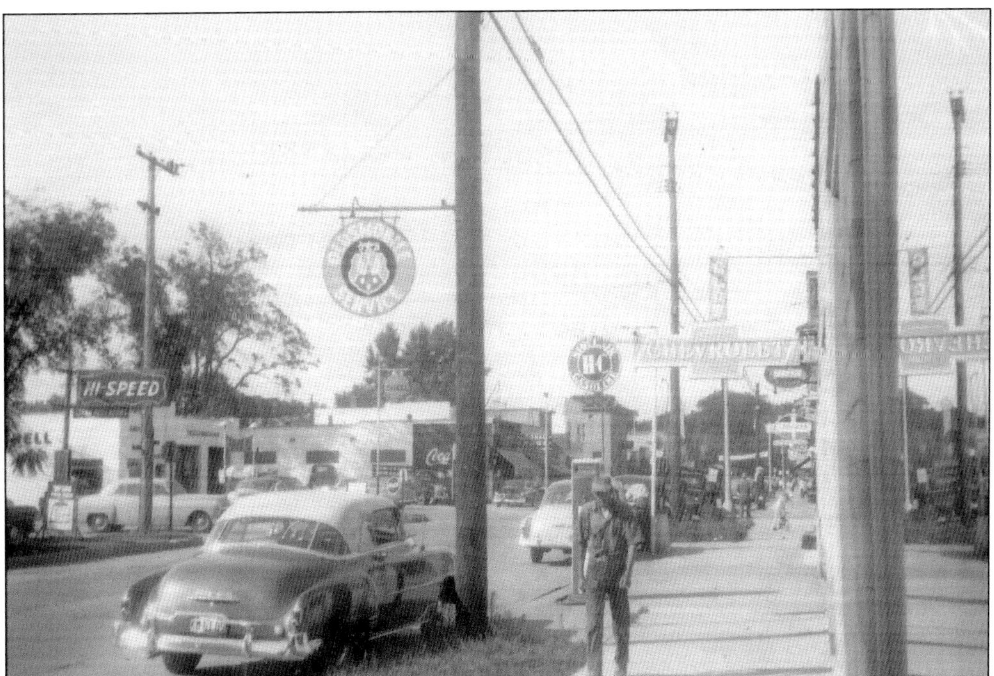

In this view of St. Clair River Drive from the early 1950s, Barker Chevrolet sells Sinclair gasoline at the curb, and Algonac Drug is located across the street after its third and final move.

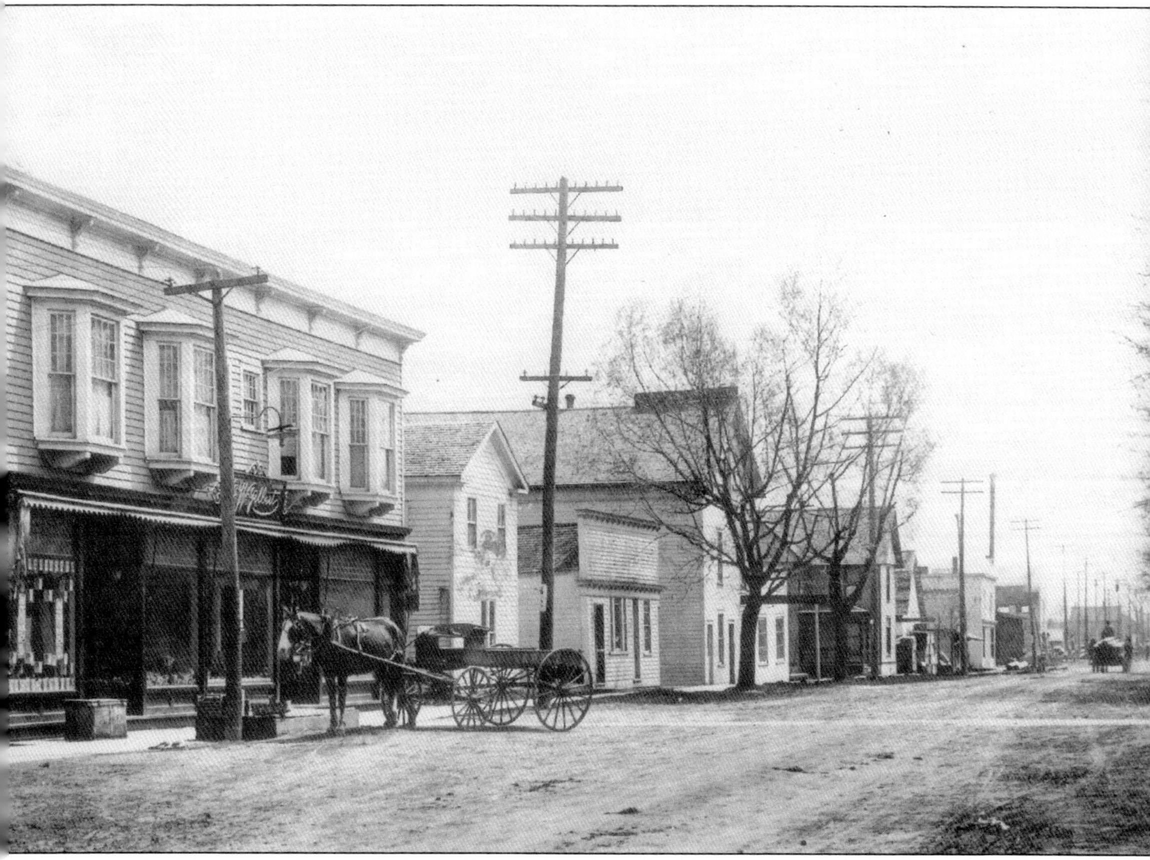

In this 1910 photograph of Algonac, an electric light is visible just above the horse's head. In 1894, gaslights with pressure tanks lighted the outside of stores, and in 1900, the village of Algonac was still burning oil for streetlamps, which had been placed on several corners. It was the marshal's job to fill, clean, and light them every day.

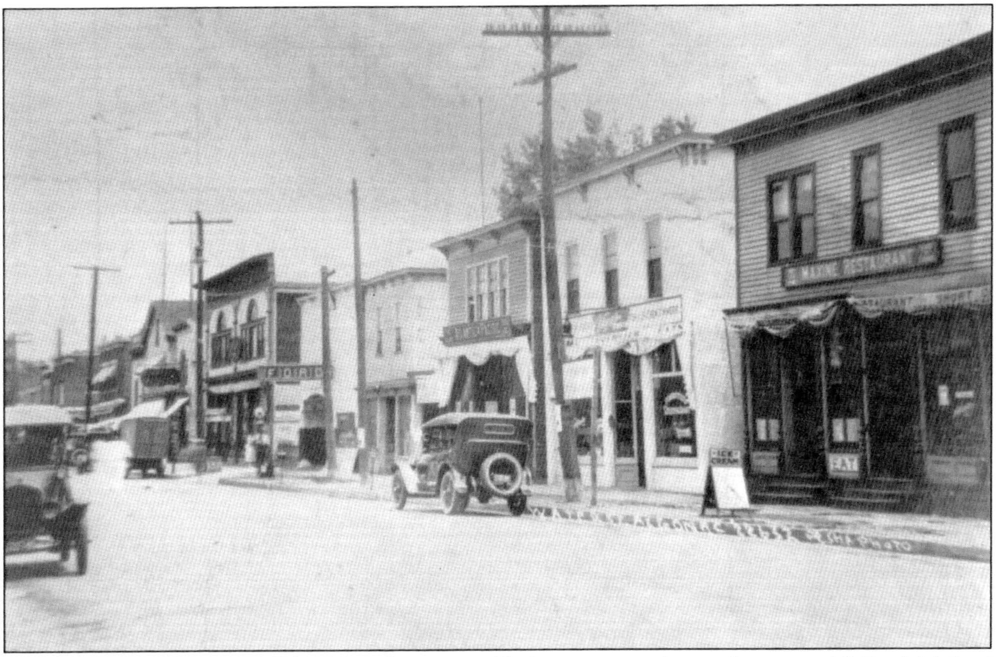

Maxine Restaurant, one of the finer dining establishments, was located next to A&P, which had three different stores in Algonac until Kroger bought the stores in the area. Note that the Ford dealer still has a gas pump at the street.

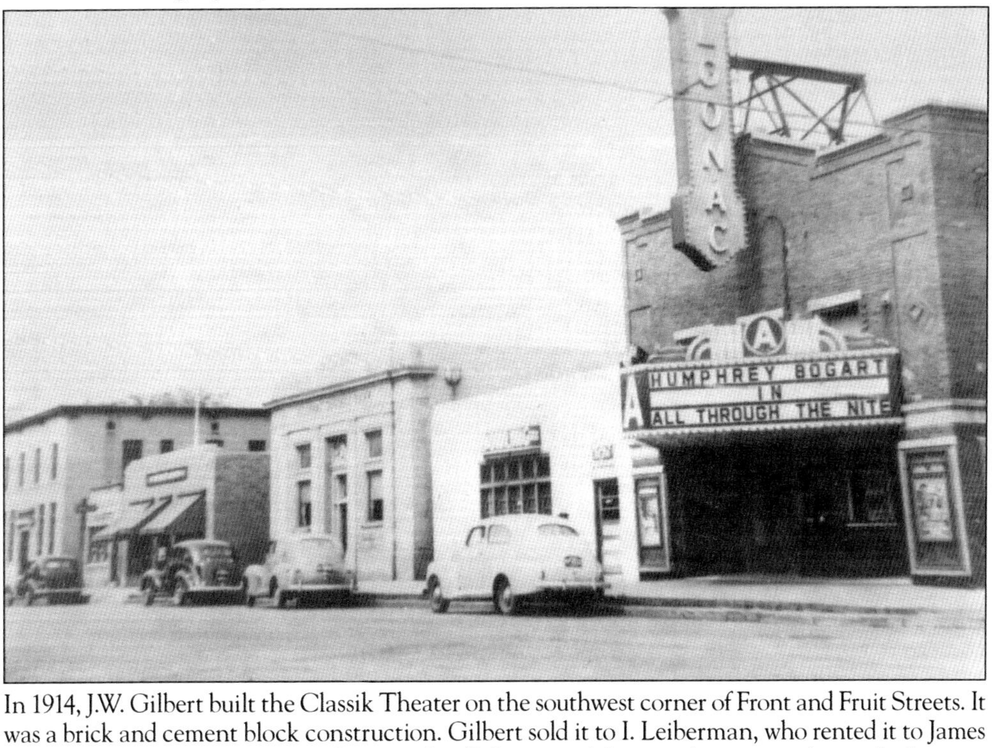

In 1914, J.W. Gilbert built the Classik Theater on the southwest corner of Front and Fruit Streets. It was a brick and cement block construction. Gilbert sold it to I. Leiberman, who rented it to James Harper. Under Harper, it operated as a vaudeville house and, later, a silent movie theater. Leiberman sold the theater to a Detroit chain owned by Shultie. It then became the Algonac Theater.

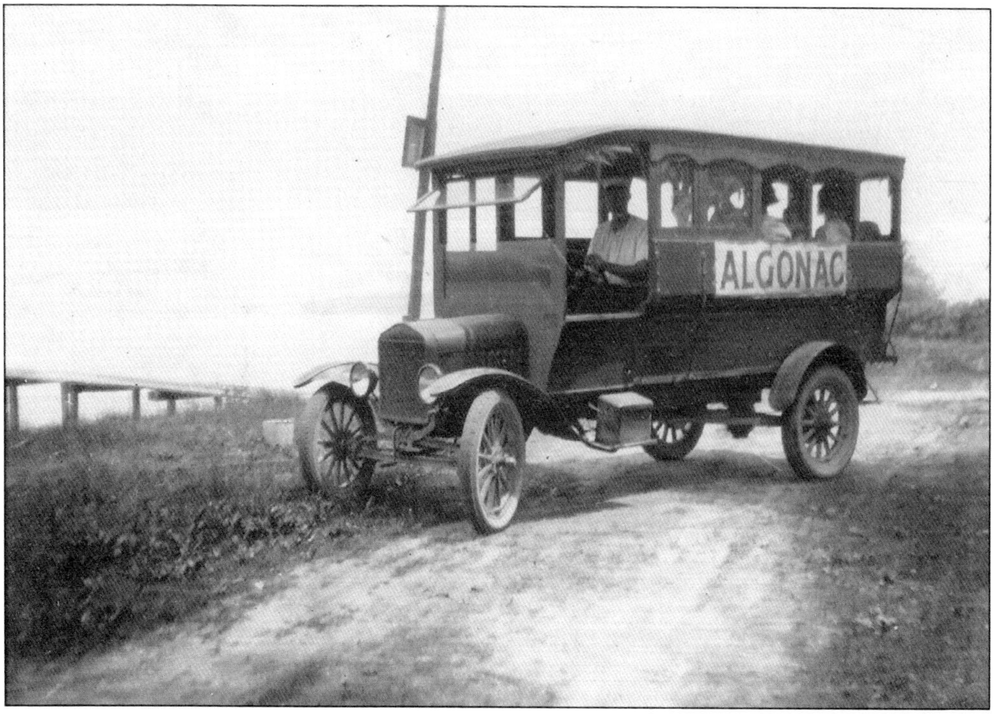

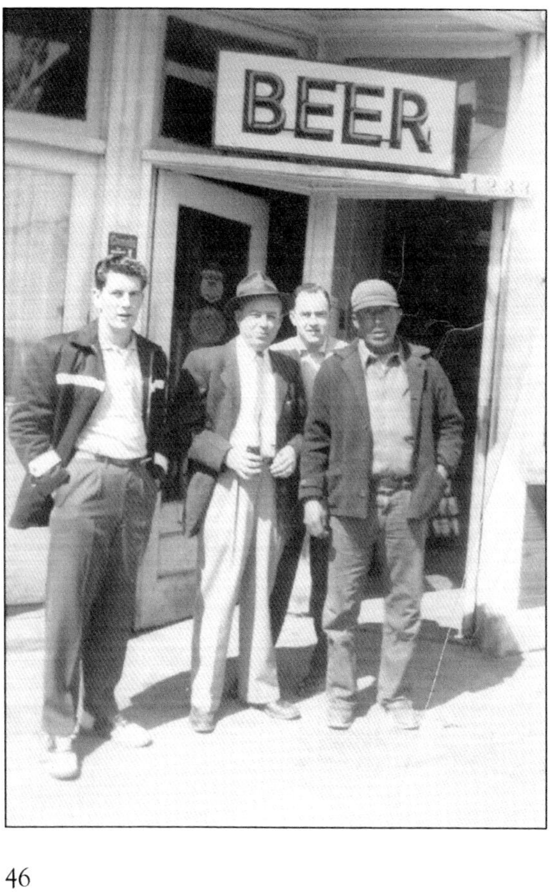

The first public transportation in Algonac was supported by local hotels to take guests to the ferries for trips to Tashmoo Park on Harsens Island or Camp Algonac on Russell Island.

Four locals stop by Jake Cole's for a cold soda and chitchat. Cole owned the gas station and beer store next to Jack Bell's barbershop for many years. In his spare time, Cole would fly his small plane around the area. He kept the plane at a landing strip alongside his home on Holland Road.

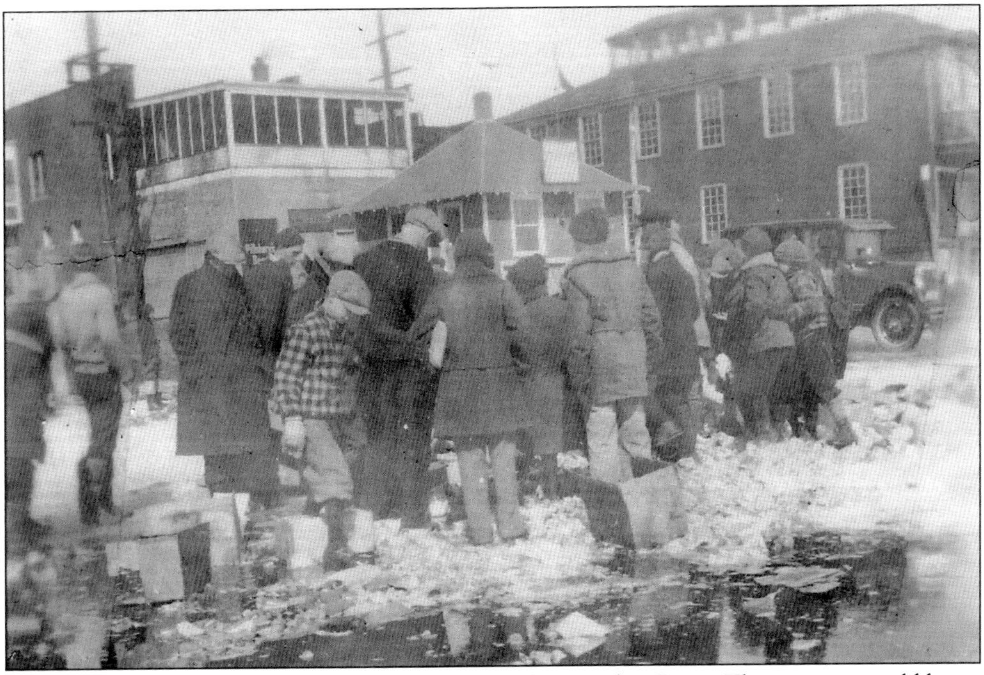

Probation was in full swing in Algonac and along the St. Clair River. The runners would bring the booze anywhere from Algonac to Fair Haven. Algonac was the shortest route. Summer or winter, the sound of boats racing across the North Channel could be heard on any moonless night. Wintertime was the most dangerous. If government agents caught them, a spectacle was made as the bottles were broken in front of them.

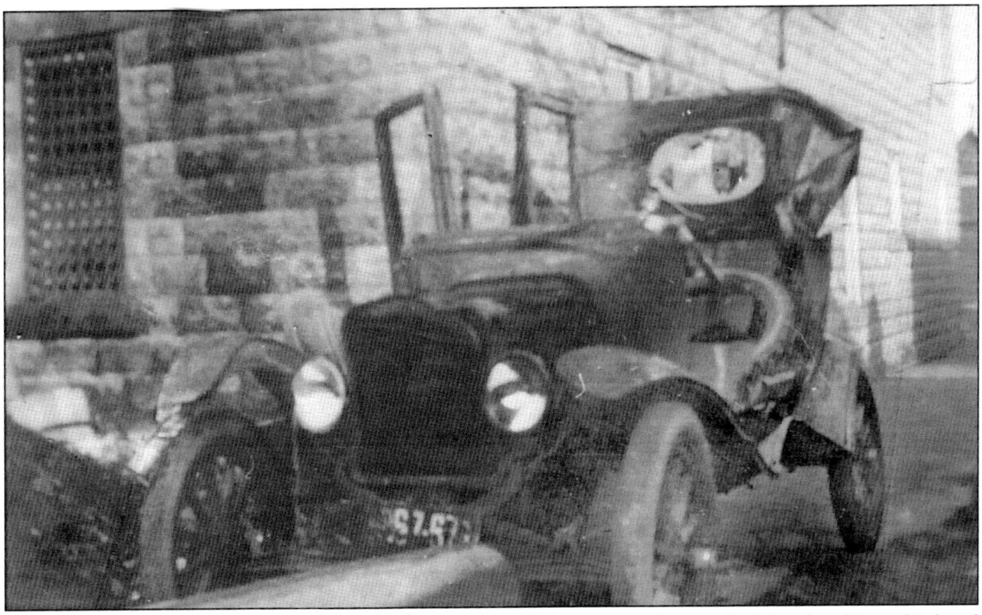

During the winter, rumrunners would drive across the ice from Walpole Island to Russel Island to Algonac. They liked Pointe Du Chene, where there were canals and plenty of brush. This vehicle might have been overloaded or crossed too early or too late in the year, as it appears the driver lost his load and the car, but hopefully not his life.

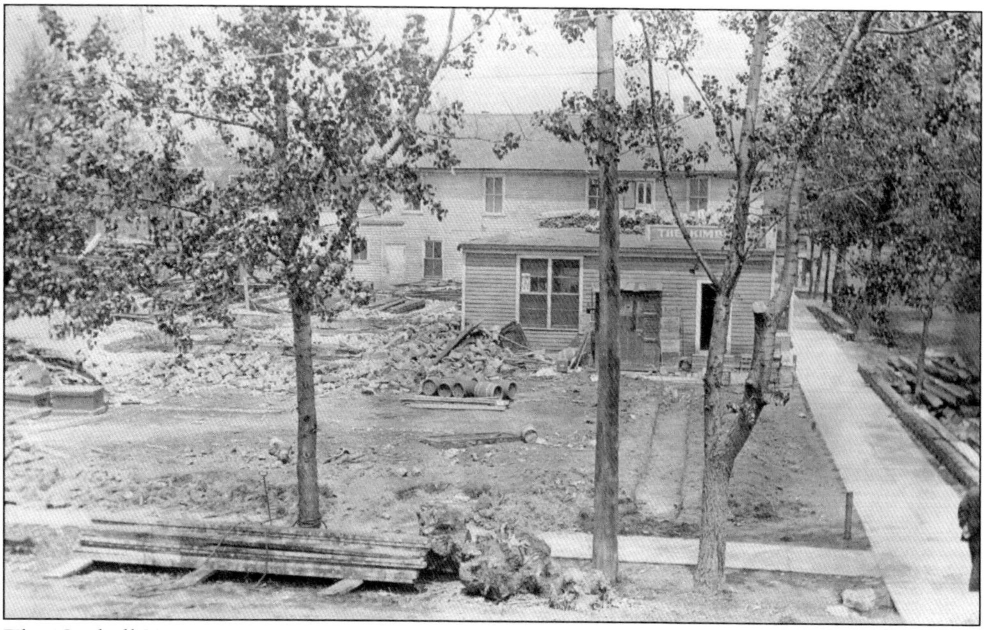

The Kimball House was torn down in 1913. Much of the materials were saved to be used for a new building.

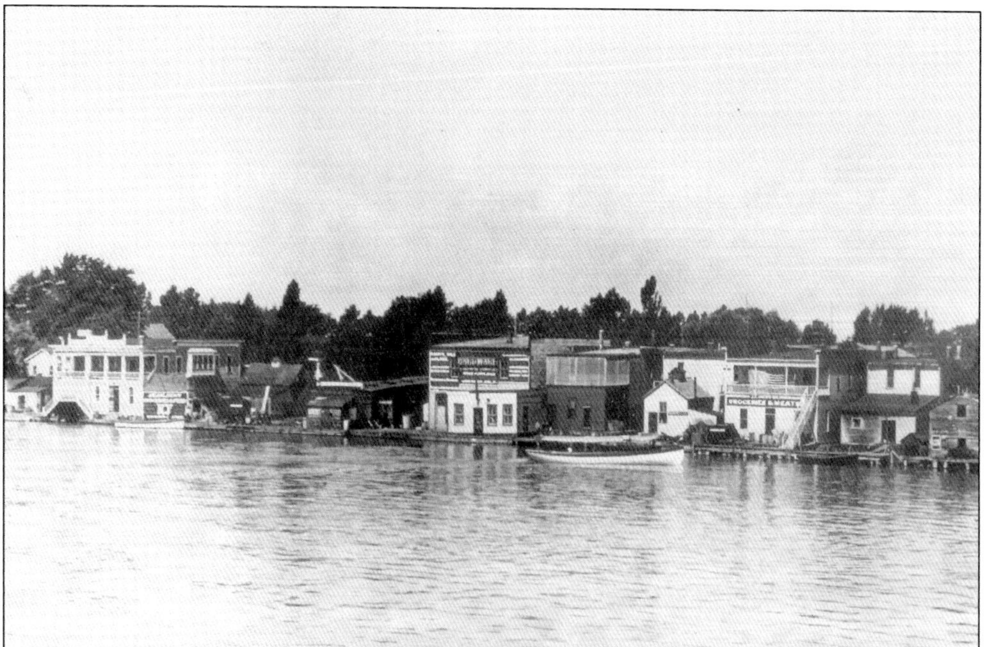

Here is the heart of Algonac as seen from the St. Clair River. Many shoppers would come by boat from Russel, Harsens, and Walpole Islands, as well as areas outside of town, to buy supplies from Gilbert's, Poole's, Gunniss Hardware, and other merchants, then row the loaded boat back home.

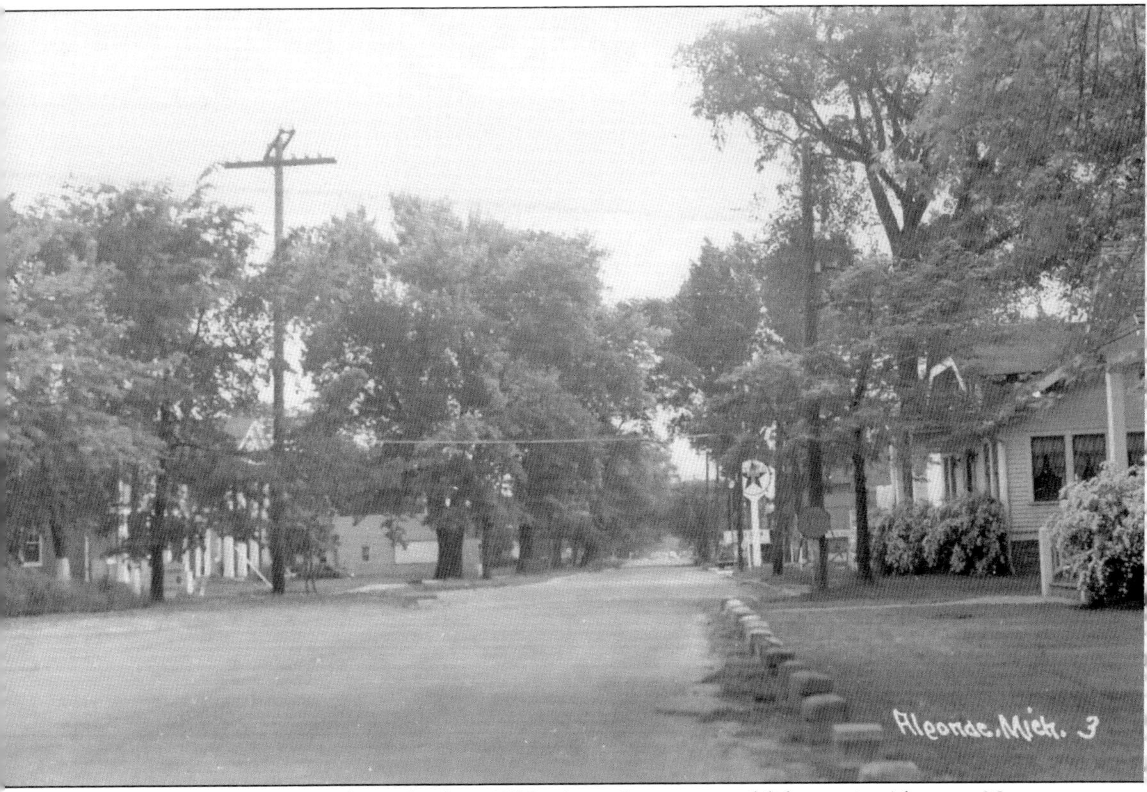

This image of Water Street from the late 1930s shows how tranquil life was in Algonac. Note the stop sign on the pole at right. During this time period, stop signs were painted yellow with glass reflectors spelling "stop."

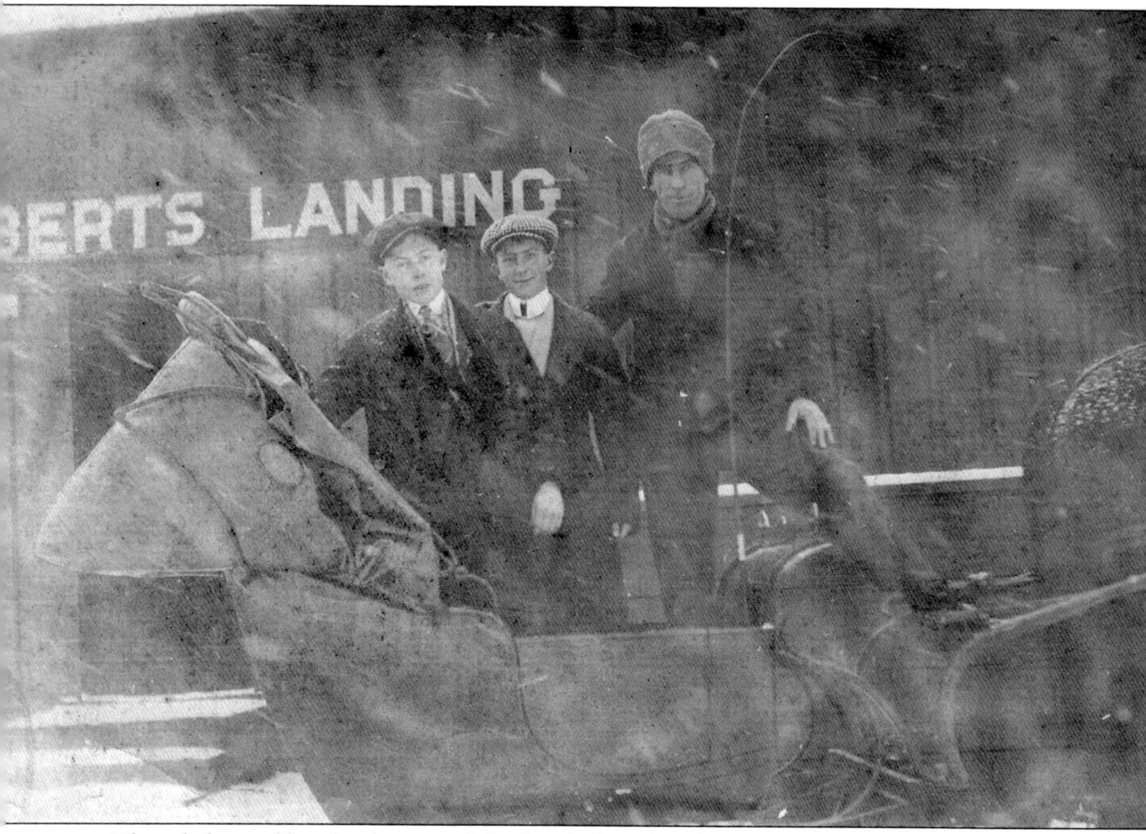

Three lads stand beside a horse and sleigh at Roberts Landing, north of Algonac. Here, there was a small store and a ferry to Canada. The horse and sleigh is set up for winter travel.

Three

Fire Department

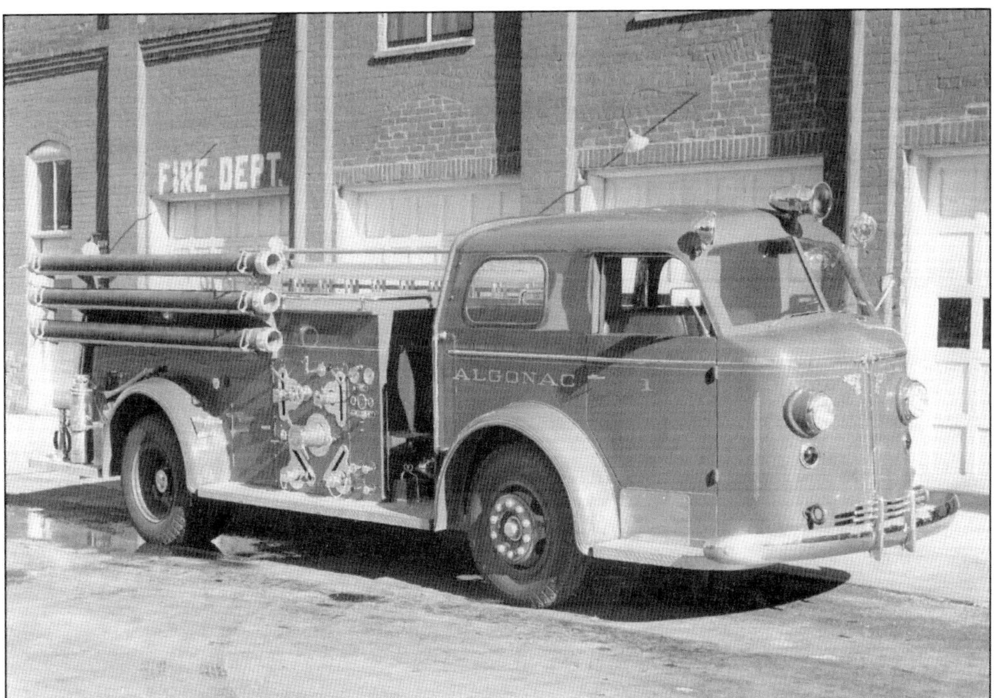

In 1900, the first fire equipment consisted of a two-wheel cart with hand pump and hose, supplemented by a bucket brigade.

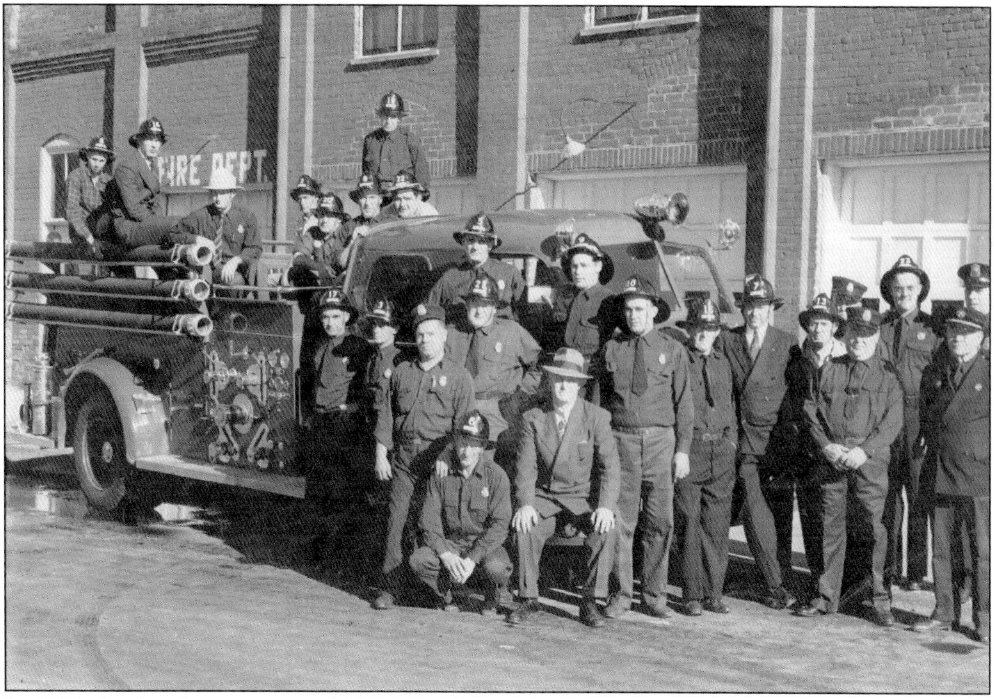

In 1899, the fire department and the city jail moved to a new site on Michigan Street where the village had exchanged land with William Hodgson.

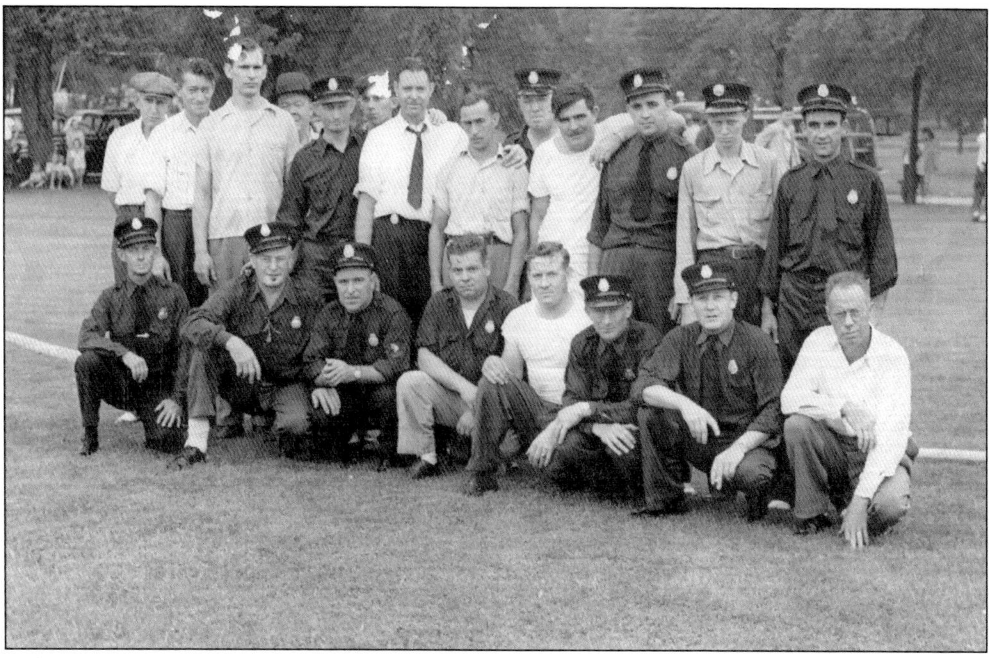

Volunteers of the Algonac Fire Department are pictured here in 1948. Most of the volunteer firefighters were returning World War II veterans.

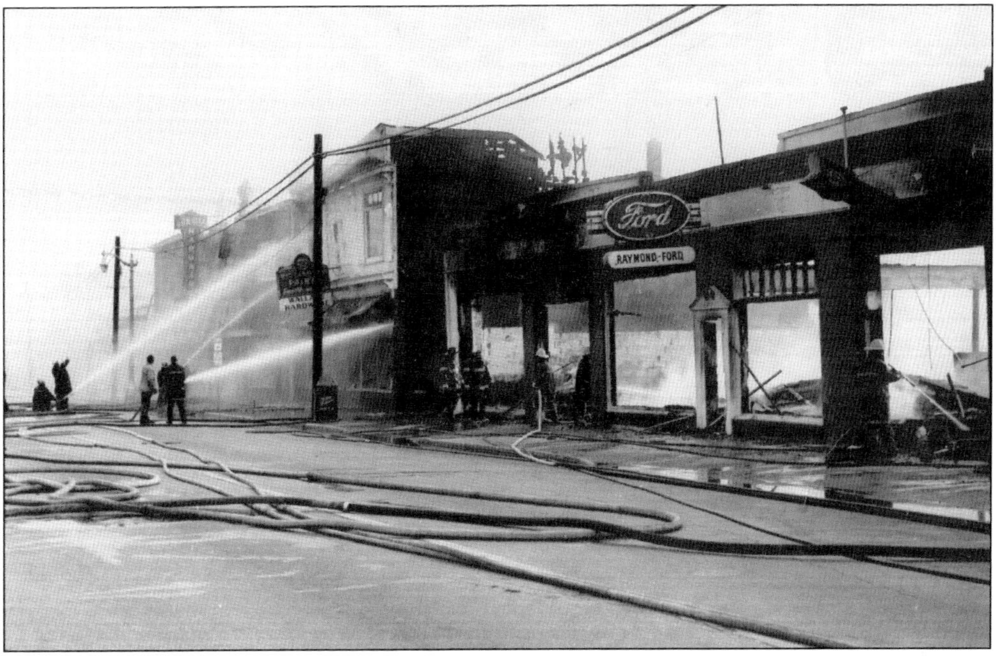

During the mid-1960s, the Algonac Volunteer Fire Department battled the largest fire of its time. An employee of the Ford dealer took his girlfriend on a date in a dealership-owned car and ran into a ditch on the way home. After returning to the garage, he saw the dents and scratches on the car and set the dealership on fire to cover up the damage.

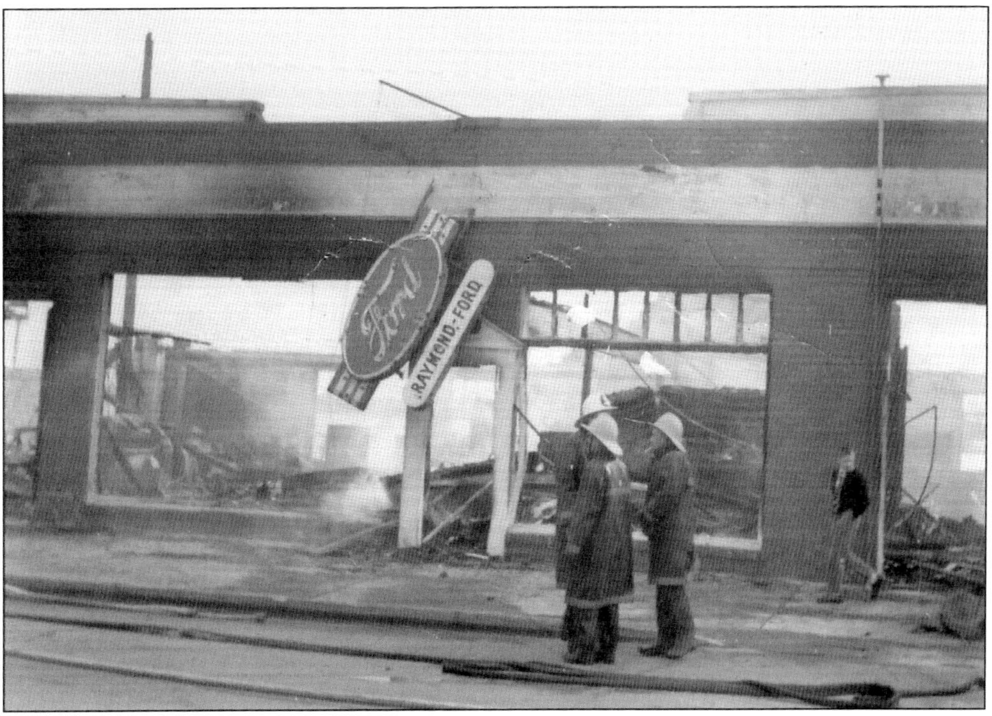

The fire destroyed not only the Ford dealer but also Wallace Hardware and damaged the Party store and Gunniss Hardware.

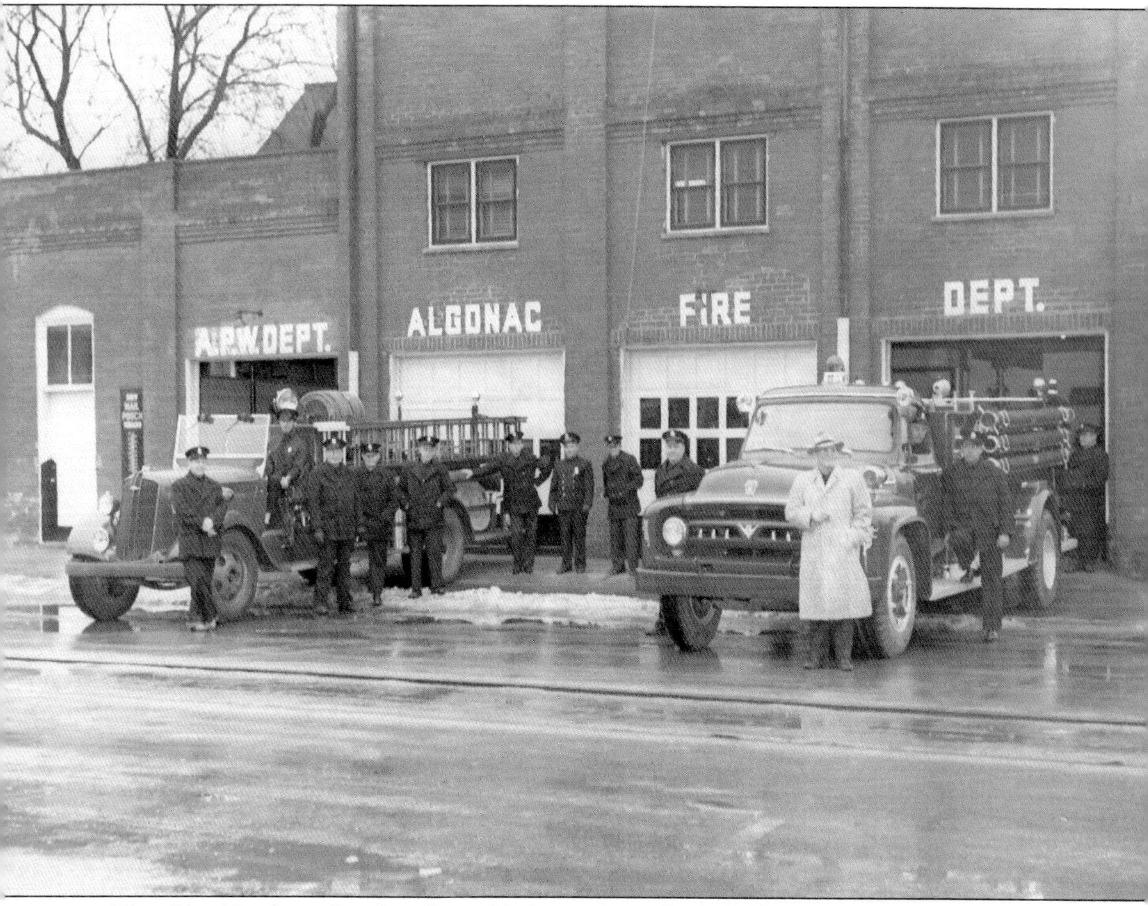

The old jail by the railroad tracks on Michigan Street had a bell on top, and whenever there was a fire, everyone gathered at the jailhouse to find out where the fire was. When four buildings, including Gunniss Hardware, burned in 1900, water was pumped from the steamer *Mary*, docked at the foot of Fruit Street.

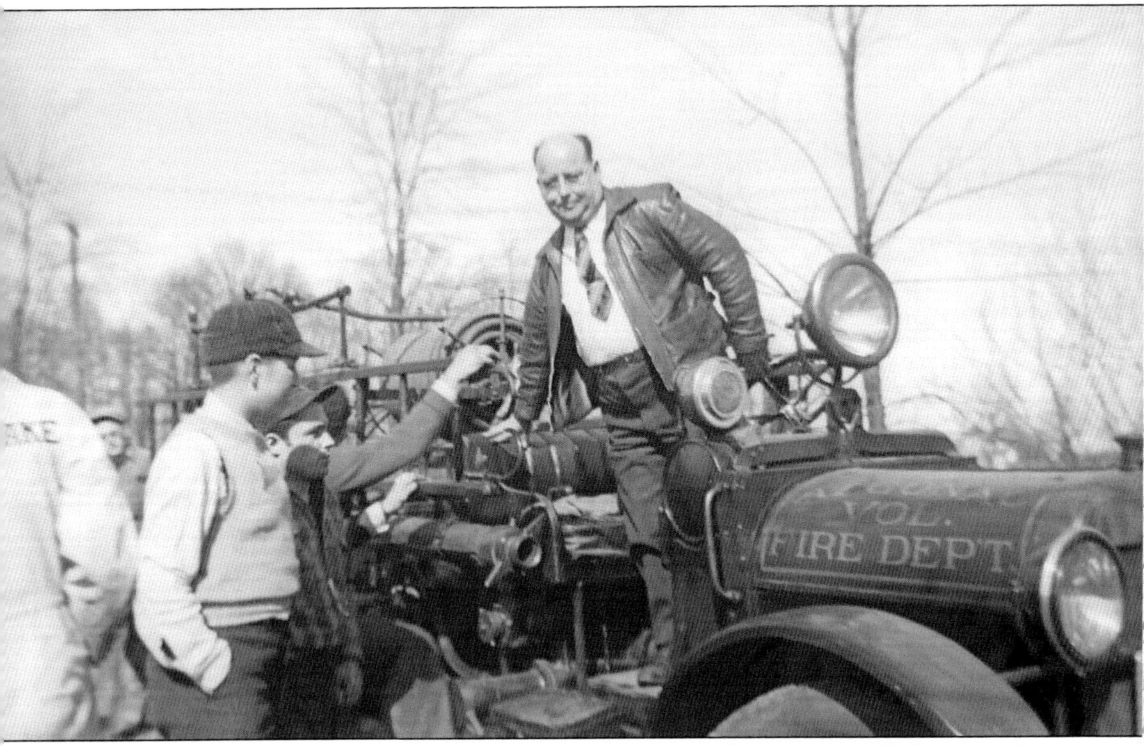

Al Robbins is seen getting off the fire truck after a run. A merchant in town, Robbins rarely missed a fire. The township of Clay was very fortunate to have the Algonac Fire Department dedicating itself to the Goodfellows, who worked unselfishly and continuously for the betterment of the community.

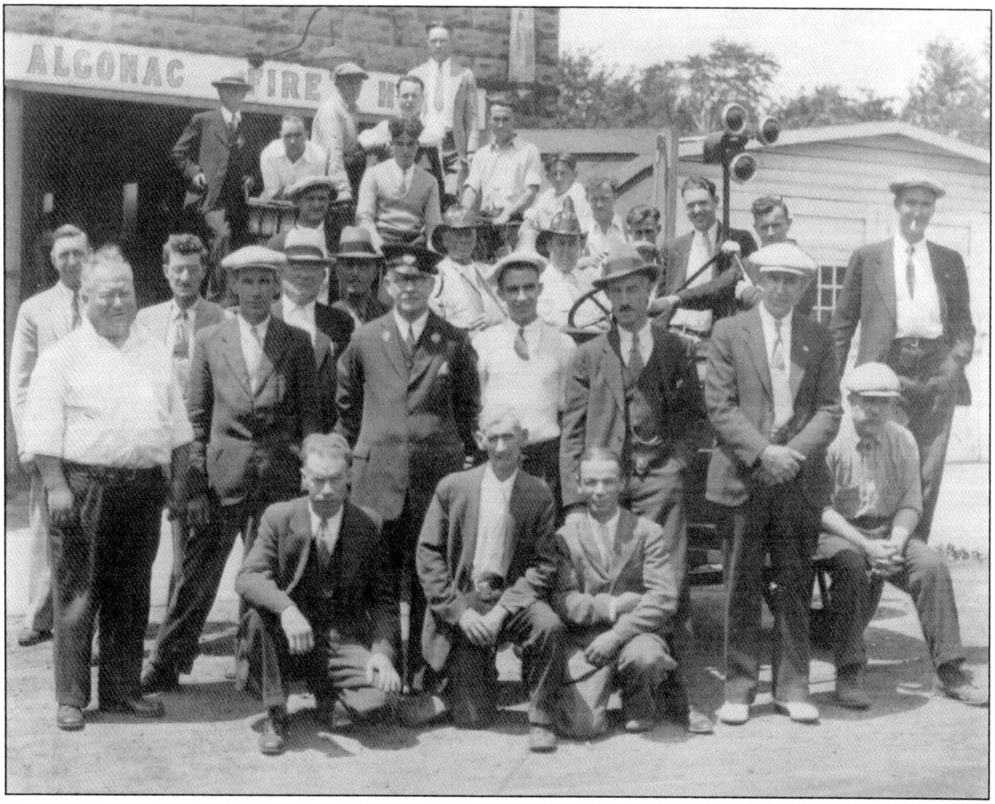

Pictured here in the 1920s, the Algonac Volunteer Fire Department station was originally the Detroit Urban Railway passenger and freight depot.

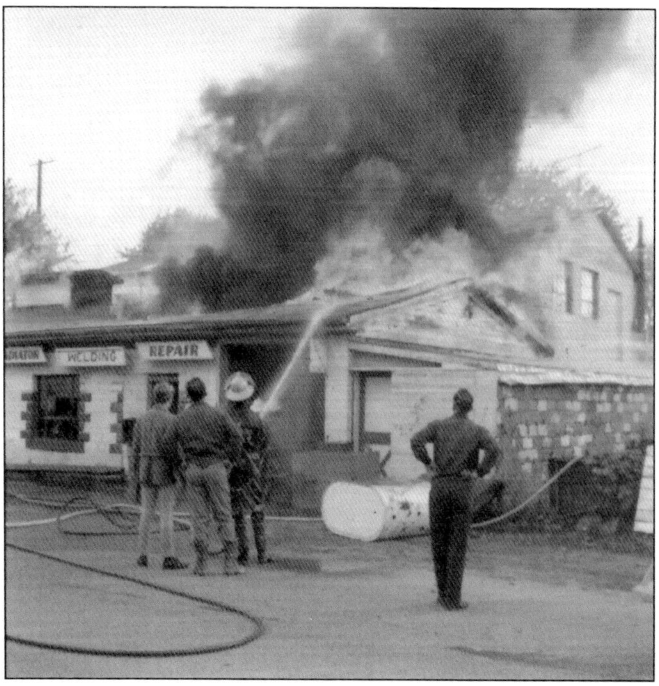

The Algonac Volunteer Fire Department brigade is seen putting out another fire. In the early 1900s, the bucket brigade would try to extinguish a fire, generally without success. Finally, a few water mains were laid, a water works was built, and a fire whistle was installed. No one could hear the whistle, however. William Chapman, who had helped organize the fire department, petitioned the council to install a new whistle that was considerably louder than the original.

Four

Schools and Churches

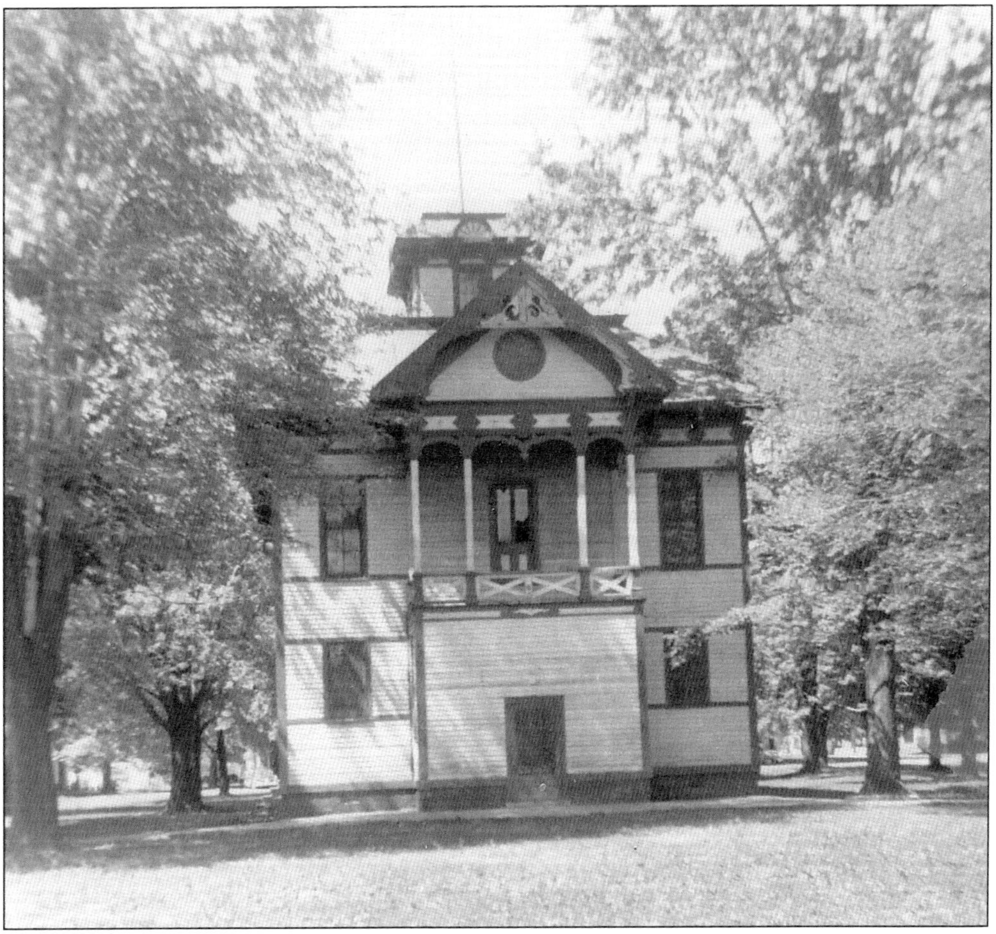

The old town hall, built between 1874 and 1875, was sold to Joe Polito for $125 with the promise to remove it from the property within 30 days.

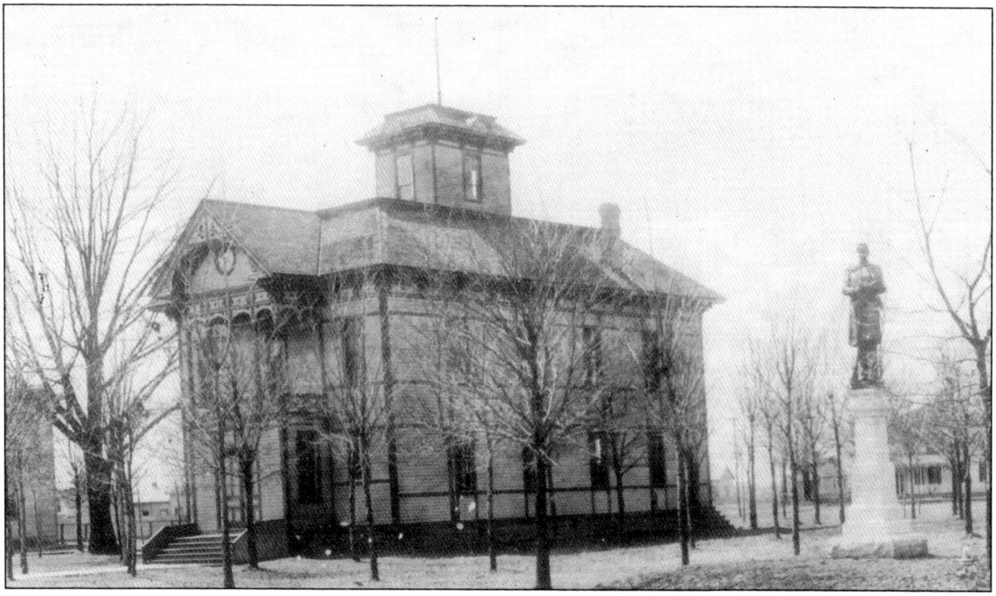

On July 7, 1905, the Soldiers and Sailors Monument was erected on the southwest corner of Washington and Smith Streets. It is presently located in the north end of Algonac City Park, next to the Algonac-Clay Historical Society Museum.

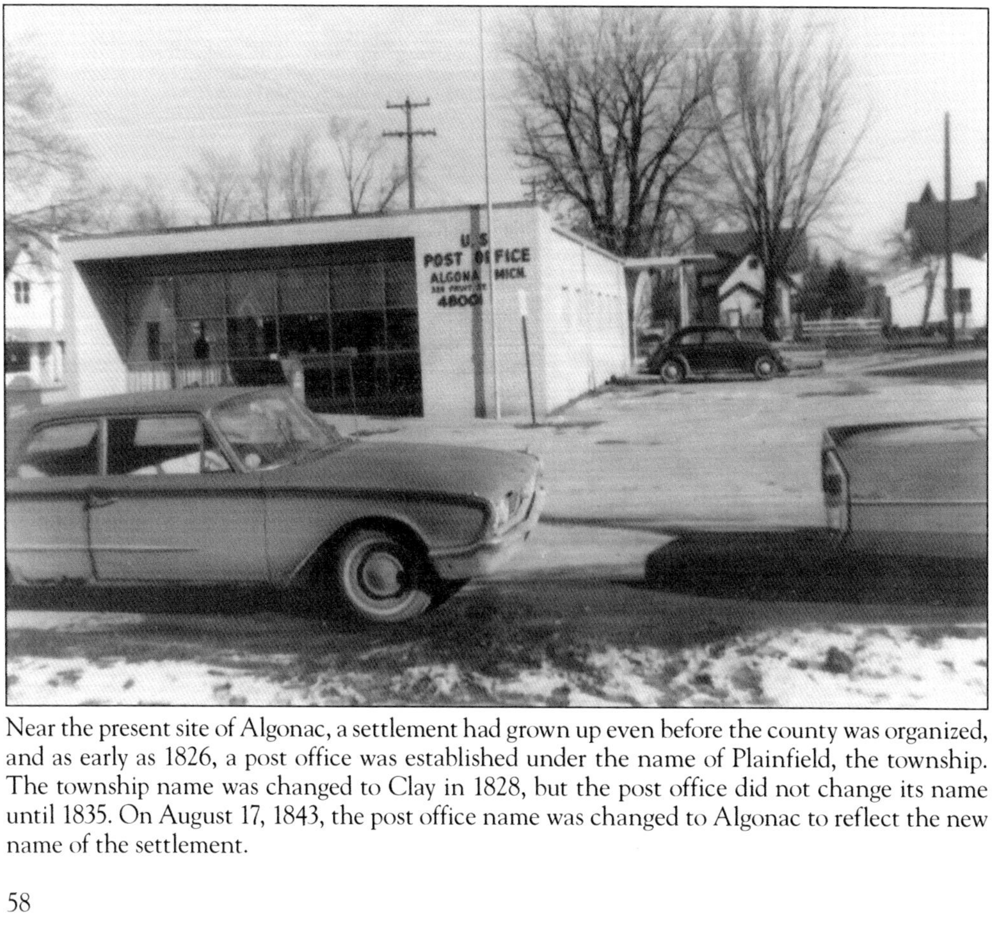

Near the present site of Algonac, a settlement had grown up even before the county was organized, and as early as 1826, a post office was established under the name of Plainfield, the township. The township name was changed to Clay in 1828, but the post office did not change its name until 1835. On August 17, 1843, the post office name was changed to Algonac to reflect the new name of the settlement.

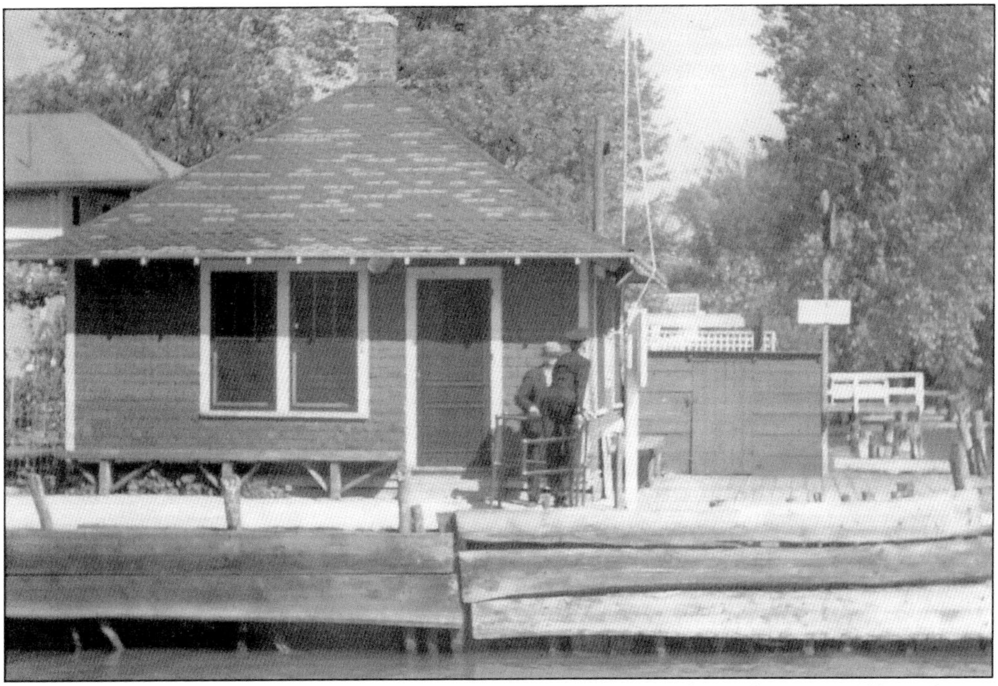

Pictured here is the original customs office based in Algonac in the early 1930s. All employees were part-time because the water would freeze over in the winter.

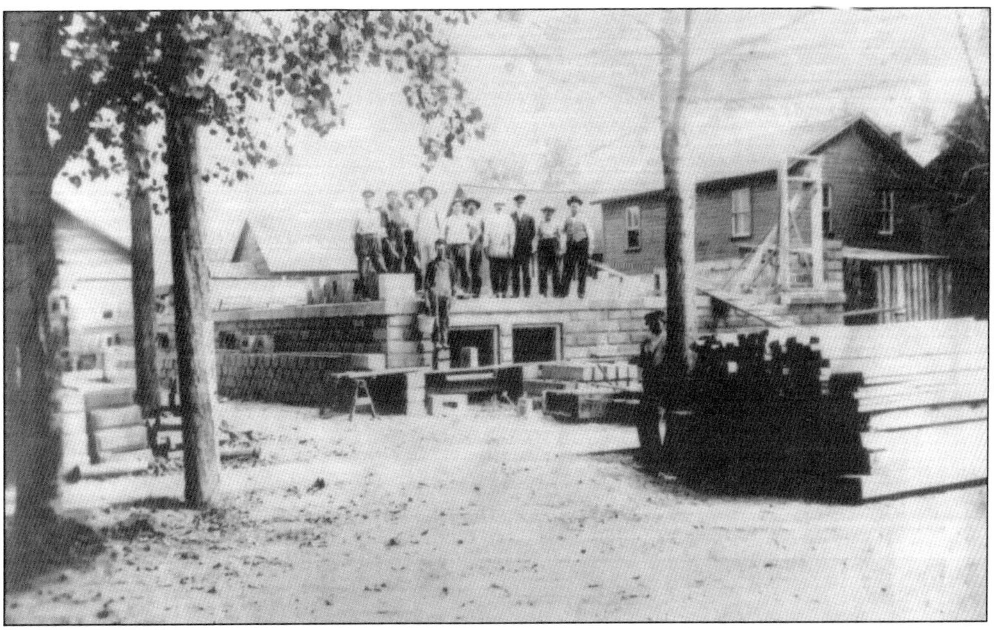

This image shows construction of the Independent Order of Odd Fellows Hall in 1908. Dancing had become so popular in Algonac that the upstairs of the hall was converted into a dance floor.

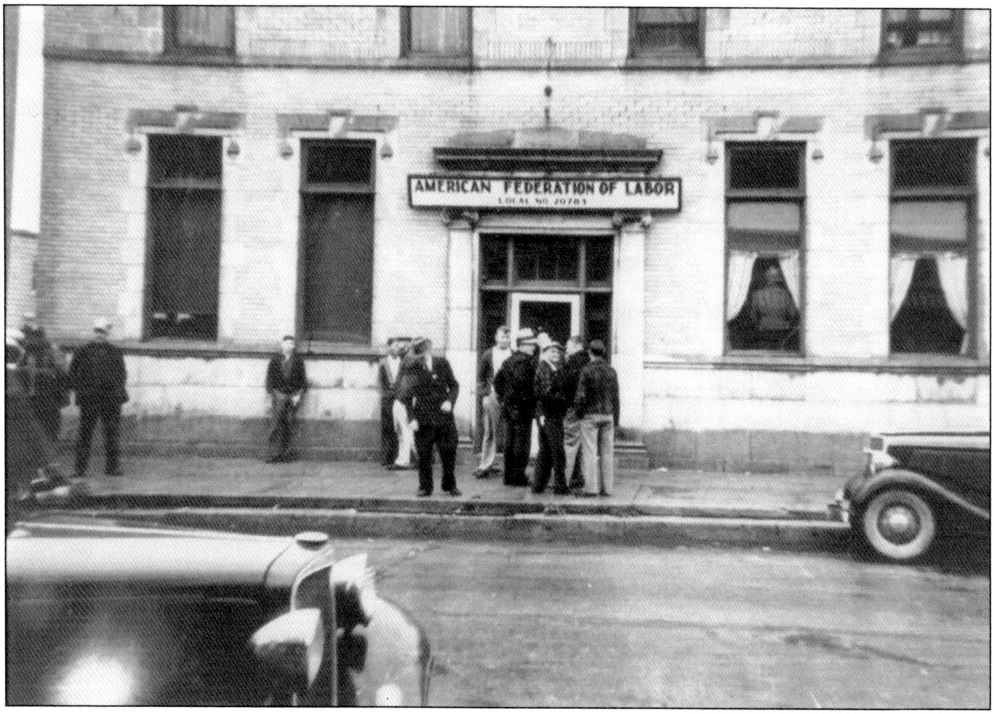

The American Federation of Labor, pictured here in the 1930s, was created by workers from the Chris-Craft factory. The workers would meet on the second of the old National Bank building, which eventually became Miles Bar.

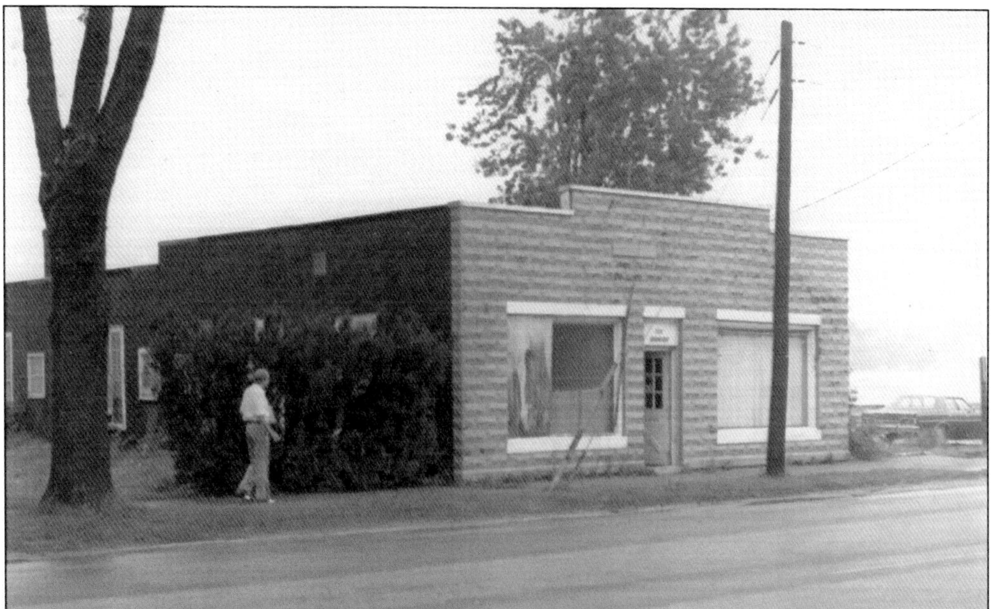

The *Algonac Courier* was established in 1894. The paper was started by J.E. Lumley and C.A. Laydon. Lumley, who was also the superintendent of schools, would eventually buy out his partner and conduct the paper by himself. After several owners, the paper was called many names, such as the Courier Publishing Company, the Speed Printing Company, and the Algonac Press.

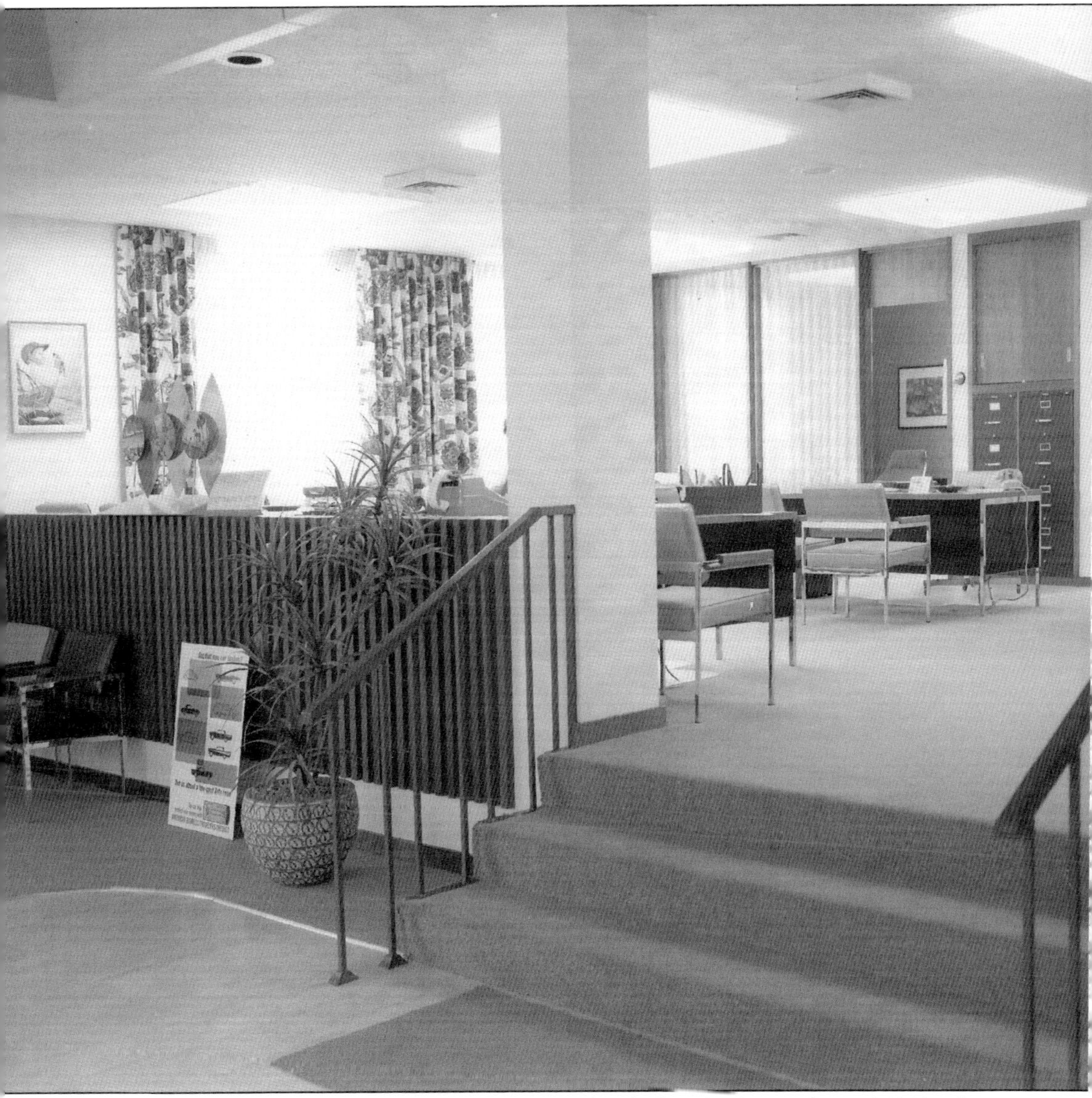

When the Algonac Savings Bank expansion was completed after the fire in the mid-1960s, the lobby was lowered to ground level, and the teller line was moved to the north side of the building. Note the sign on the half wall advertising a 10 percent discount on Canadian currency.

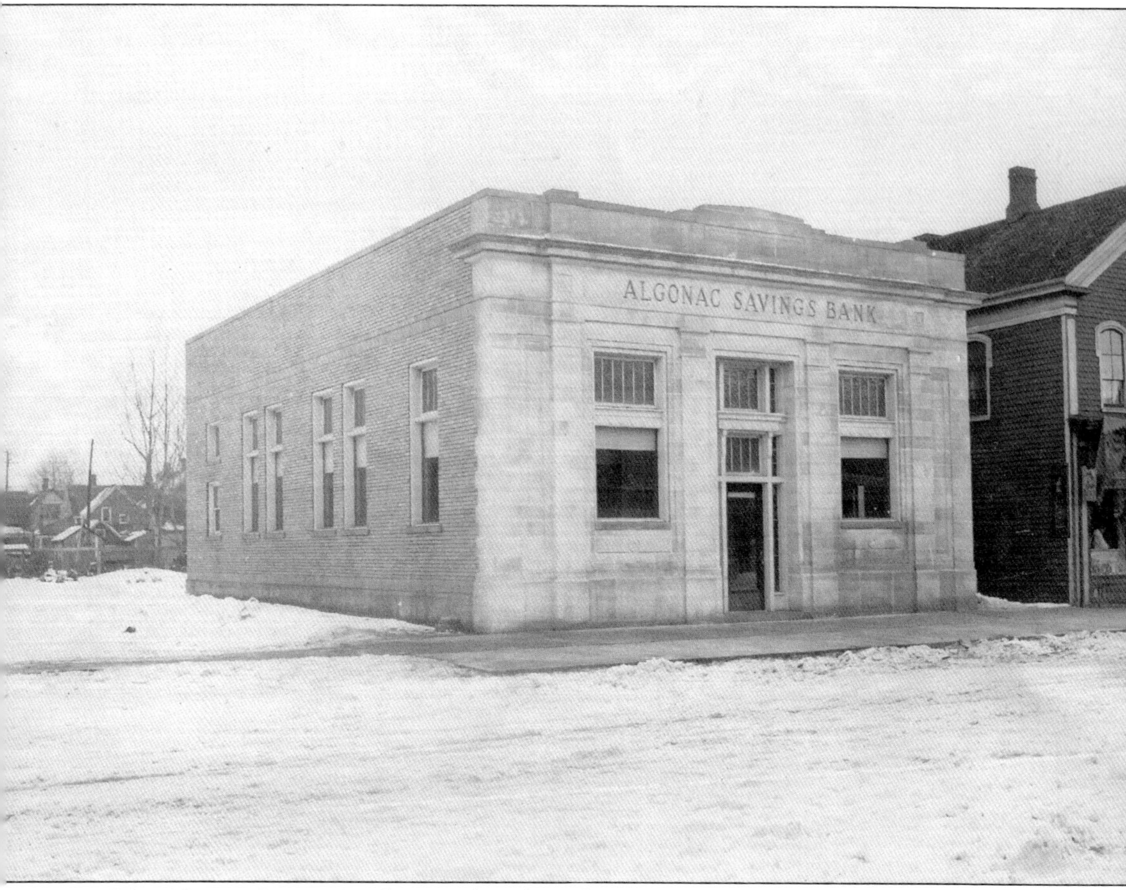

The Algonac Savings Bank opened its doors for business on April 18, 1912. It expanded in the 1920s, and after the bowling alley and the Classik Theater burned down, the bank expanded yet again and installed a drive-through window.

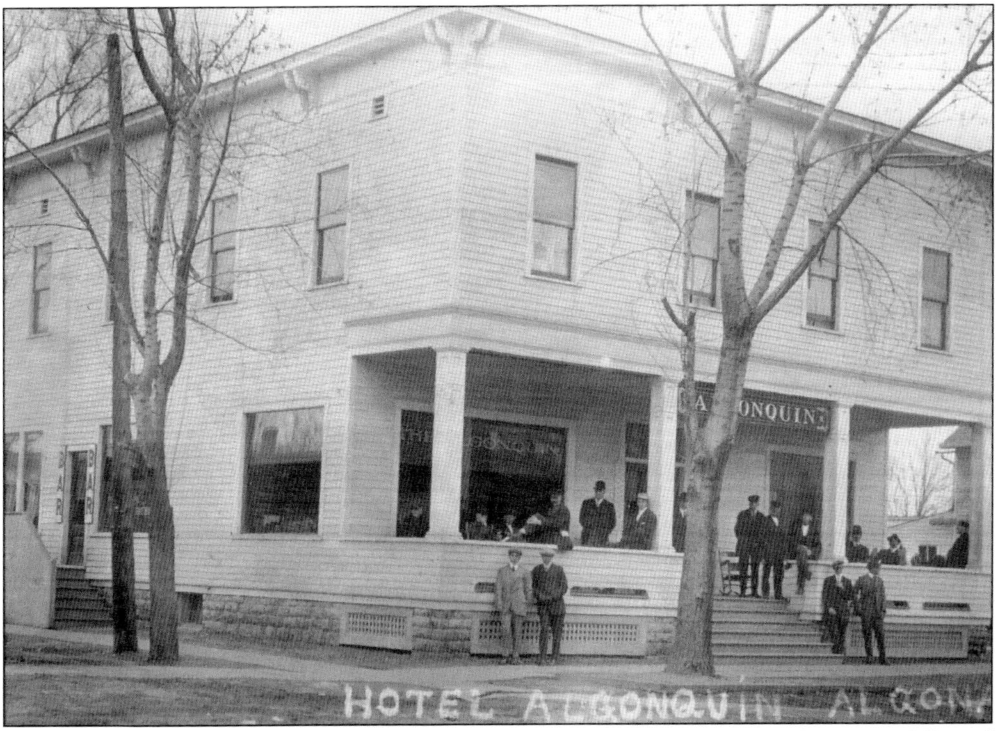

The Algonquin Hotel replaced the Kimball House in 1913. Gus Harsen was the owner, followed by Max Quimet and Robert G. Hillen. This site would later become the location of the First National Bank.

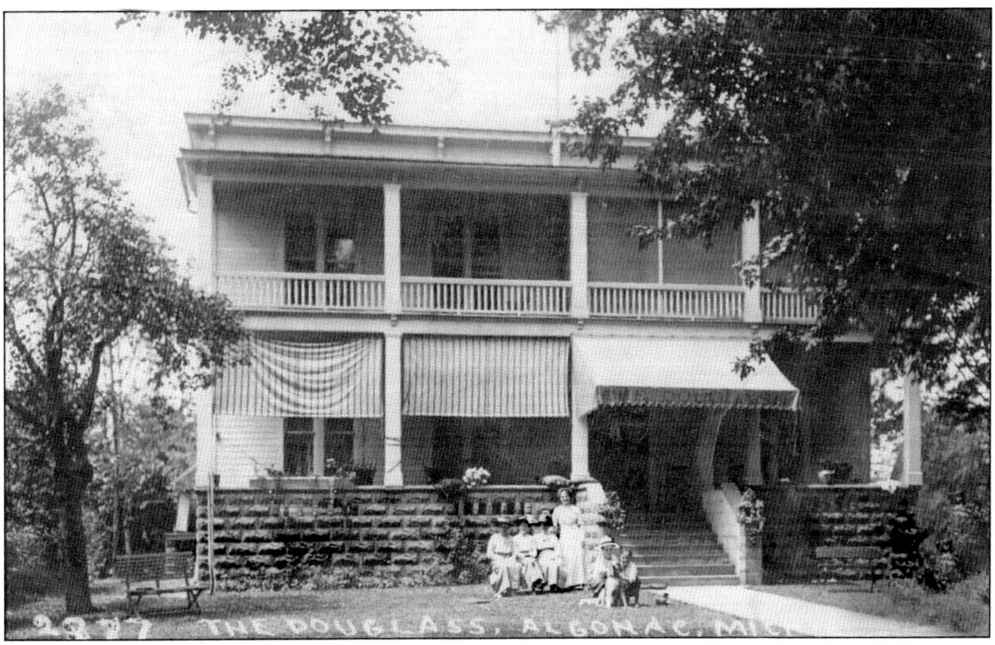

The Douglass House, pictured here in the early 1890s, was used as a hotel and then as a boardinghouse. Many of the hotels during this time would ultimately become boardinghouses after the Detroit Urban Railway was dissolved.

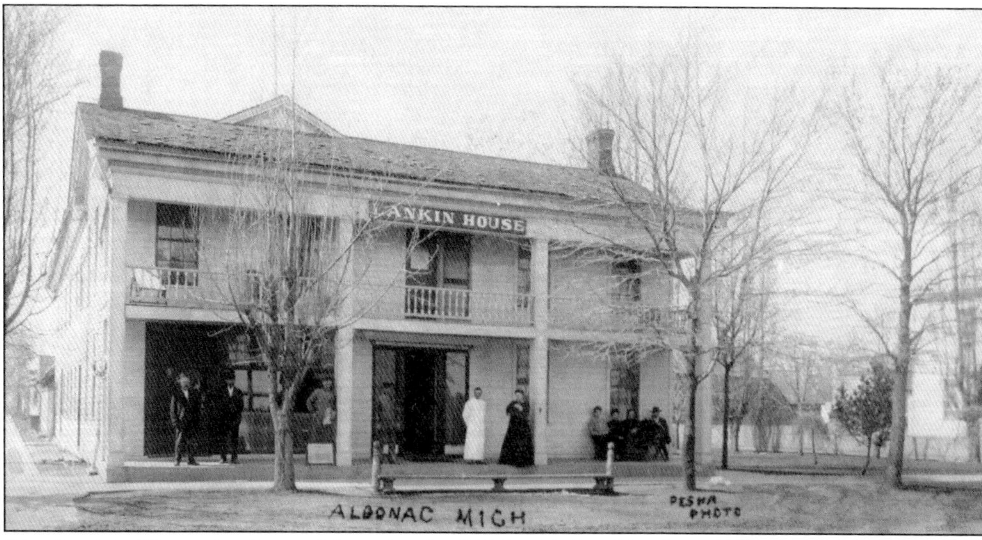

The Lankin House is pictured here in the 1900s. Michael Jackson, who came to Algonac in 1836, ran the Jackson House on the corner of Water and Summer Streets until his death in 1883. It would later become the Riverview Hotel, Johnson House, Parker House, Lankin House, and Sherwood Hotel.

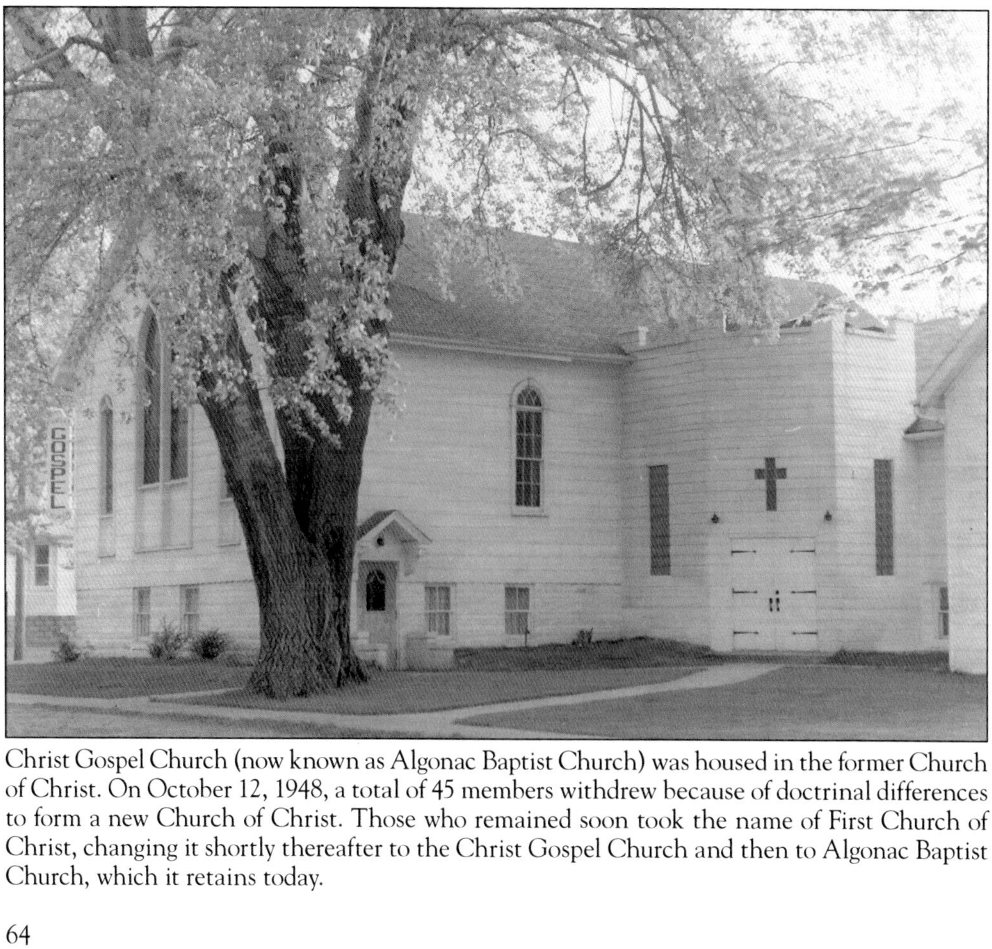

Christ Gospel Church (now known as Algonac Baptist Church) was housed in the former Church of Christ. On October 12, 1948, a total of 45 members withdrew because of doctrinal differences to form a new Church of Christ. Those who remained soon took the name of First Church of Christ, changing it shortly thereafter to the Christ Gospel Church and then to Algonac Baptist Church, which it retains today.

The Church of Christ traces its history back to 1872 when an itinerant preacher of the Restoration Movement organized a congregation in Algonac. In 1914, preacher Harry Kellogg moved the church to its present location on the northwest corner of Washington and Summer Streets.

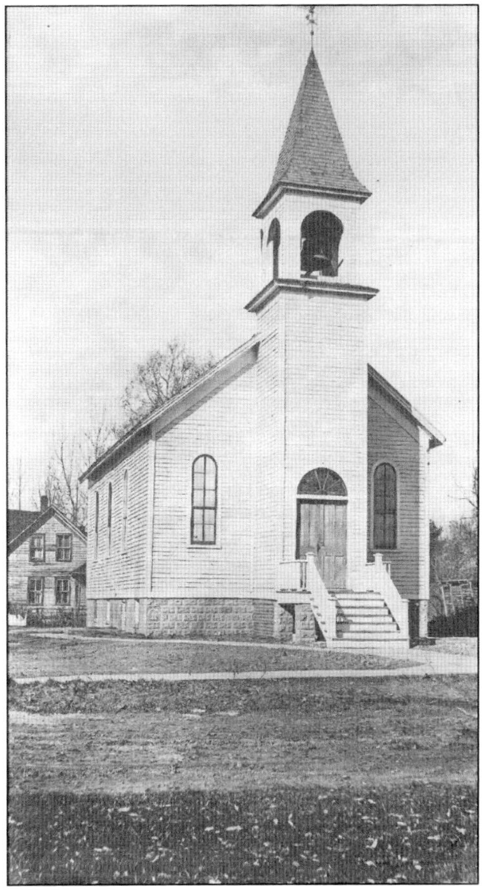

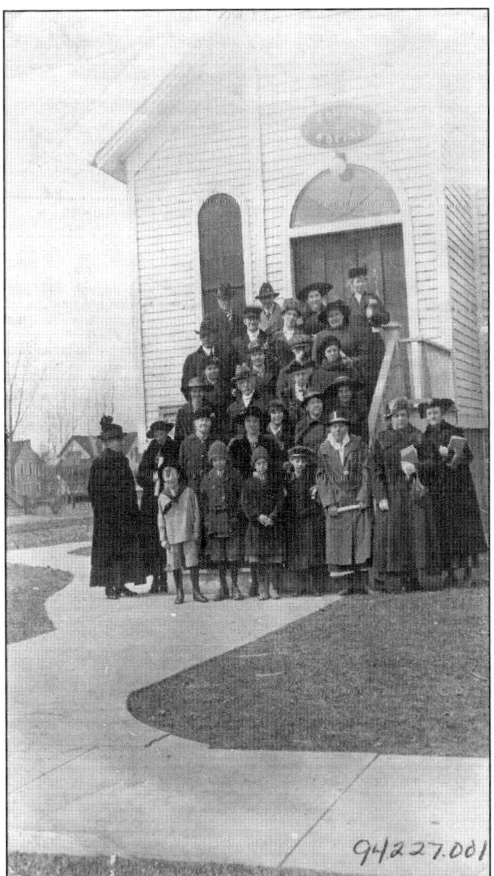

Reverend Haydon from the Church of Christ was a pastor from 1916 to 1926, during which time a parsonage was built. In 1928, the first wing was added to make room for more Sunday school facilities.

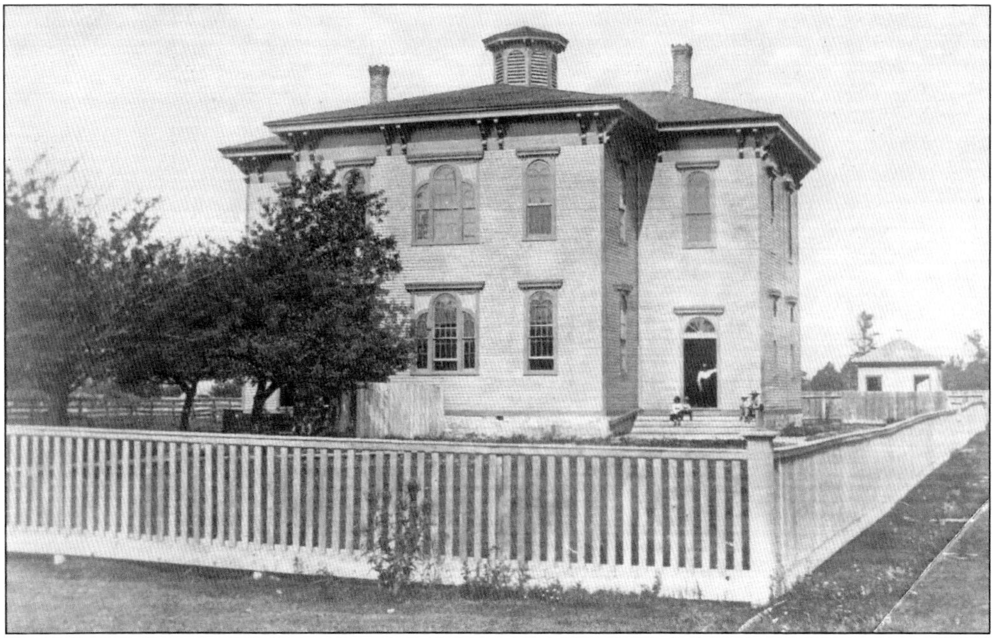

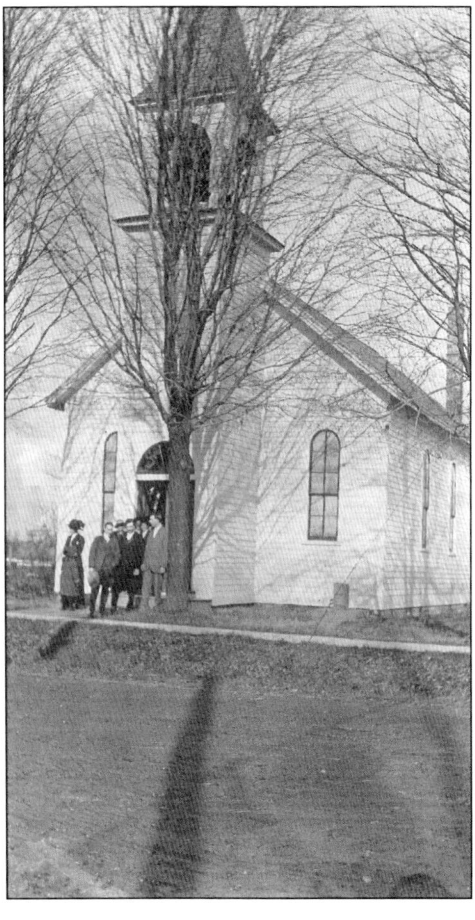

This is an 1880s photograph of the Union School (also called the Algonac Wooden School). Peter F. Brakeman opened the first school in Algonac in the winter of 1827–1828. The "Painted Red" school at 600 Mill Street had stumps for the foundation, wide boards for flooring, and a woodstove for heat. The "Painted White" school was the second school to be built and was located at 1011 Michigan Street. Both schools were replaced by the Union School around 1860.

The Church of Christ is pictured here in the 1920s when it was located at the corner of Market and Smith Streets. Later, the church moved to Washington and Summer Streets, where it was built on a basement foundation for more room.

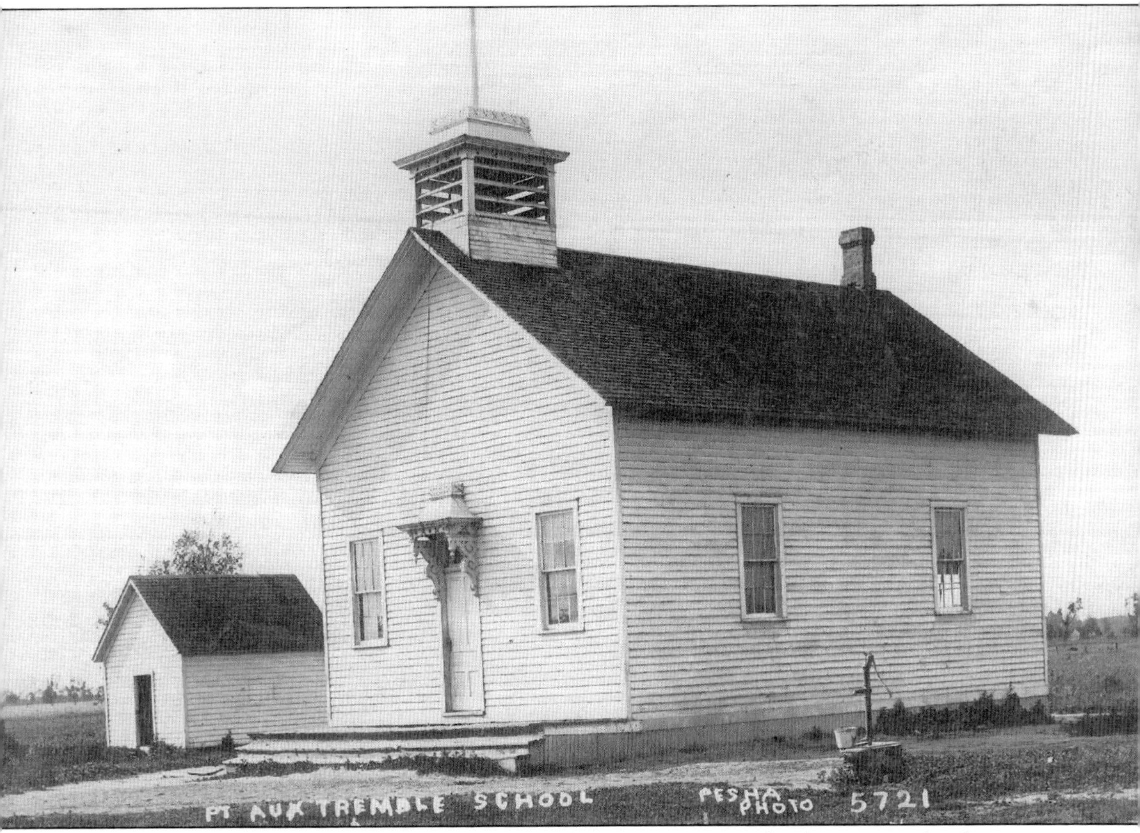

The Pointe Tremble Elementary School is pictured here in 1900. In 1954, three new schools were built in Fair Haven, Pointe Tremble, and Algonac. The school district purchased 80 acres of land on Taft and Ainsworth Roads, adjacent to the Pointe Tremble Elementary School. In 1964, the high school was moved to a new building on the acquired acreage. The vacated high school was then designated as the Gilbert Junior High School.

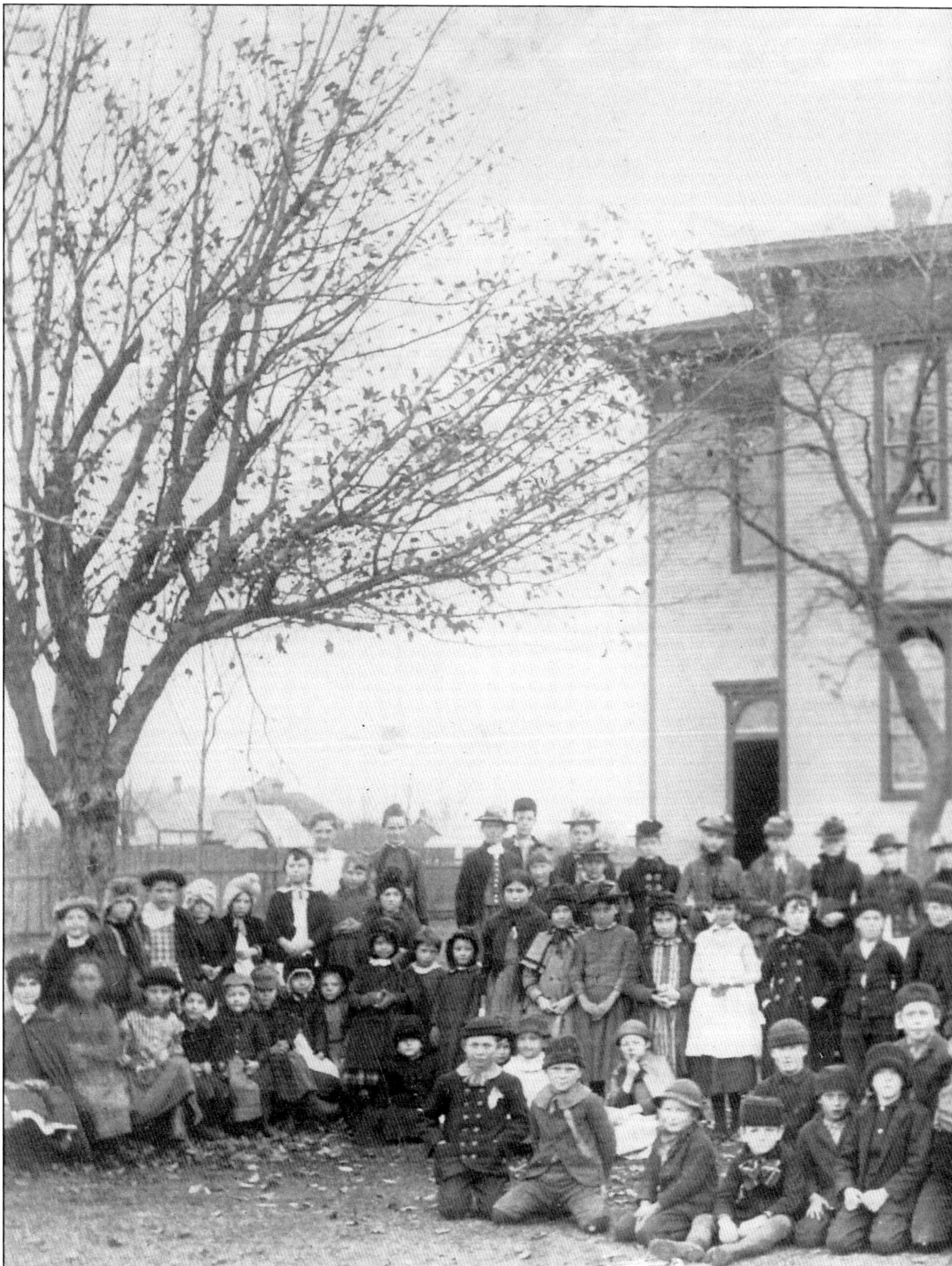

A group of students from kindergarten to 12th grade have gathered for a photograph in front of the Union School in 1890. In the 1880s, the school year was eight months long. The salary was $40 for a male teacher and $20 for a female teacher. Often, evening classes in ciphering,

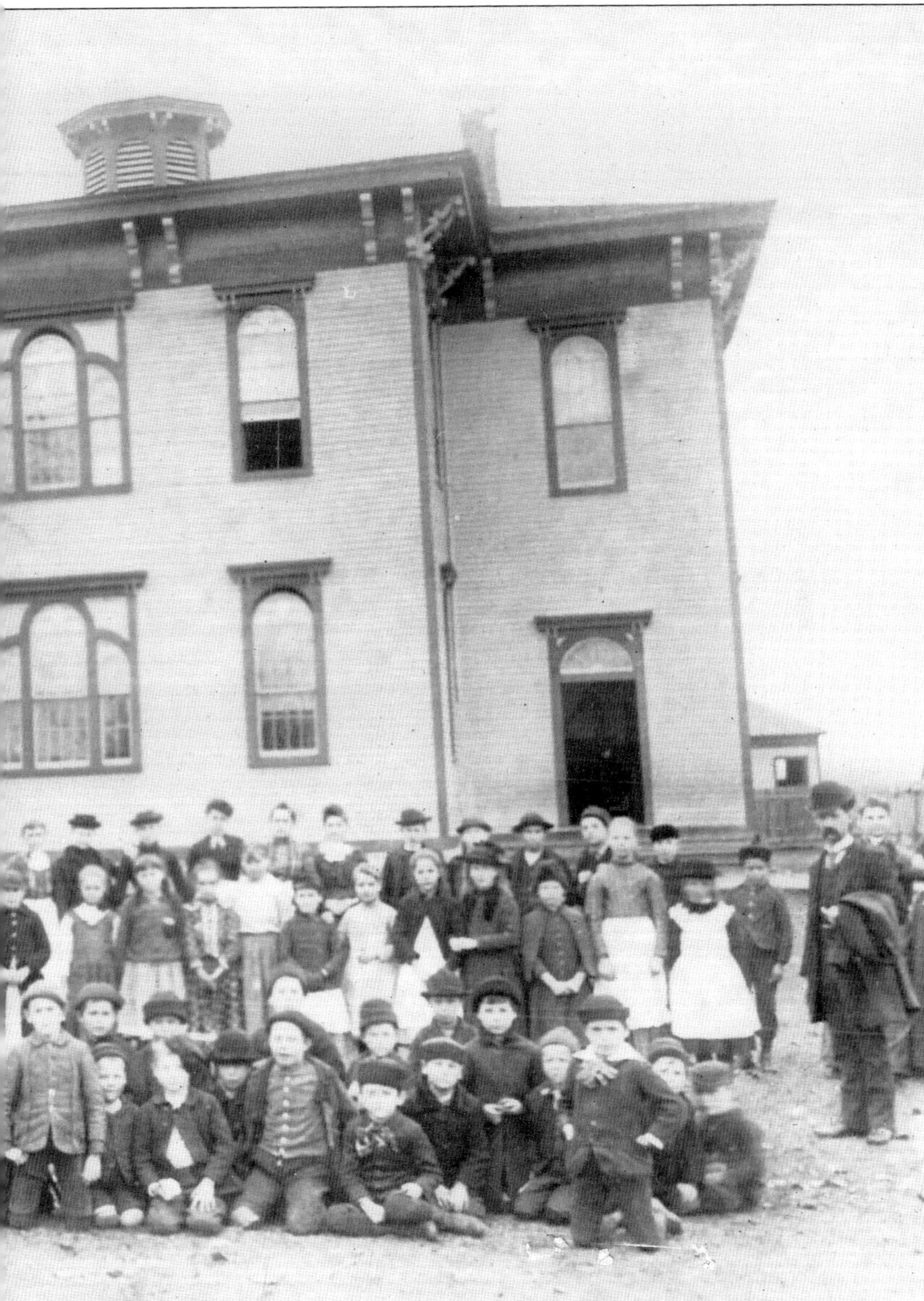

penmanship, and reading were held for adults. When the first graduation was held in 1890, the graduates were Russel Hemenger, Eliza McComb, Katie Cartwright, Lillian Doswell, and Grace Hamet. By 1892, the graduating class had doubled to 10 students.

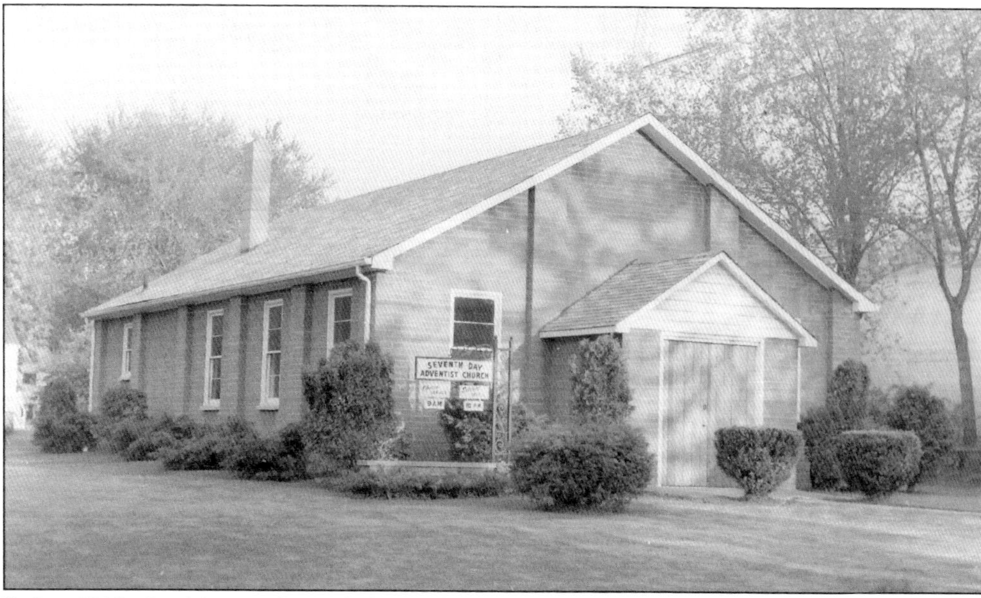

Before 1948, the Algonac Seventh Day Adventist Church met in Starville. The Starville M.E. Church was a branch of the Sabbath School and an affiliate of the Port Huron Seventh Day Adventist Church. After formal organization under the guidance of pastor H. Hosford at Starville, the congregation met in public buildings and homes while the Algonac church was being built on Market Street. It was ready for occupancy in 1957, with pastor James Cunningham helping in the completion.

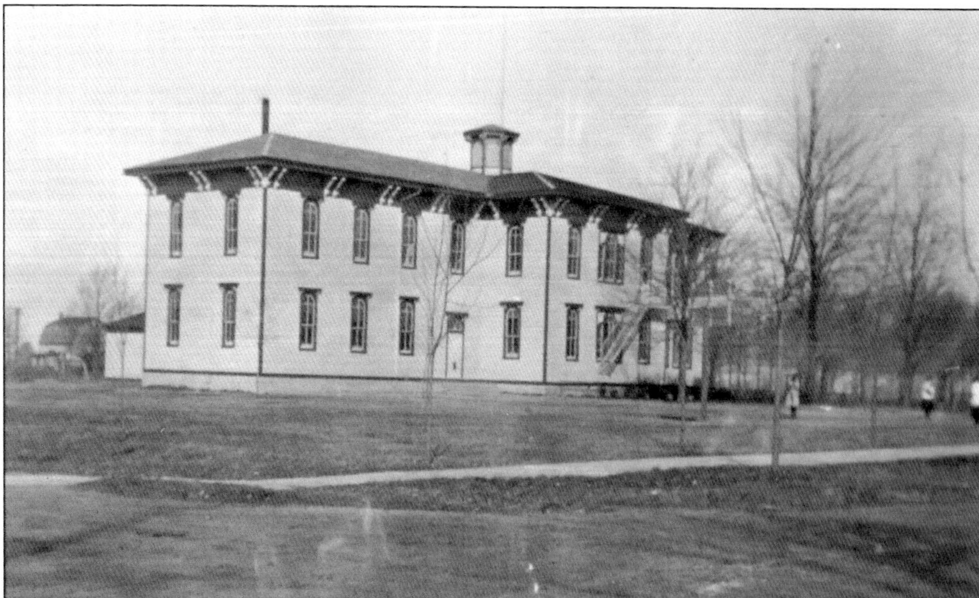

The Algonac School is shown here as it appeared in the 1890s. Effective August 15, 1913, every child under the age of 16 in the state of Michigan was required to attend school or maintain regular employment, without regard as to whether he or she had passed eighth grade. Prior to this time, children who had satisfactorily passed eighth grade were exempt from the provisions of the law, regardless of age.

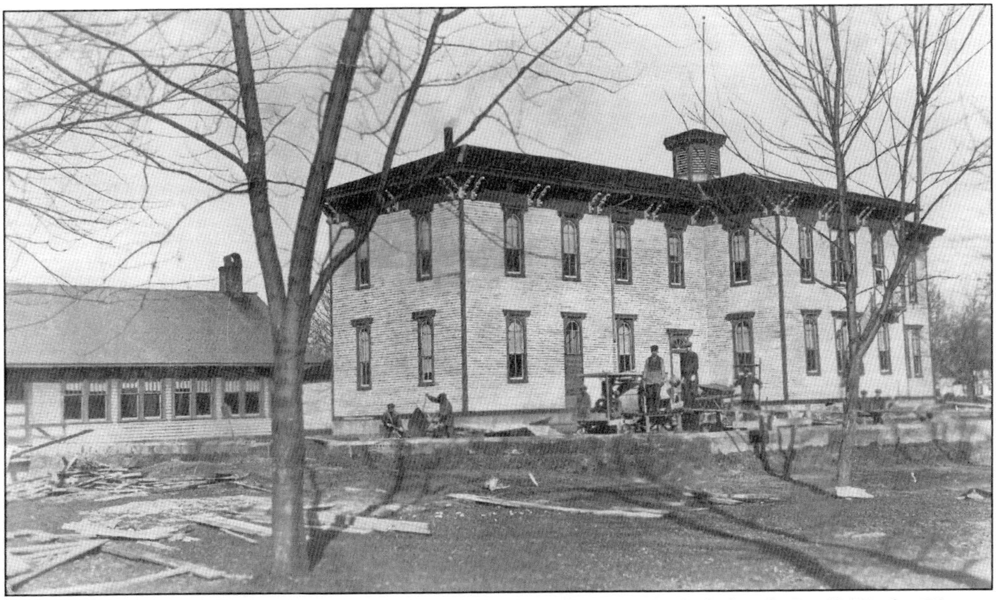

In 1923, workers laid the cornerstone for the new Algonac High School. In 1927, the Union School (pictured here) was replaced by a new brick building. This school included kindergarten through 12th grade. The school was built at a cost of $178,000. In 1941, the Starville School was encouraged to send students to Algonac High School. In 1942, the Algonac School Board voted to continue the practice of taking students from surrounding districts without tuition as long as overcrowding did not become an issue.

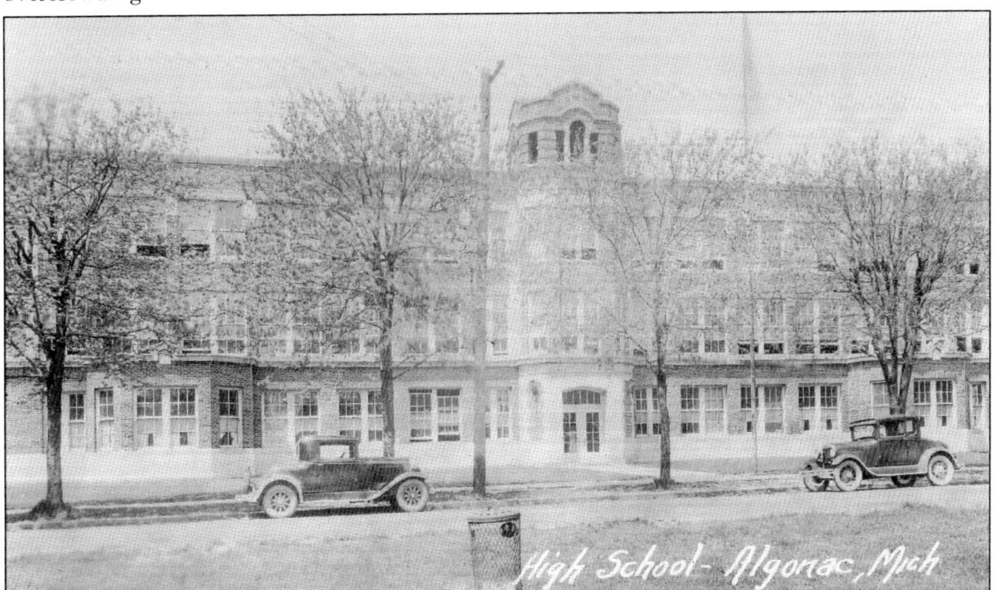

This is a photograph of Algonac High School from the 1930s. On January 12, 1948, the Algonac School Board considered the purchase of a bus to transport students who lived outside a one-mile radius to and from school. In 1952, the Algonac School District was enlarged through the annexation of the Harsens Island, Pointe Tremble, Swartout, and Fair Haven and became the Algonac Community School District.

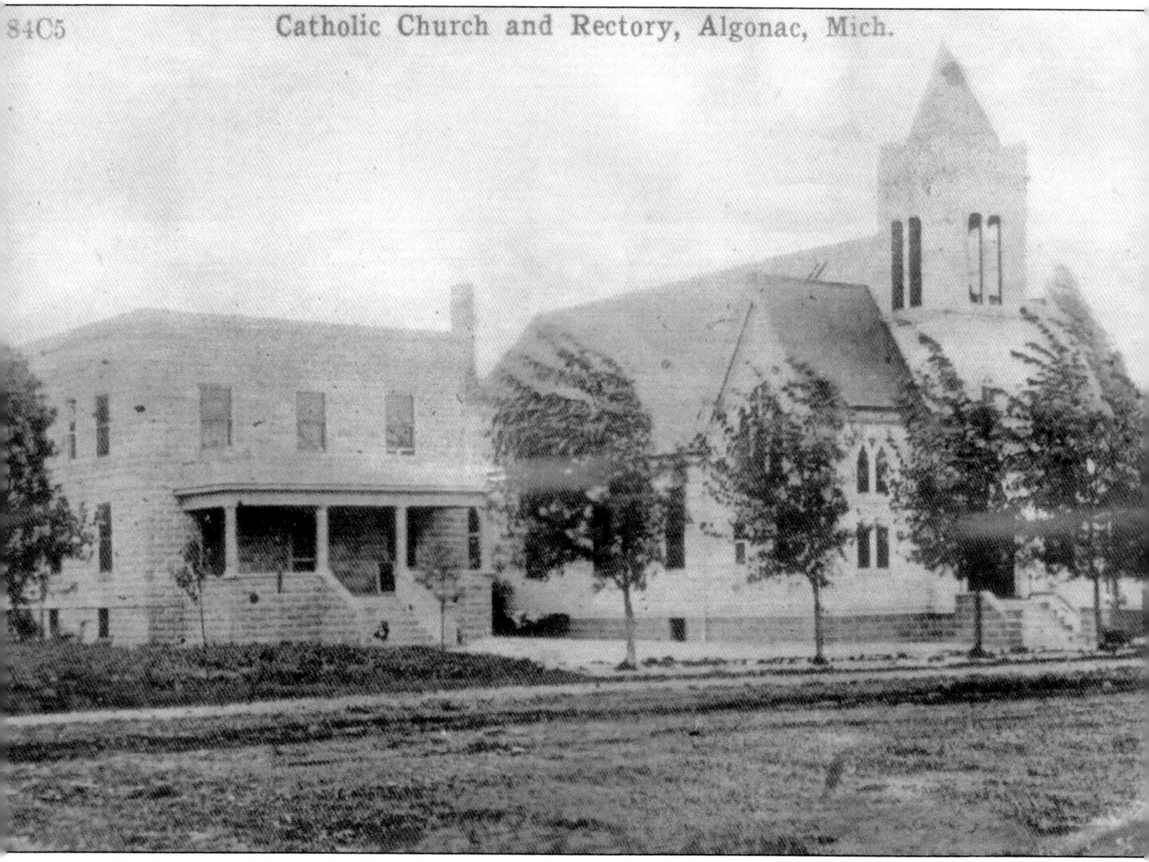

St. Catherine's Catholic Church is pictured here in 1895. This Algonac church was first established as a mission of the Marine City parish, which is mentioned for the first time in the Catholic Directory of 1873. However, Fr. Aloysius Lambert had regularly visited the French inhabitants of the settlement much earlier. The deed to the church was property executed by Charles Gilbert on September 4, 1866. Three years later, Father Lambert erected the first church, but no resident pastor was appointed until 1894, when Fr. Francis Kemper was given the charge. It was one of 29 missions established between 1870 and 1888.

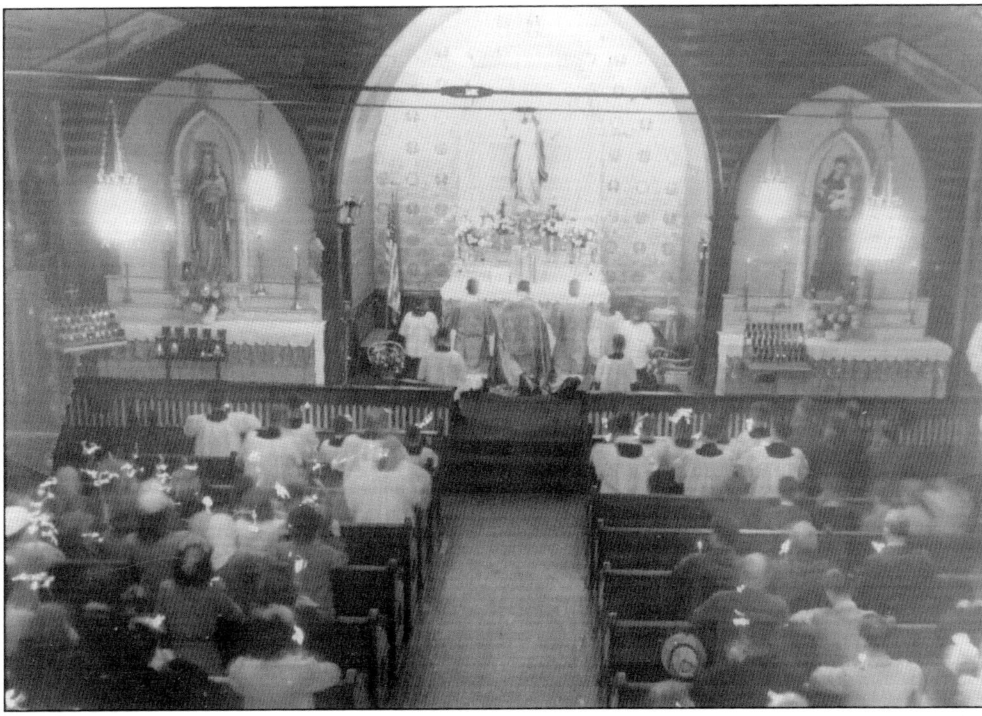

Mass is being held at St. Catherine's Church. The first church burned to the ground on November 30, 1895. At this time, Fr. Francis Kemper was succeeded by Fr. Benoit Gery, who immediately began building a church on the southeast corner of Fruit Street and St. Clair Boulevard.

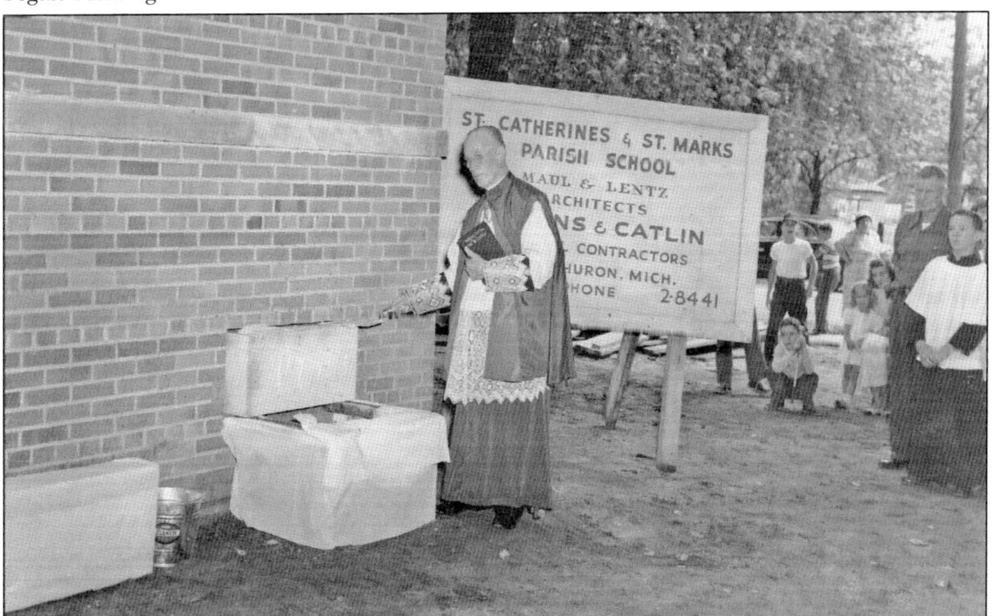

Archbishop John F. Dearden is pictured here laying the cornerstone for the new St. Catherine's and St. Mark's Parish School in 1951. The parish and convent was dedicated to the soldiers who had fought and died during the Korean War and World War II. A new church and rectory was erected on St. Clair Boulevard in 1959.

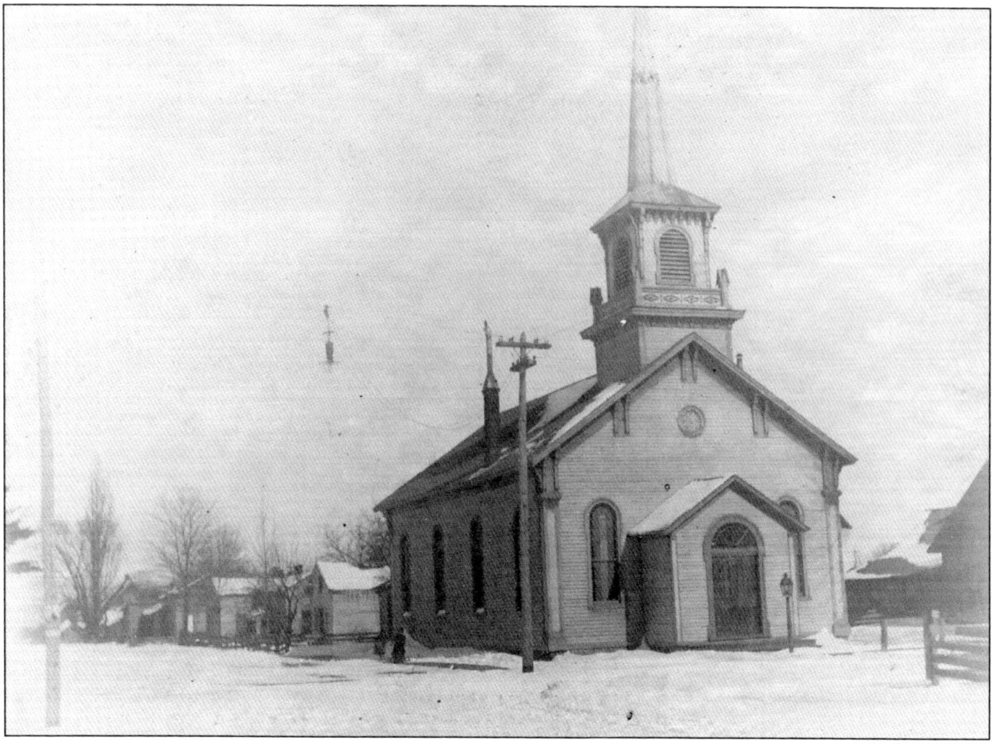

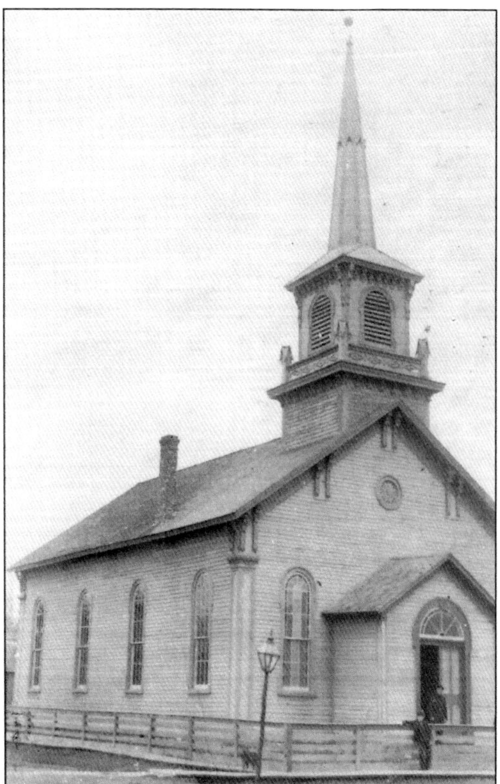

The First Methodist Church in Algonac was organized by the Reverend Griffith in 1821. Ebenezer Westbrook donated the land in 1830, and the original church was erected at 603 St. Clair River Drive. A stone marker has been placed at the site to commemorate its humble beginnings. The total cost of the building was $179,733, of which only $49 was paid in currency, the balance coming from subscriptions of grain, produce, and labor. When the church burned down in 1866, it was replaced by a new building at the corner of Smith and Washington Streets (its present location) the following year.

The First Methodist Church is shown as it appeared in the 1890s. When the Great Storm of 1913 demolished the steeple and twisted the church building, services were held in the annex.

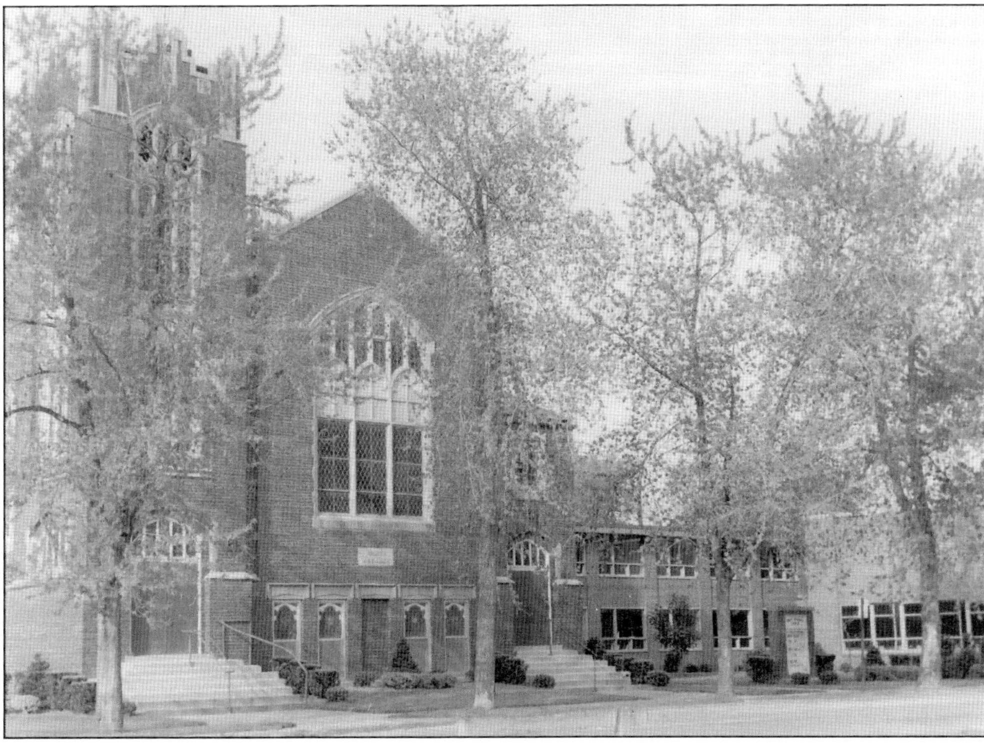

Pictured above is the Trinity Methodist Church from the early 1930s. On the evening of Easter Sunday 1922, the last meeting was held in the old church.

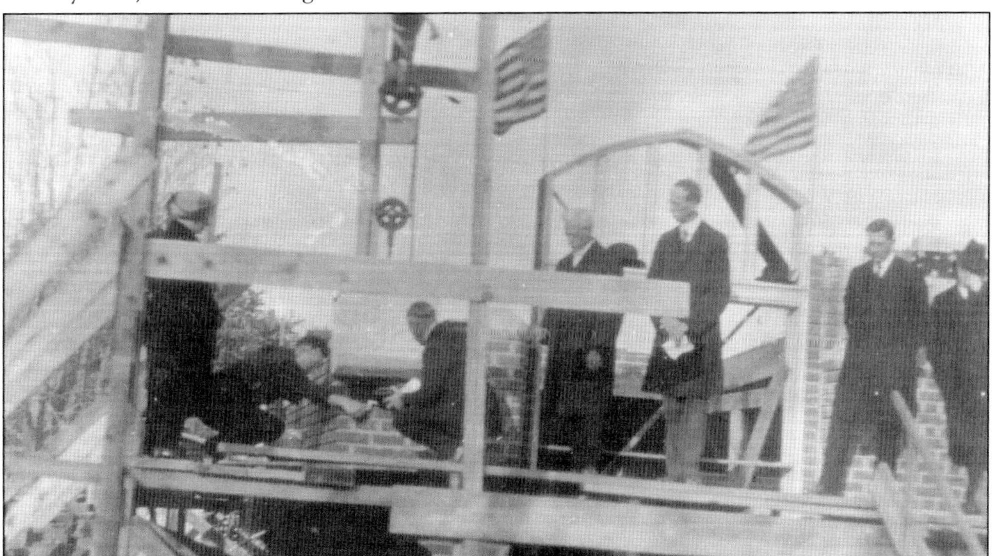

Members of the Trinity Methodist Church are pictured here laying the cornerstone on October 22, 1922. Ground was broken for the new church on July 1, 1922, and Bishop Theodore Henderson conducted dedication services on November 25, 1923. The church had a seating capacity of 350, and in 1957 a three-stage building program was launched to create a two-floor educational wing, a new church parsonage, and a chapel. In 1942, the family of Joseph Clark donated the chimes in his memory.

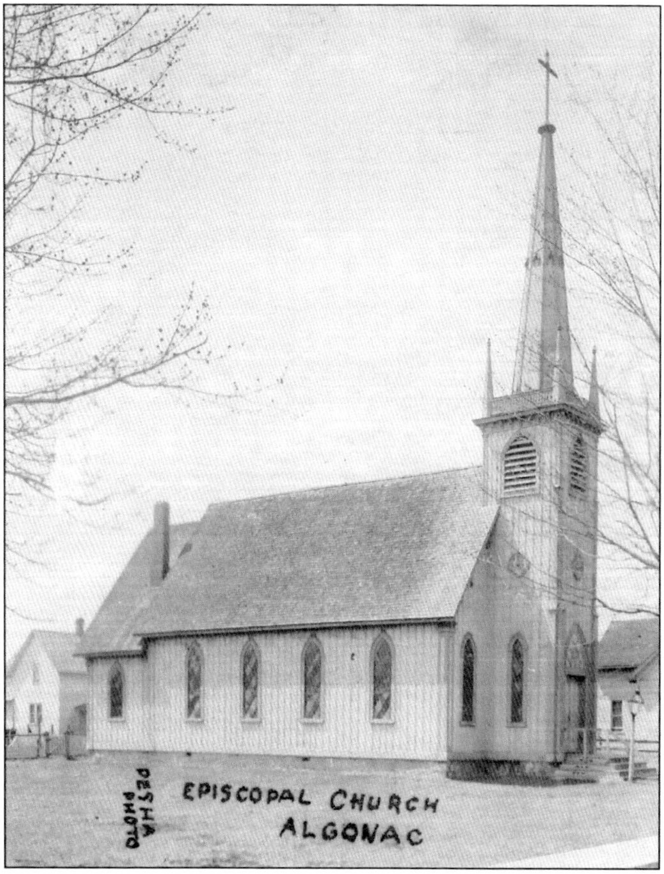

St. Andrews Episcopal Church is pictured here around the turn of the 19th century. The original church was completed and dedicated in 1867 and consecrated in 1872.

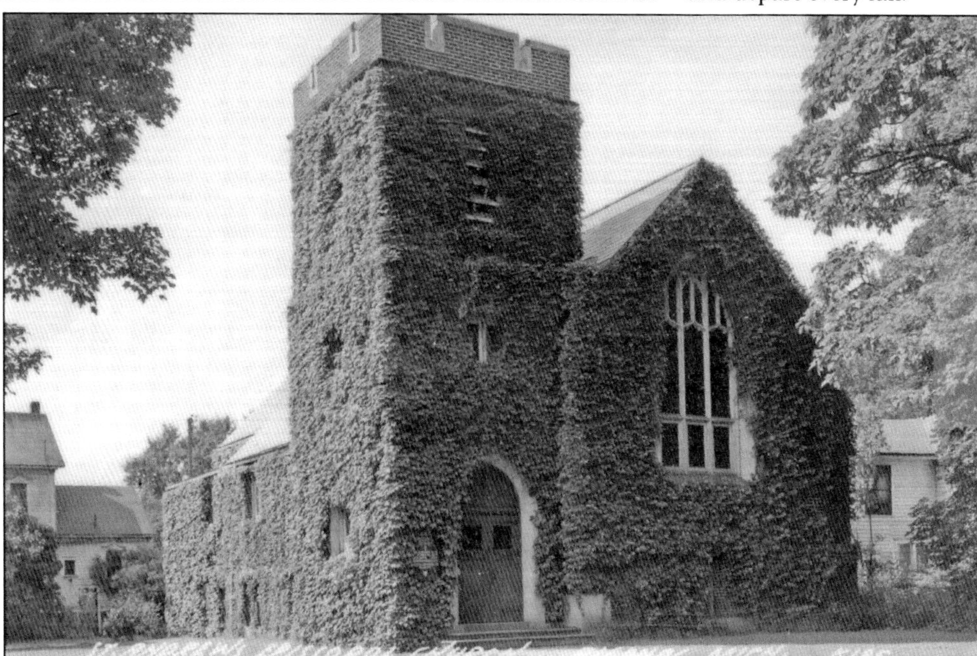

Named for the first disciple, St. Andrew's Episcopal Church imitated early Christian practices of holding services in the homes of various parishioners. The present church building on St. Clair River Drive was started in 1915 and consecrated on May 7, 1916. The church has become nationally known as "the Church of the Wrens" because, for so many years, wrens arrive each spring and depart every fall.

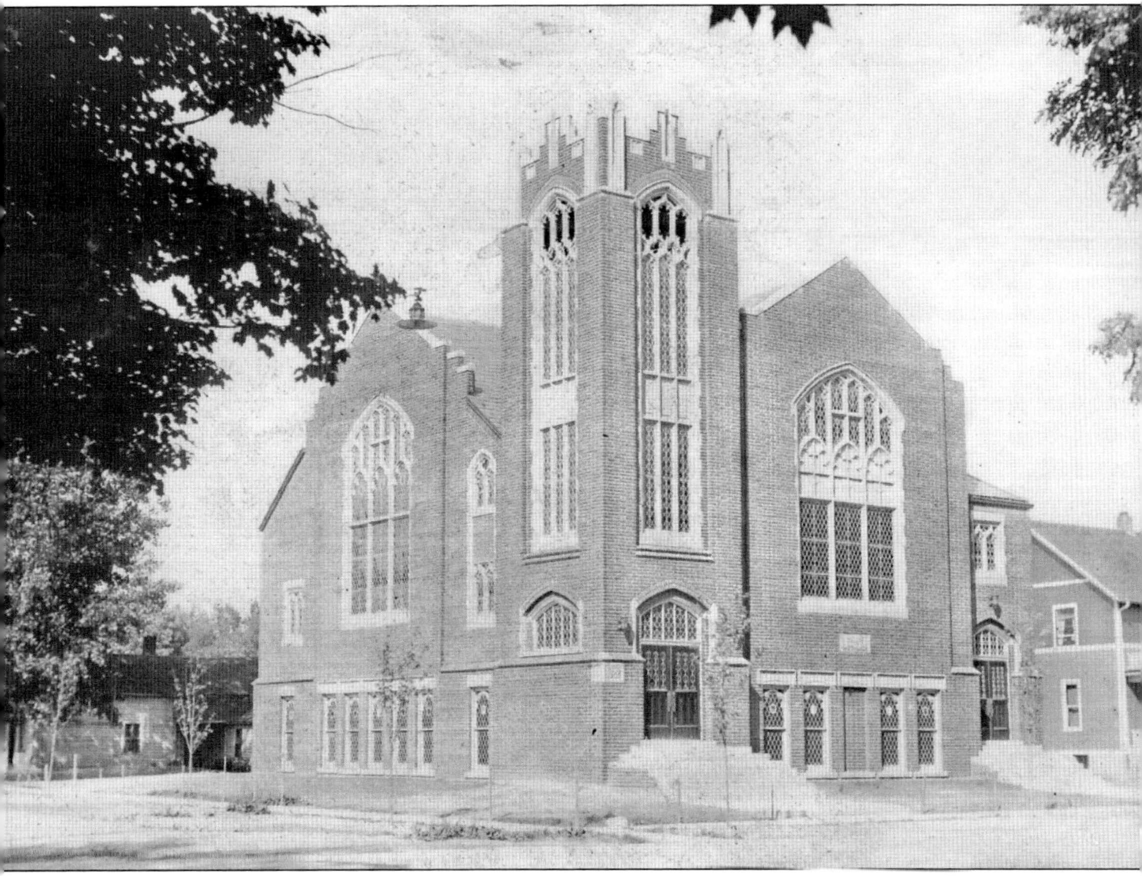

St. Andrew's Episcopal Church is pictured in the 1920s, soon after it was built. Note how different the church appears without the ivy.

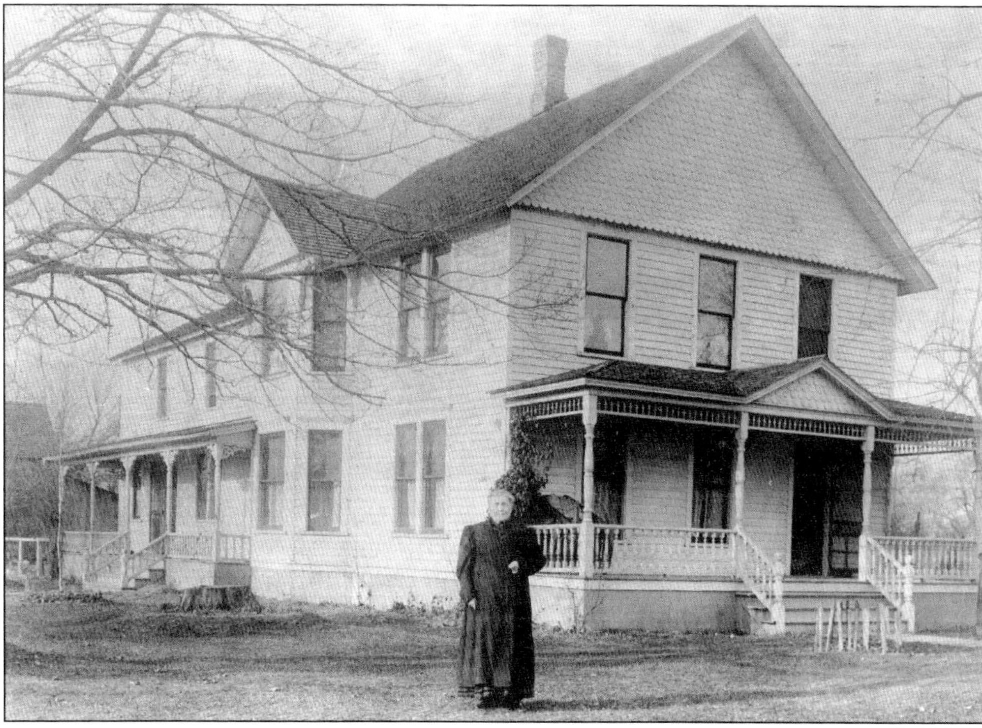

The First Evangelical Lutheran Church of Algonac traces its beginnings to 1943. The first service was held in the town hall of the village and was conducted by the Rev. E. Schade of St. Peter's Lutheran Church of Fair Haven. In 1945, a large two-story frame house was remodeled to provide an attractive first-floor chapel, which was dedicated on July 22, 1945.

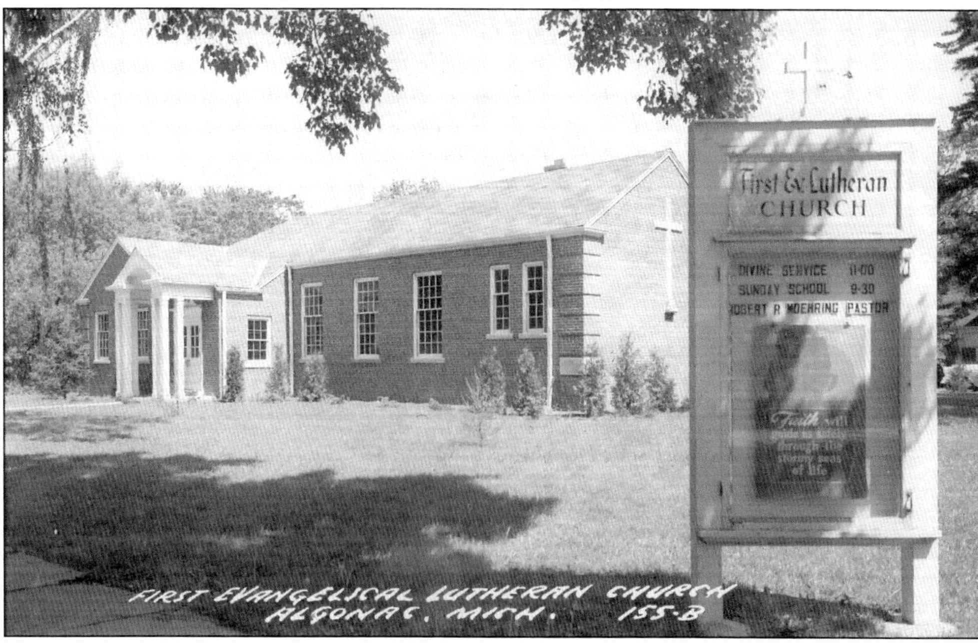

Construction of the present First Evangelical Lutheran Church and parsonage began in June 1953, and the church was dedicated on September 12, 1954.

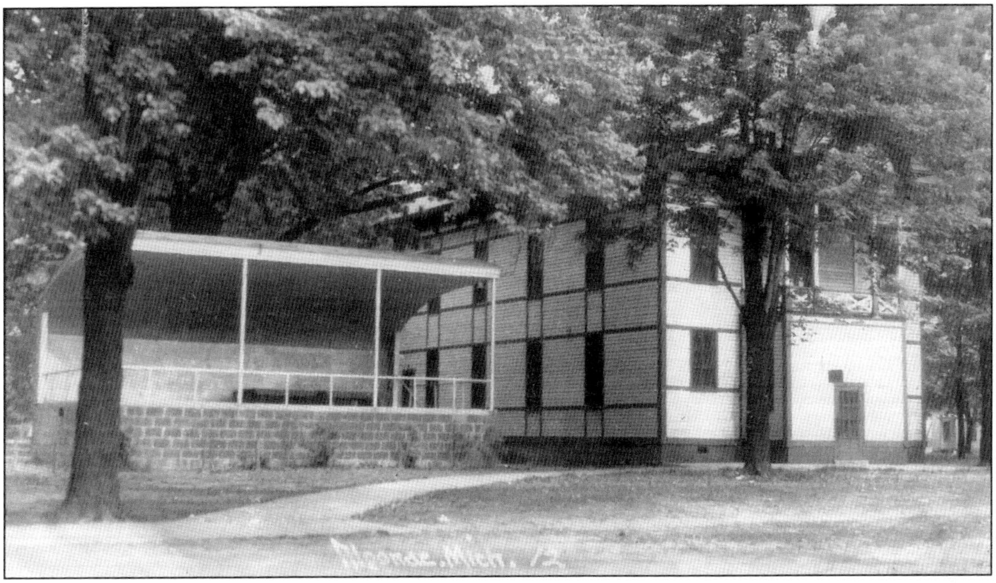

The Clay Township City Hall was built in 1876. It was torn down in 1956 to make room for a new elementary school.

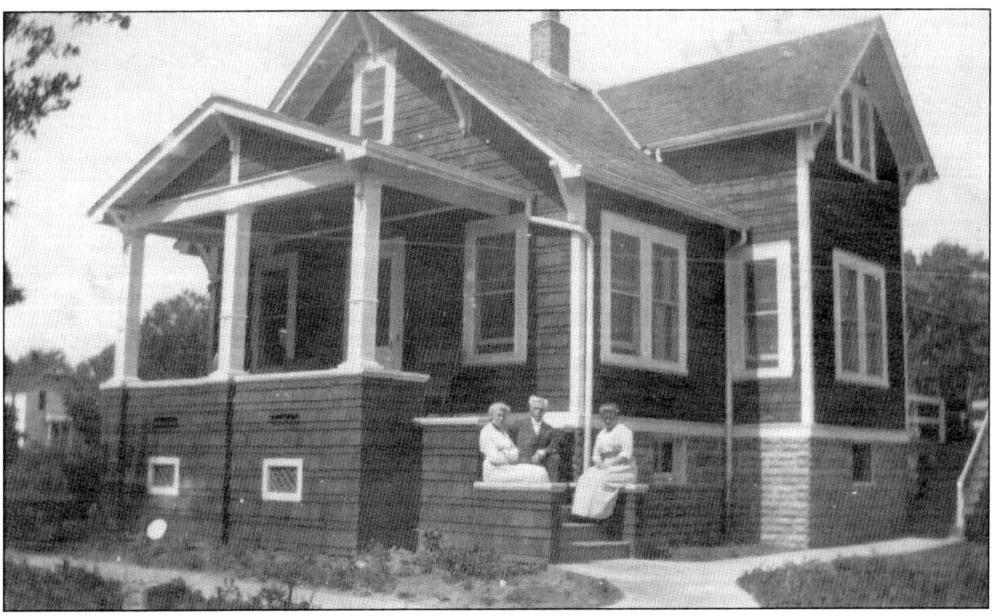

This photograph from the early 1920s shows the parsonage of the Church of Christ. Later, it would become the parsonage for the Algonac Baptist Church.

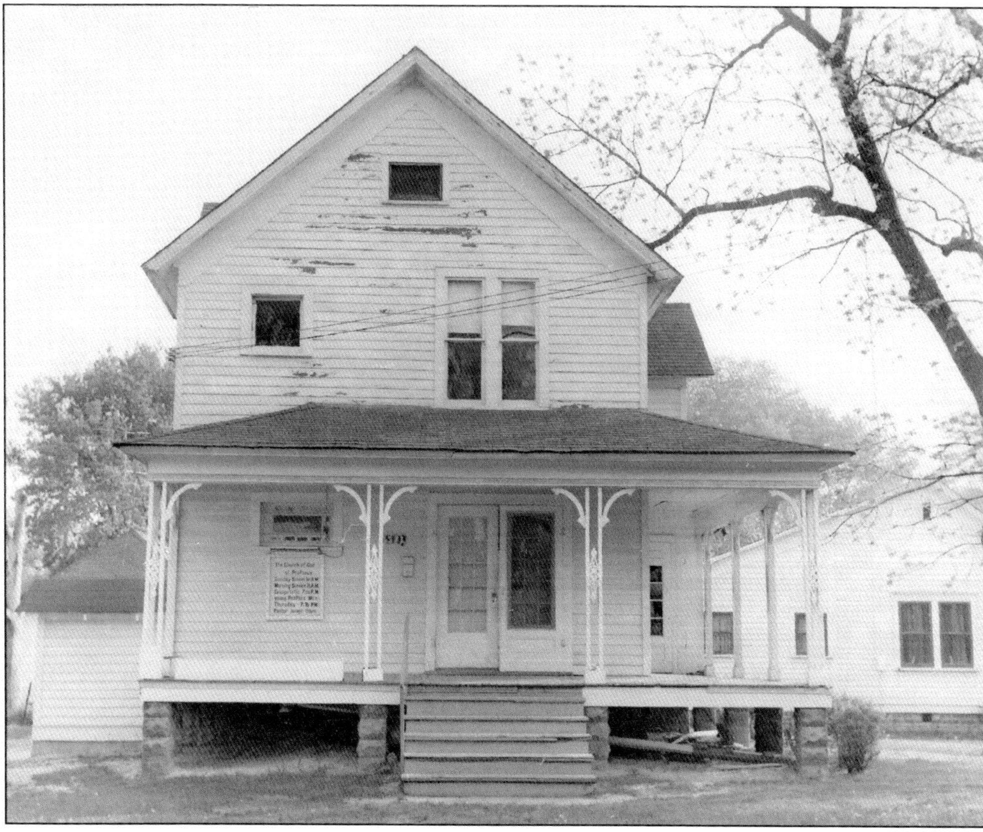

The Church of God of Prophecy was organized in 1963, with Rev. Hermas Grubbs serving as its first pastor. Members of the congregation accept the whole Bible as their rule of theocratic faith and doctrine. The present site of the church is 531 Mill Street, while the parsonage is located on Folkert Road.

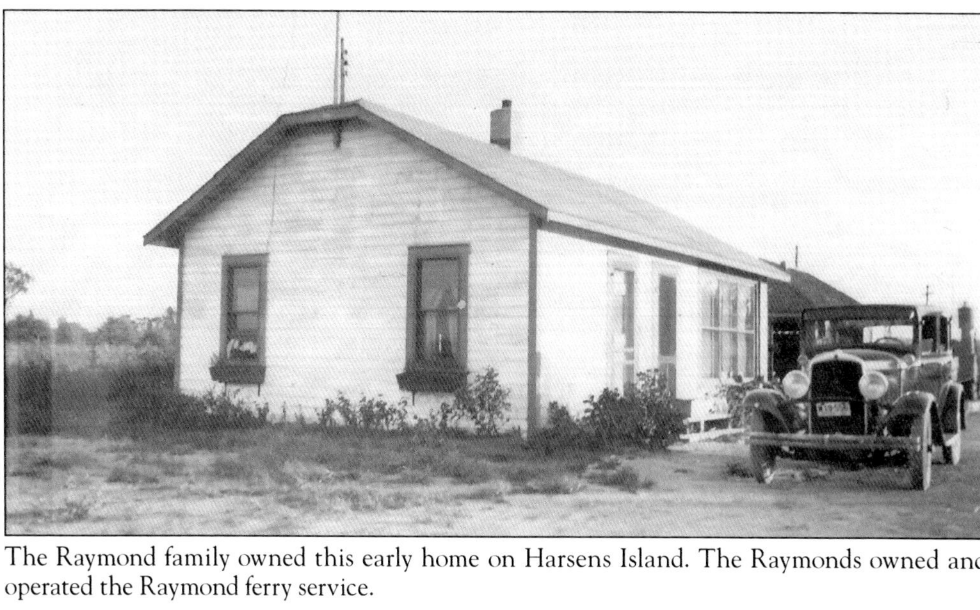

The Raymond family owned this early home on Harsens Island. The Raymonds owned and operated the Raymond ferry service.

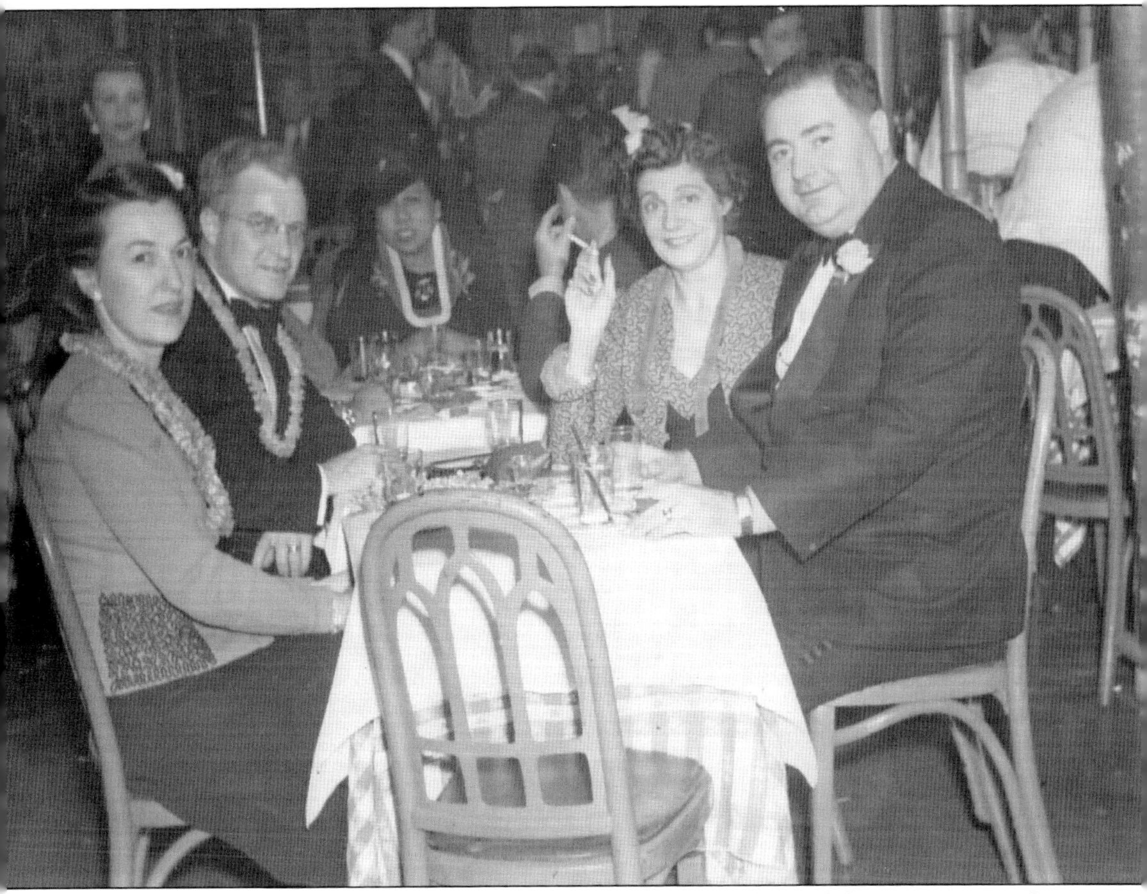

Postmaster general James A. Farley appointed Helen Kane (seated at right) as postmaster of Algonac on July 10, 1934. She retired on July 5, 1968, after serving for nearly 34 years.

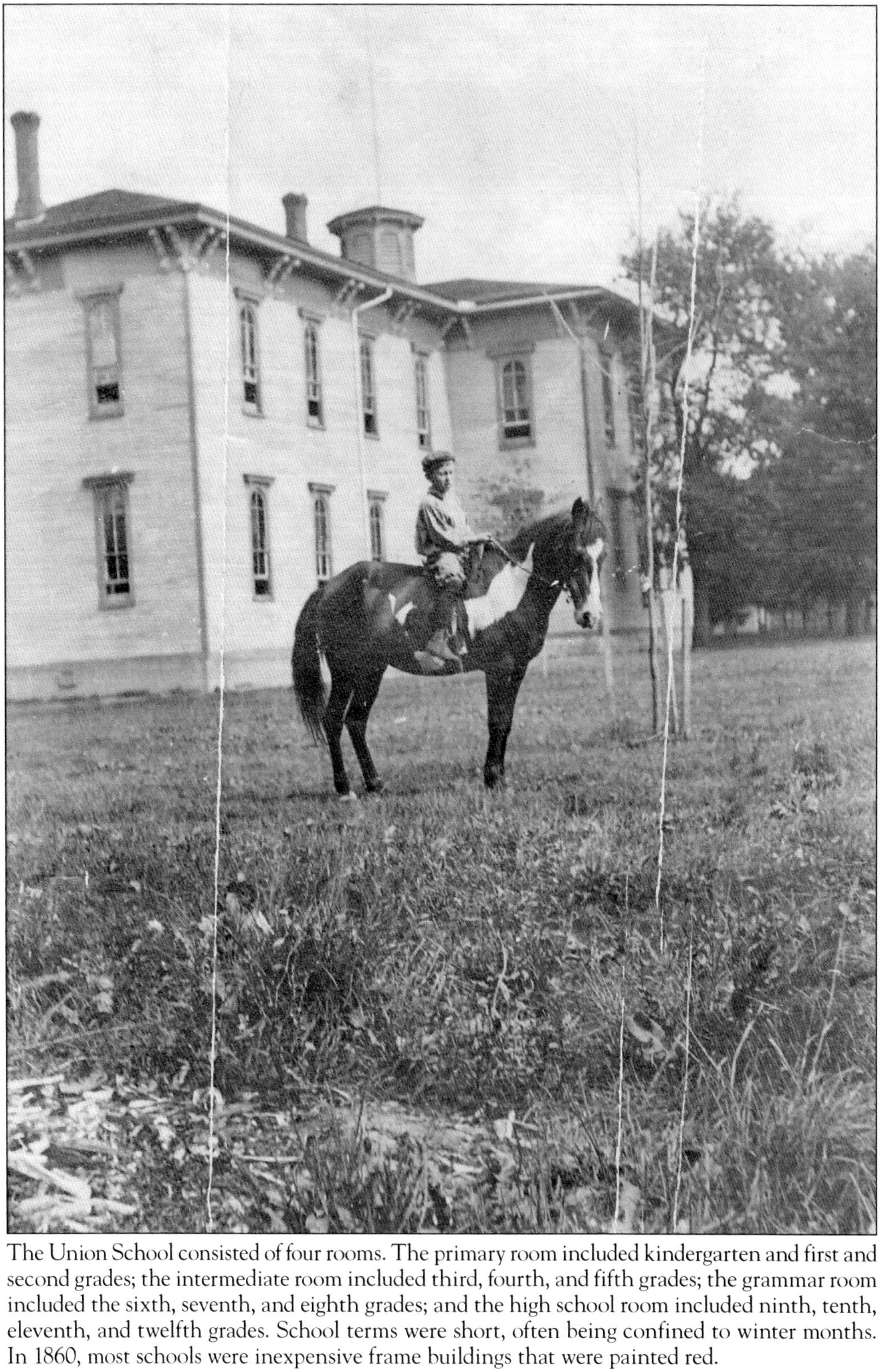

The Union School consisted of four rooms. The primary room included kindergarten and first and second grades; the intermediate room included third, fourth, and fifth grades; the grammar room included the sixth, seventh, and eighth grades; and the high school room included ninth, tenth, eleventh, and twelfth grades. School terms were short, often being confined to winter months. In 1860, most schools were inexpensive frame buildings that were painted red.

Five

Sports and Entertainment

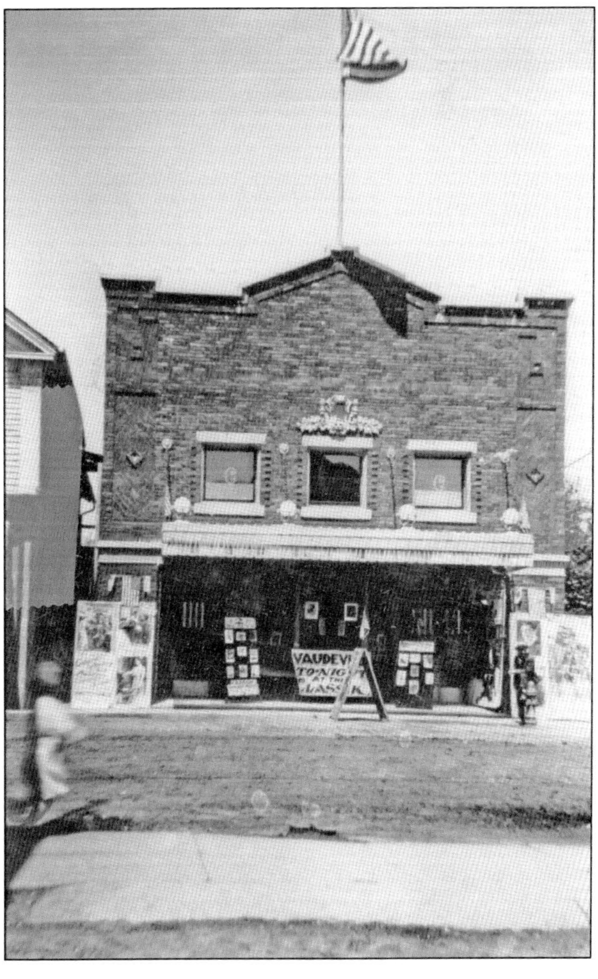

The Star Theater was later moved to the east side of Front Street and bought or leased by James Harper, who used it for a vaudeville house.

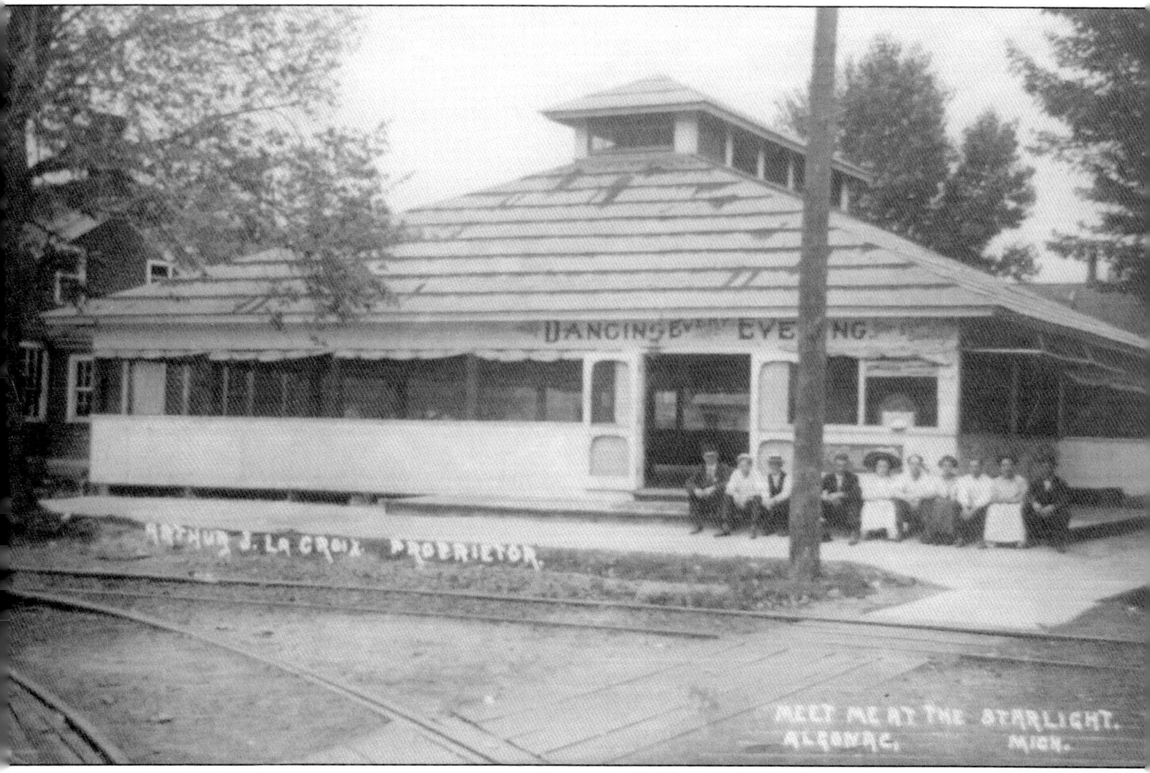

The Starlight Dancing Pavilion, pictured here in 1915, was located on the southwest corner of Michigan and Pleasant Streets. Note that the dance hall was completely screened in, including the cupola.

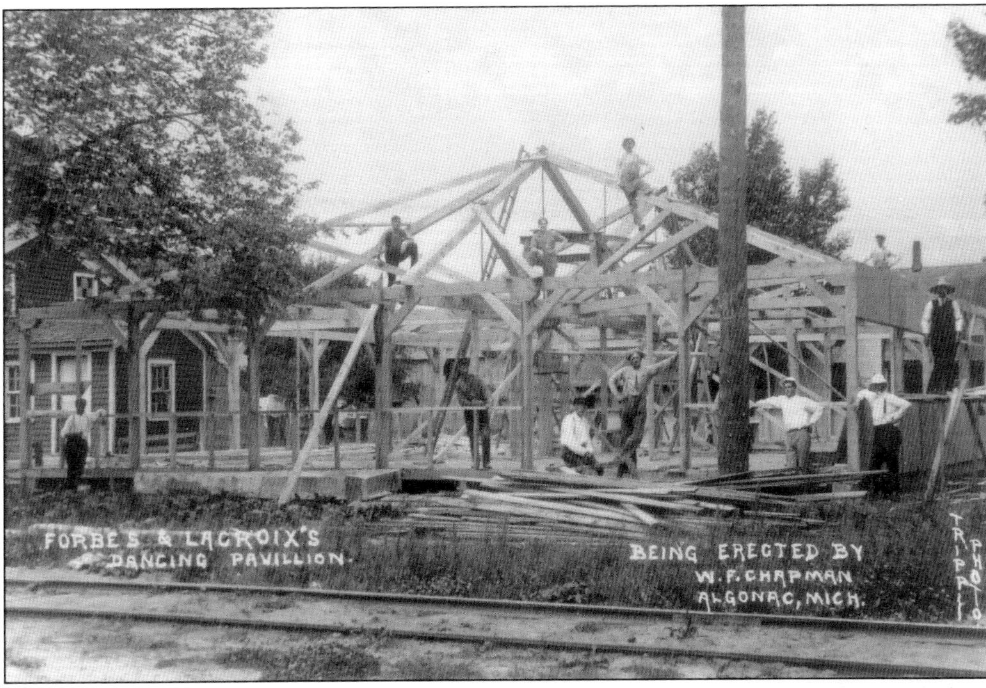

Forbes & Lacroix's Dance Pavilion is pictured here being built in the late 1800s. It would later become the Starlight Dancing Pavilion in 1900. A favorite saying of the day was "Meet me at the Starlight."

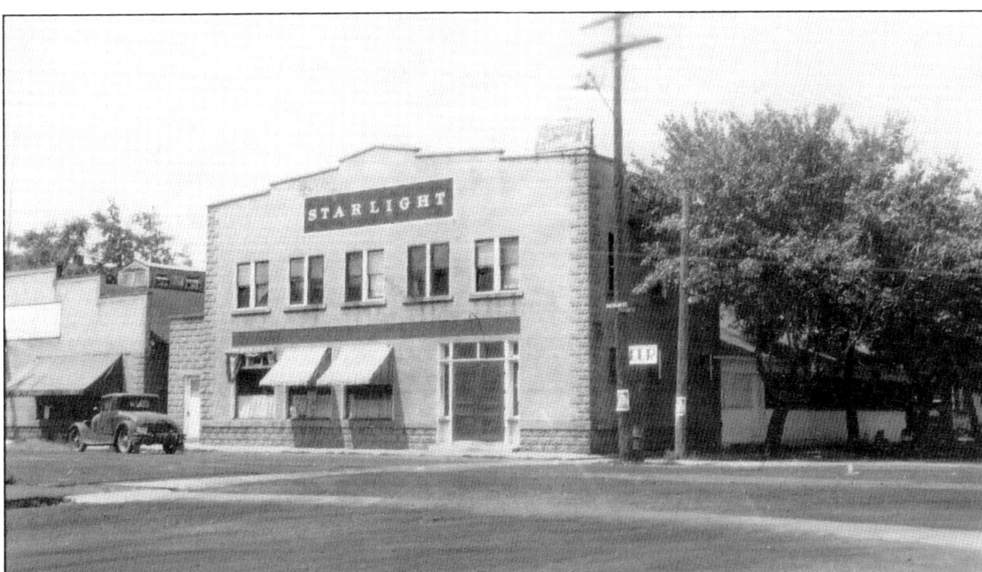

The Starlight is shown as it appeared in the 1920s. The front had been changed from a wood facade to brick. Later, the front was removed, and the building was converted into a roller rink. It would also become an IGA store and then a VFW hall in later iterations.

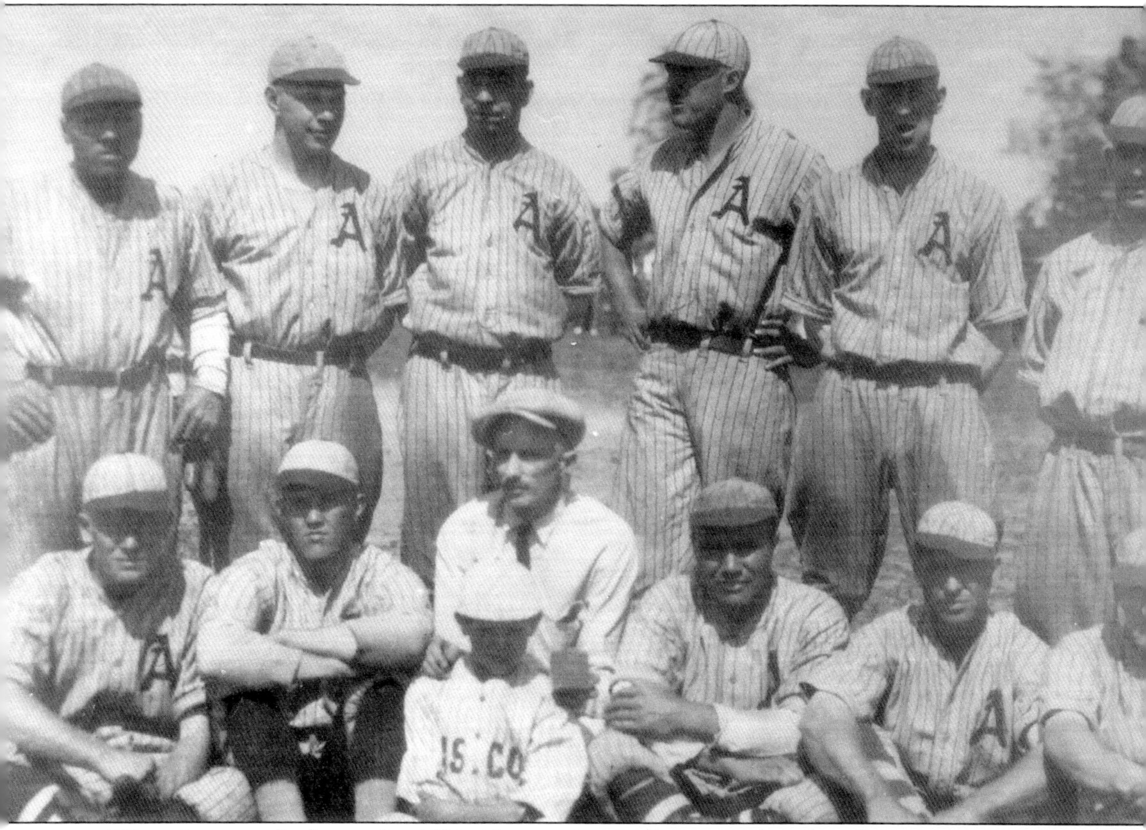

This photograph shows the 1921 Algonac baseball team, who played the Detroit Tigers at Steward's Ballpark.

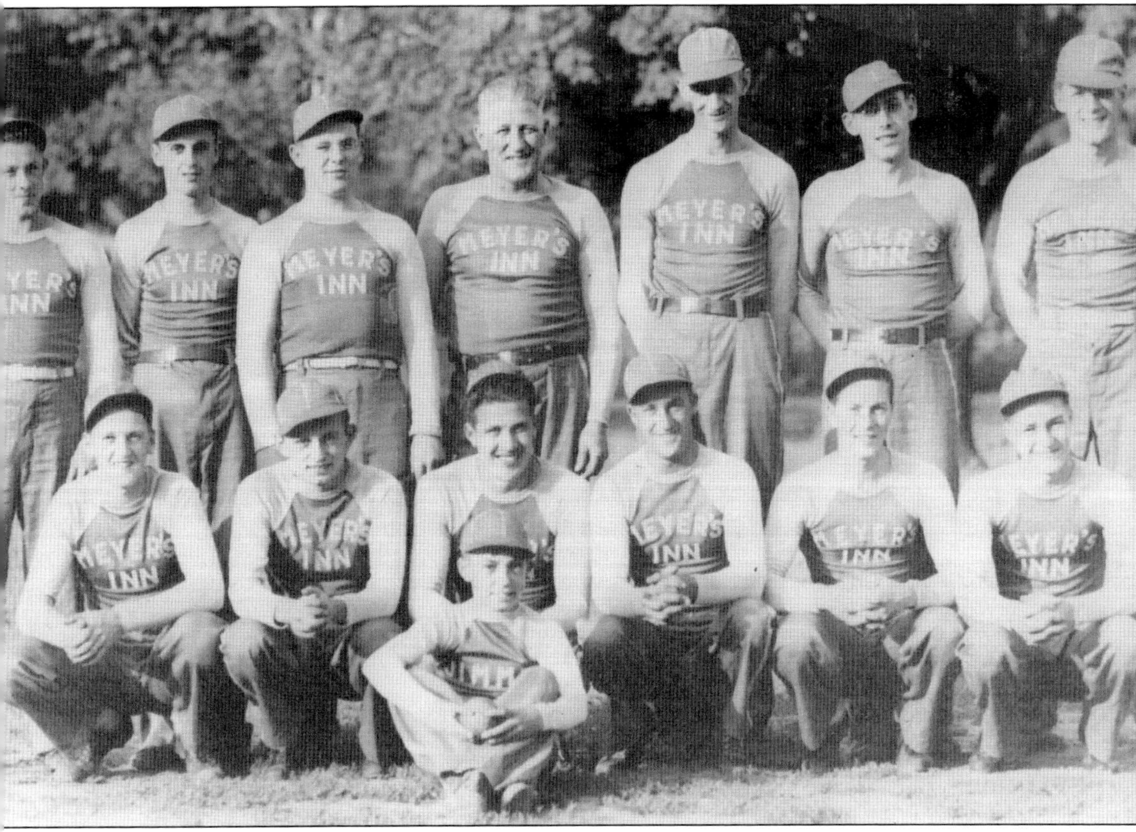

Pictured here is the Meyer's Inn baseball team from the 1940s. Many businesses in Algonac sponsored local teams.

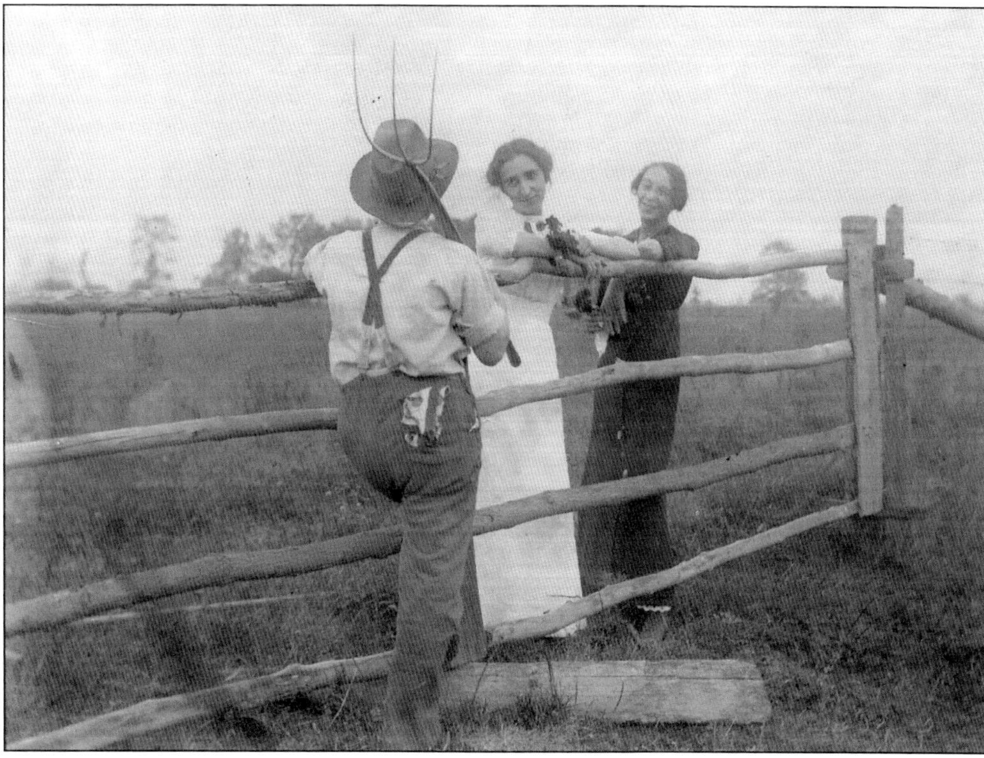

The Cartwright family is pictured here in the 1890s. Although difficult, the way of life for early pioneers developed men and women of courage and self-reliance. Each family was mostly economically independent, and farming was crucial.

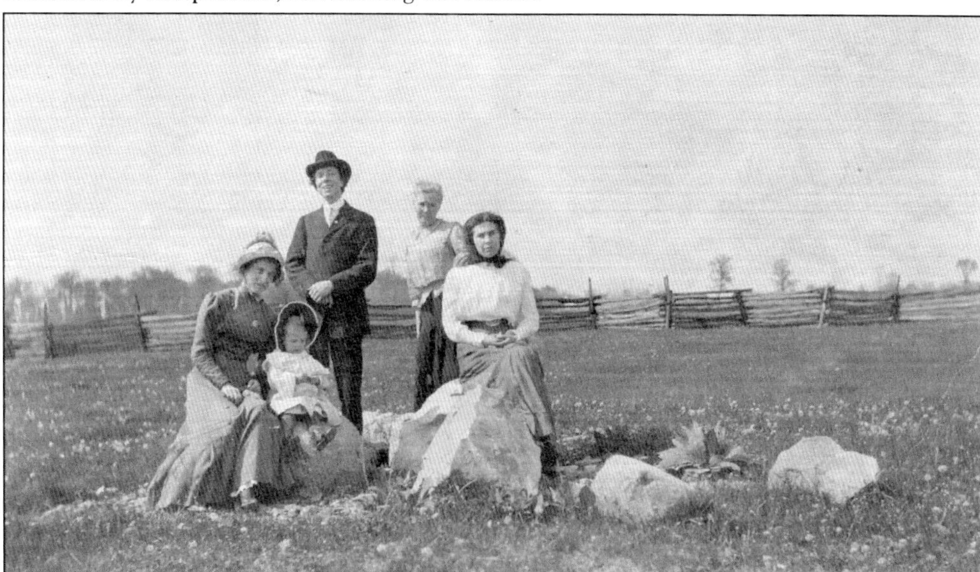

The Pangborn family is pictured here in 1910. After the trees had been chopped down and cut into size, neighbors came from miles around to help erect a cabin. The roof was made out of bark or long, wide strips of wood, called shakes. Floors were made of thick hewed planks, and a ladder led to the loft.

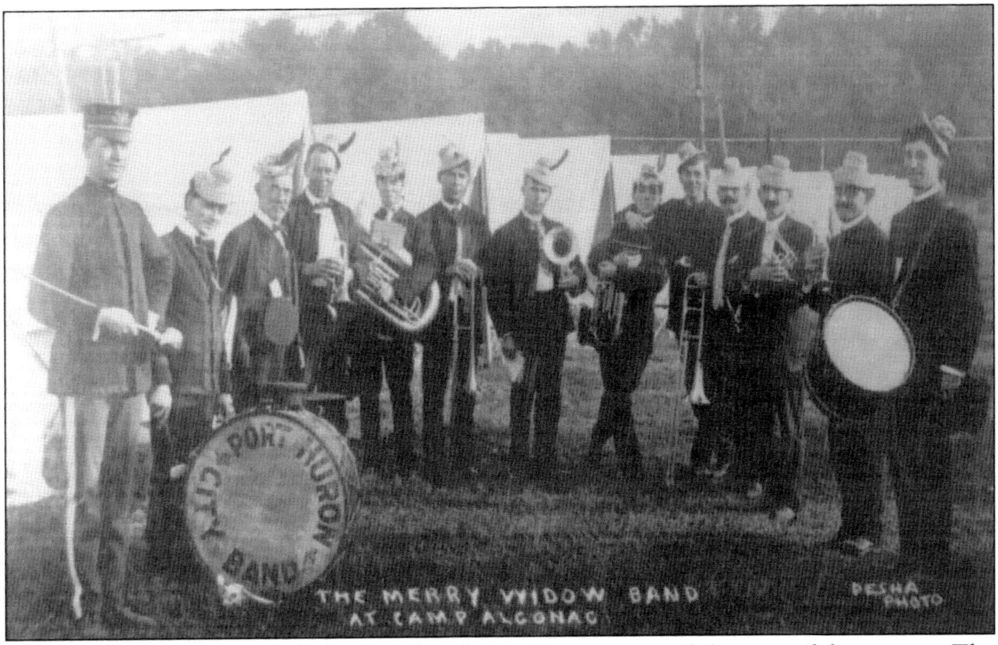

Pictured here is the Merry Widow Band at Camp Algonac around the turn of the century. The island was described as "the Gem of the Great Lakes." The camp was approximately 187 acres. In the center was a beautifully shaded oak grove of 43 acres with walkways, a swing, and rustic seats. Those who desired activity found boating, bathing, fishing, tennis, croquet, bowling, and billiards. There was a constant moving panorama of steamships passing the island, averaging one every four minutes. It was common to see 12–20 huge freighters passing up and down the South Channel at one time.

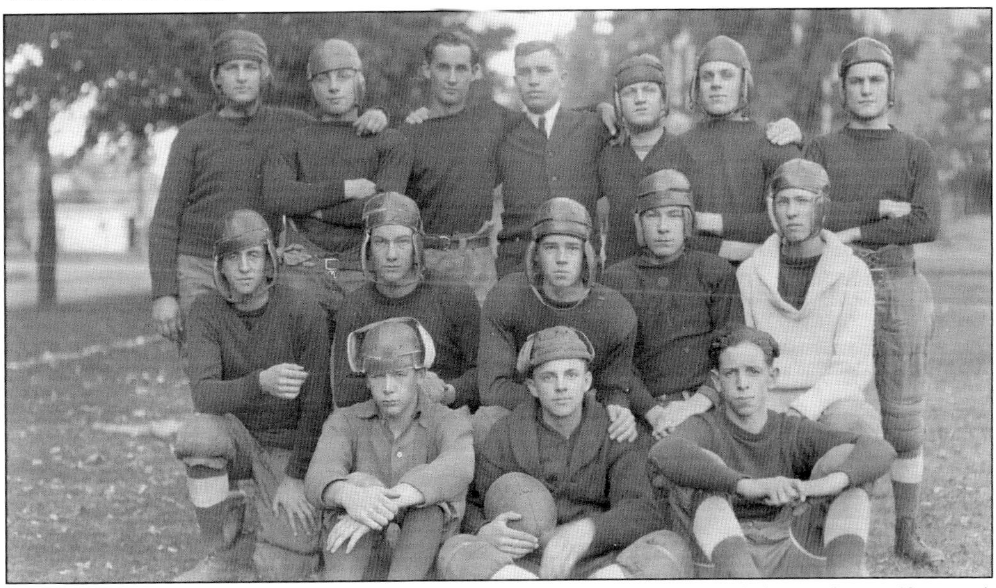

Pictured here is the Algonac High School football team from 1925. From left to right are (first row) ? Simpkins, Kermit Zaetsch, and Theodore Newkirk; (second row) Ed Kane, W. Warner, A. Woods, and John Plonkey; (third row) Harvey Bell, Ted Zaetsch, Bill Thompson, coach Loren Eyler, Chuck Smith, Clarence Nugent, and Harry Bell.

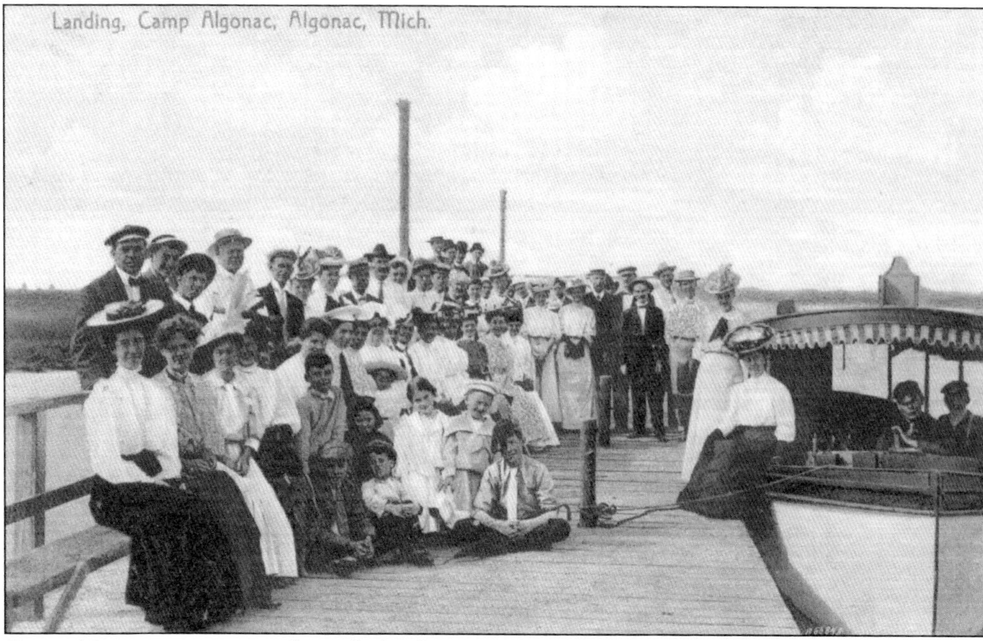

Camp Algonac, a tent city also called White City, was constructed on Russell Island. Excursions ran from Pittsburgh, Pennsylvania; Cincinnati, Ohio; Terre Haute, Indiana; and other inland cities. The passengers arrived in Detroit by train, took the steamboats to Algonac, and were ferried to the island in small motor launches to the dock at Camp Algonac. An advertisement boasted, "In All The World, No Trip Like This."

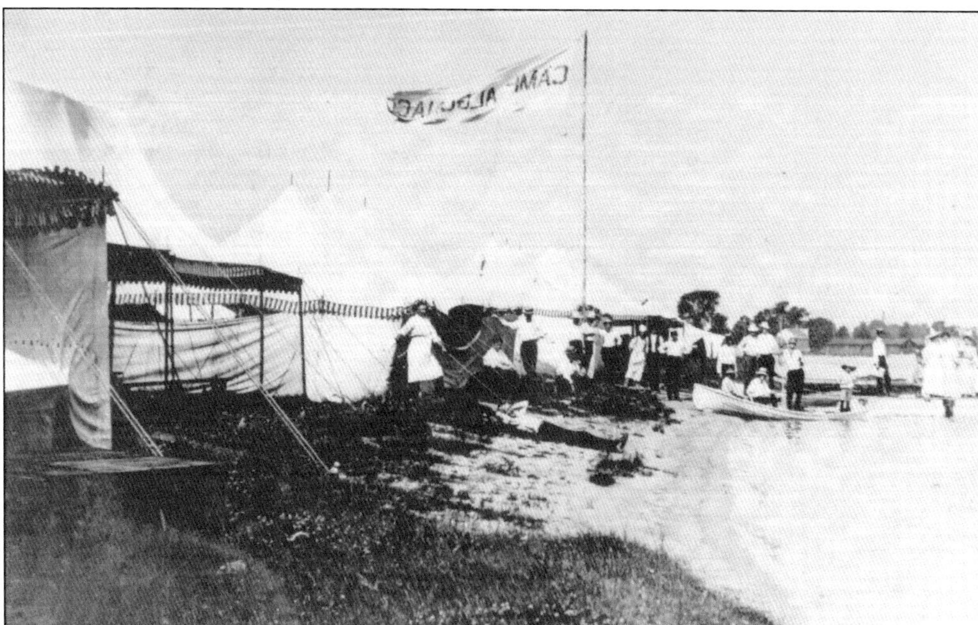

Russell Island is located between Algonac and Walpole Island and separates the St. Clair River into the North and South Channels. In 1905, Algonac merchants gathered $1,700 obtained through voluntary subscriptions and taxes to secure control of Russell Island from the Detroit, Belle Isle & Windsor Ferry Company to create a summer resort.

Six

Detroit Urban Railroad

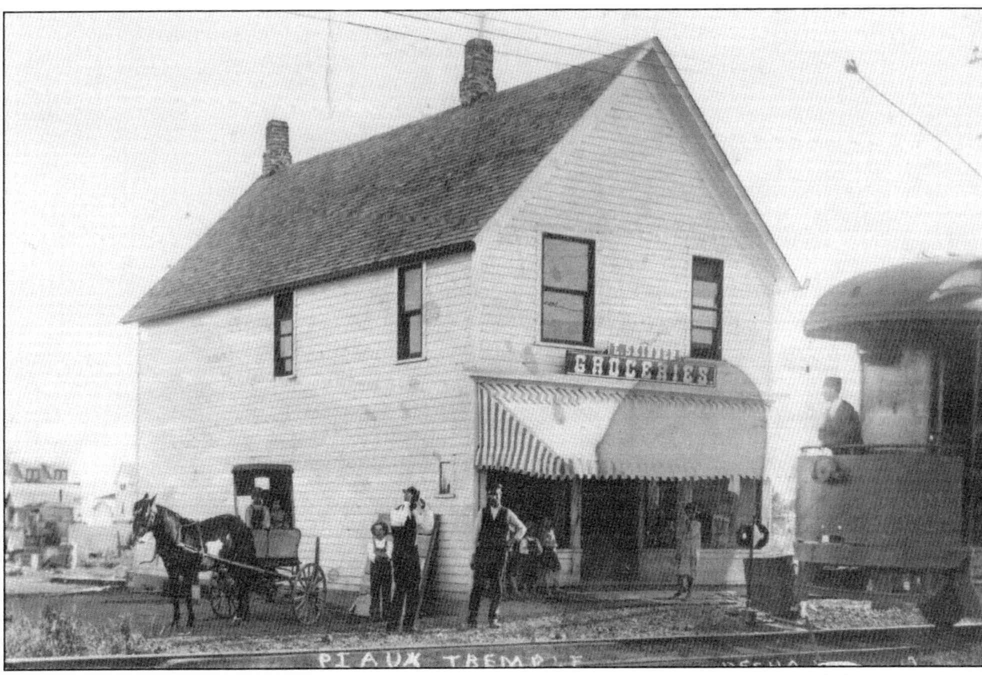

Travel was difficult in the early 1800s. There were no land routes in the area until the completion of the Gratiot Turnpike from Detroit to Fort Gratiot in 1833. The Grand Trunk Railroad was built between Detroit and Port Huron, and when residents of Algonac wanted to go to Detroit, they would drive by horse and buggy to the nearest train station, located at the corner of Gratiot Avenue and 23 Mile Road in Chesterfield.

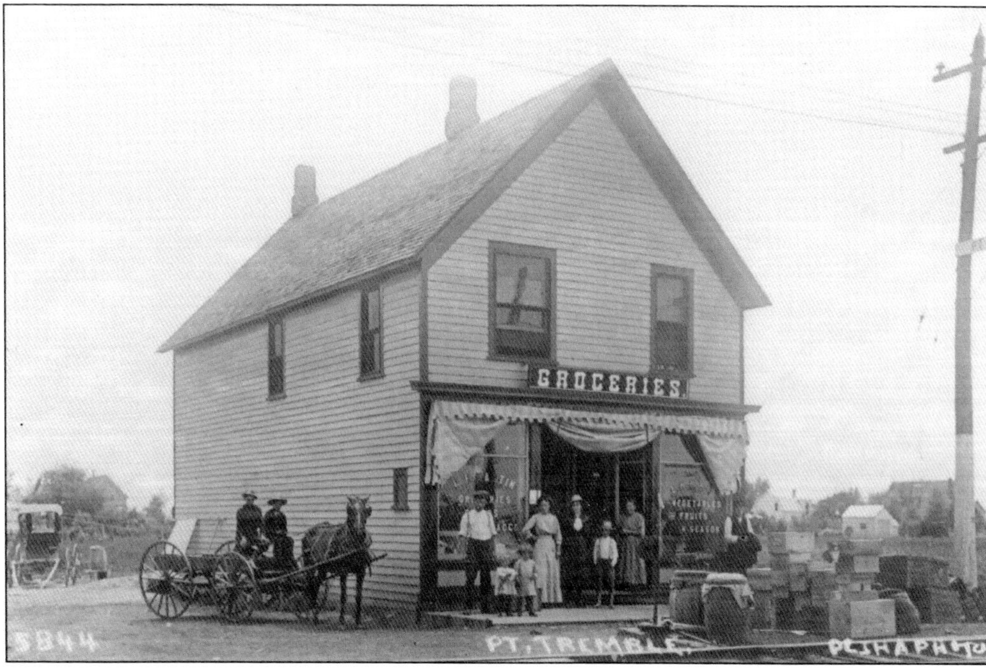

L.H. Martin's grocery store, pictured here in the late 1890s, also served as a depot of the Detroit Urban Railway. Steam railroads could not be bothered with the short-haul passenger, nor did they want the half dozen cans of milk a farmer might send to town if pickup required a stop midpoint on their line. Streetcar barons saw an opportunity and took it.

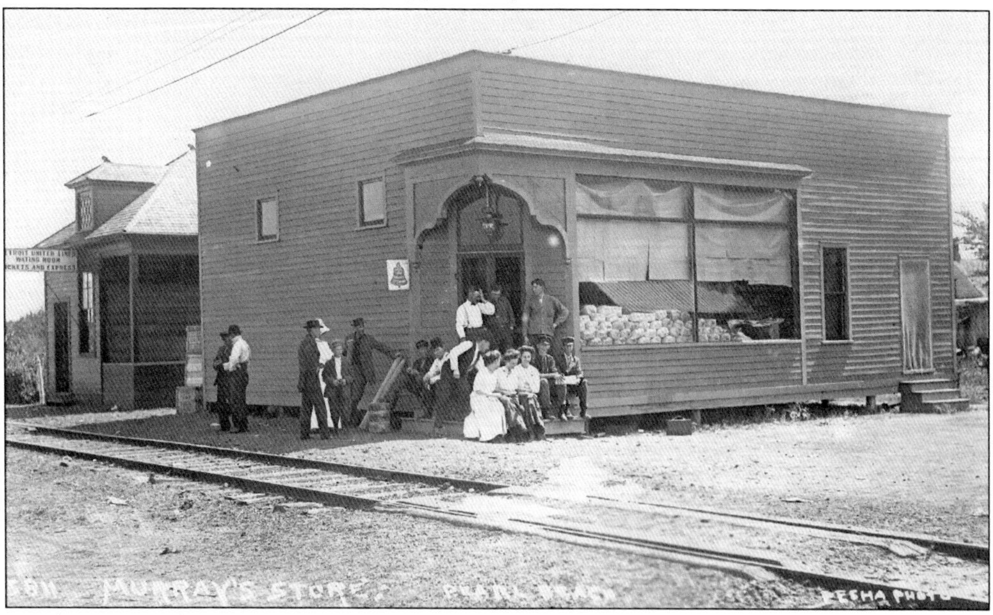

People are seen here waiting for the train at Murray's Store in Pearl Beach. At its peak, the Detroit Urban Railway severed 159 communities within a 75-mile radius of Detroit. The success attracted competition. The Shore Line System built a line from Detroit, along Jefferson Avenue through Grosse Pointe, to Mount Clemens in 1900. It then extended the line along the St. Clair River to Port Huron.

This image of the Martin grocery store, pictured in the early 1960s, shows what gas prices were like during this era. The grocery store had originally been a depot for the Detroit Urban Railway.

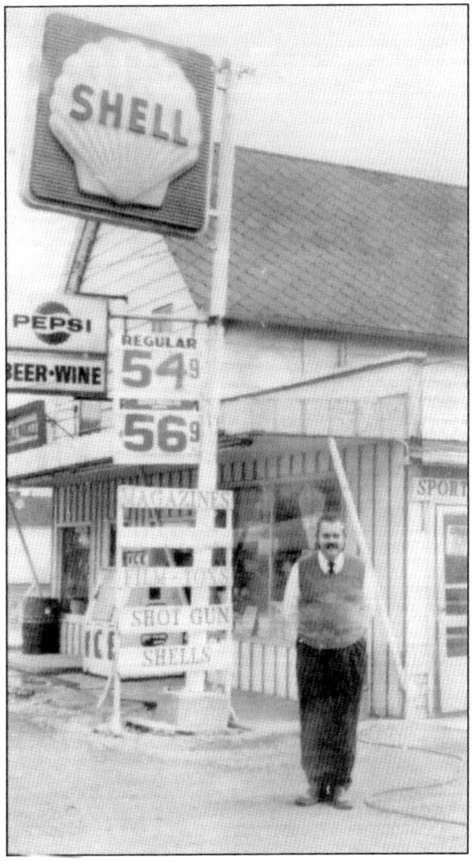

Pictured here is the DUR station at Pearl Beach. The interurban made its debut in the late 1800s, and the Detroit Urban Railway system became one of the most extensive in the country. In 1900, the Detroit Urban Railway had a double routing, one by way of Algonac and one by Anchorville to Marine City. The advantages of this railroad were quickly realized, and summer residents began to build permanent homes and cottages.

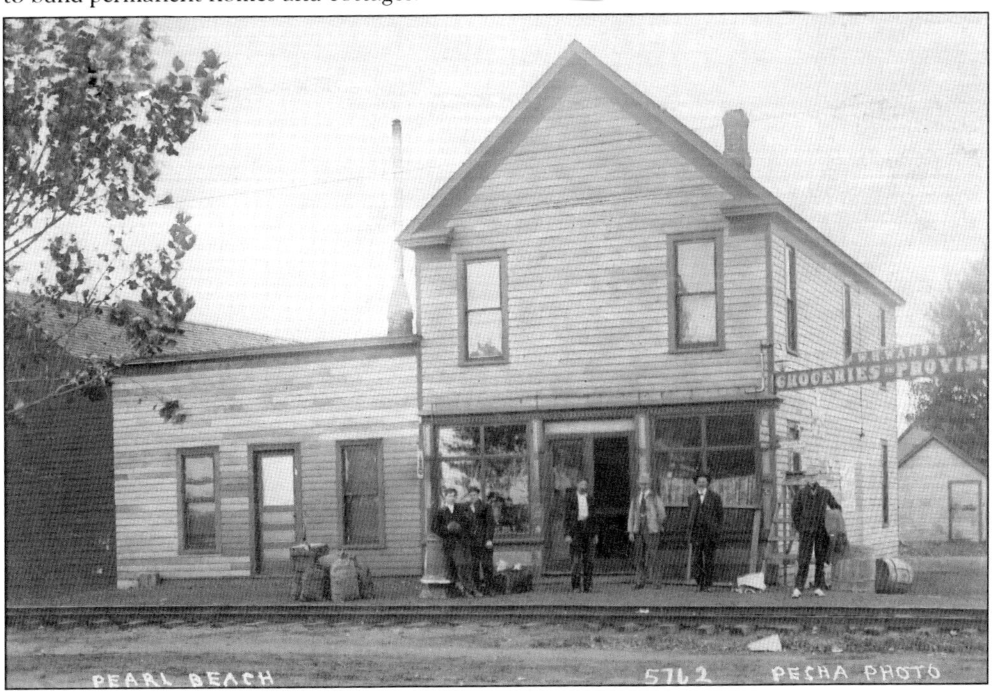

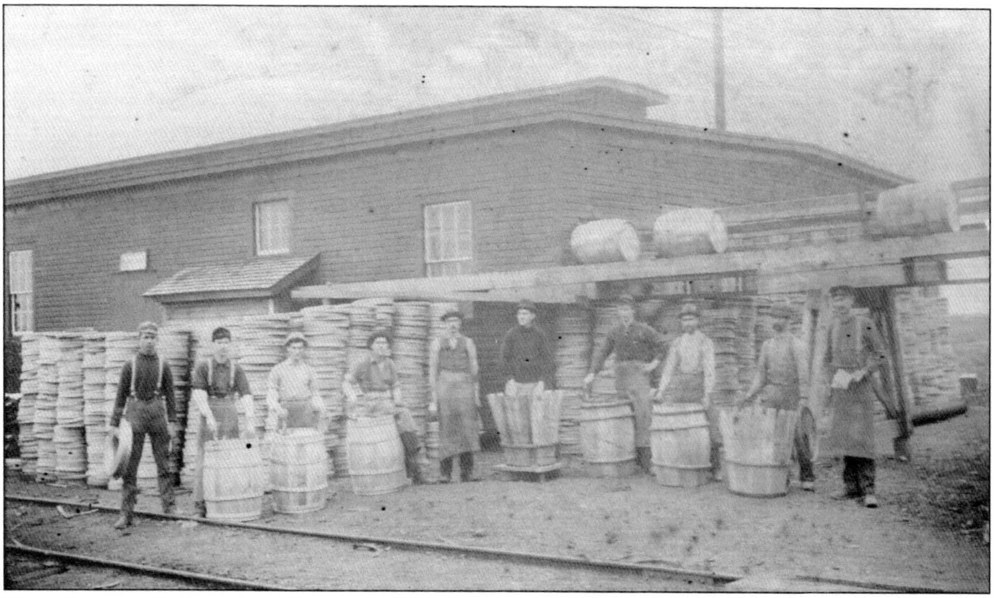

This photograph shows barrel makers along the Detroit Urban Railway. In 1915, the Detroit Urban Railway had 1,403 closed passenger cars, 263 open passenger cars, 247 freight and construction cars, 36 line cars, and 84 express cars in service. Patrons soon learned that the express cars were faster than the local cars and made fewer stops. The limited cars were the fastest and could reach 90 miles per hour.

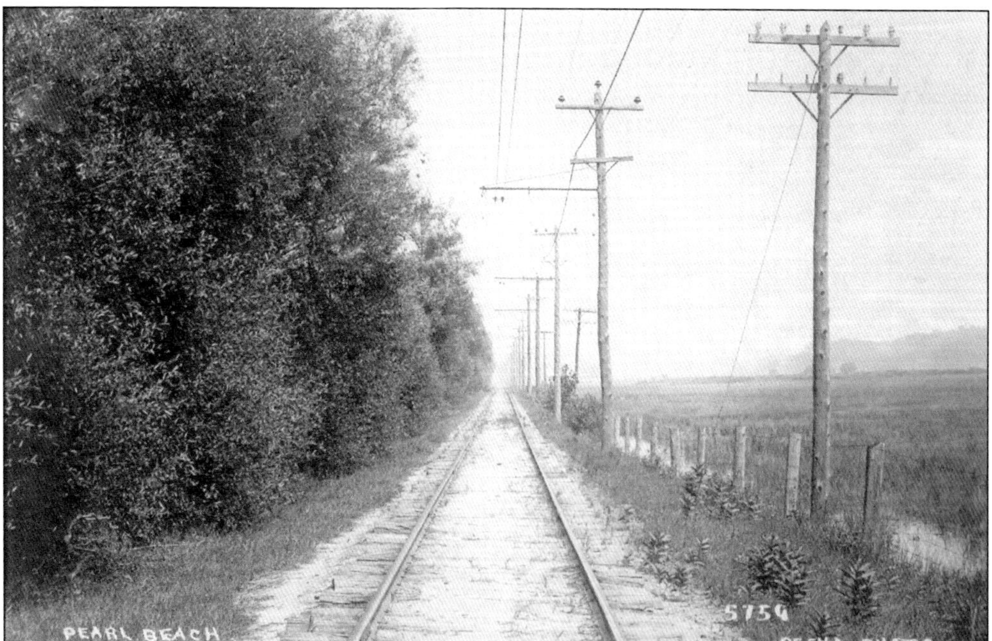

Here, the Detroit Urban Railway crosses the marsh coming into Pearl Beach. The availability of low-priced automobiles for working people was a main factor in the interurban's demise. Another factor was ground transportation between the municipalities provided by the bus companies. As the roads improved in the 1900s, the Greyhound and Goose Bus companies were becoming more popular. By 1932, all DUR operations had been discontinued.

Seven

BOATS AND CAR FERRIES

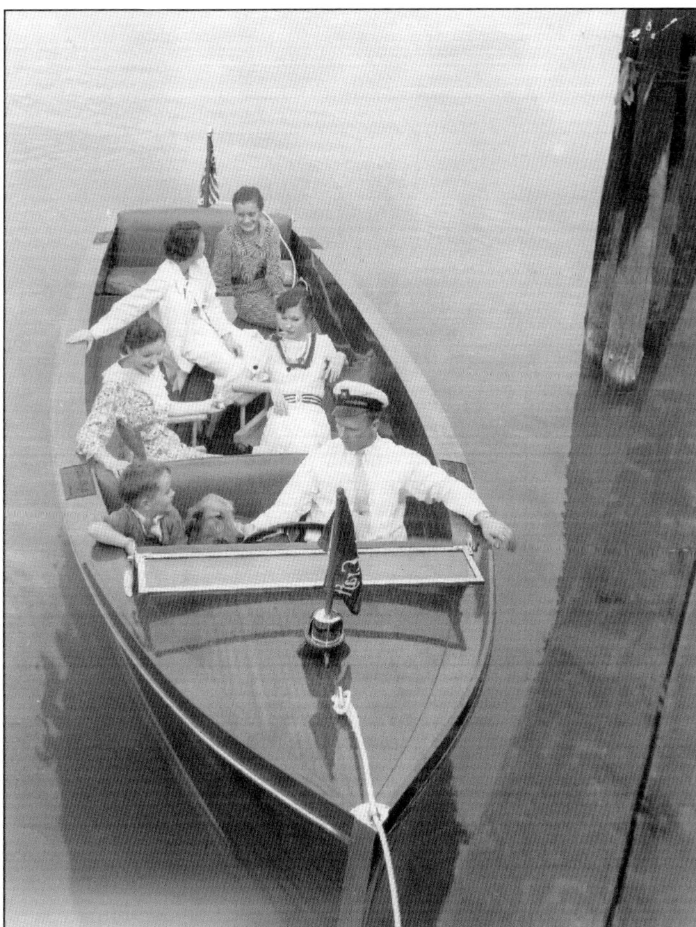

This photograph portrays the social importance of Chris-Craft boats in the 1930s. The women who appear in the image were all models for the Chris-Craft Corporation. In 1929, Chris-Craft solidified its niche in the cruiser and yacht market by offering 18 models.

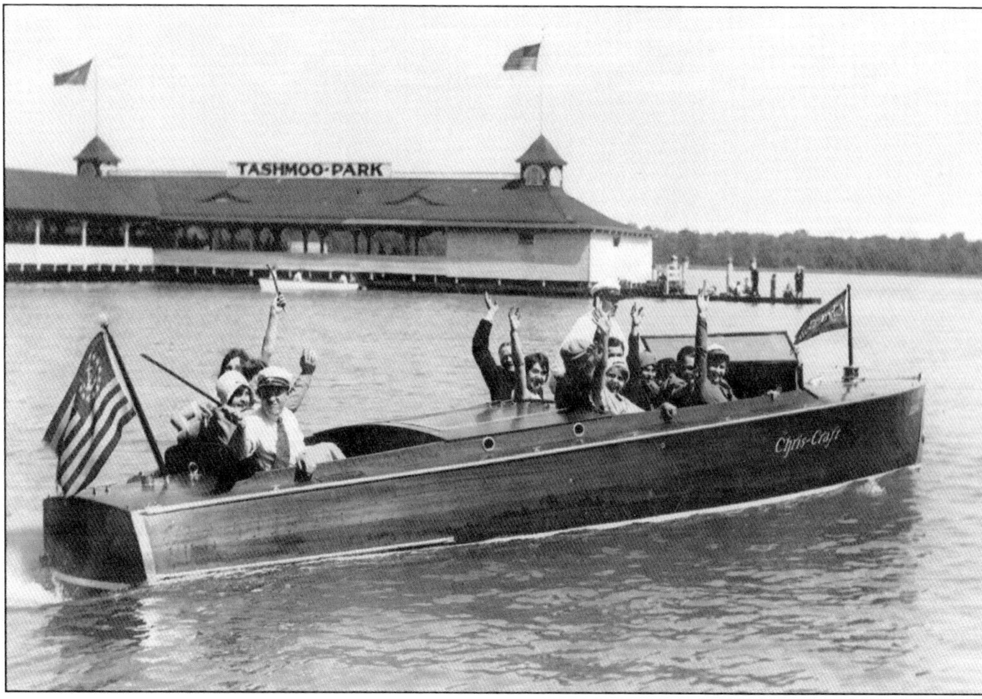

Floyd Gibbons is pictured in his 22-foot Chris-Craft runabout. Tashmoo Park, seen in the background, was located on Harsens Island and was a favorite vacation spot in the 1920s and 1930s.

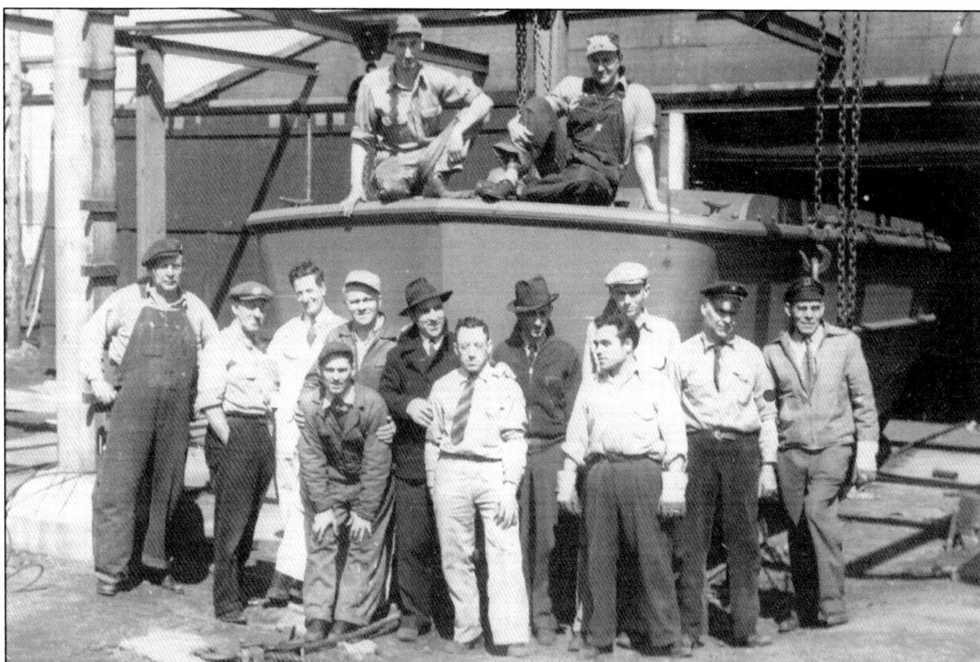

Chris-Craft workers pose next to one of the many boats that were produced to support the war effort during World War II. Chris-Craft manufactured more than 12,000 craft for the armed services between 1942 and 1945.

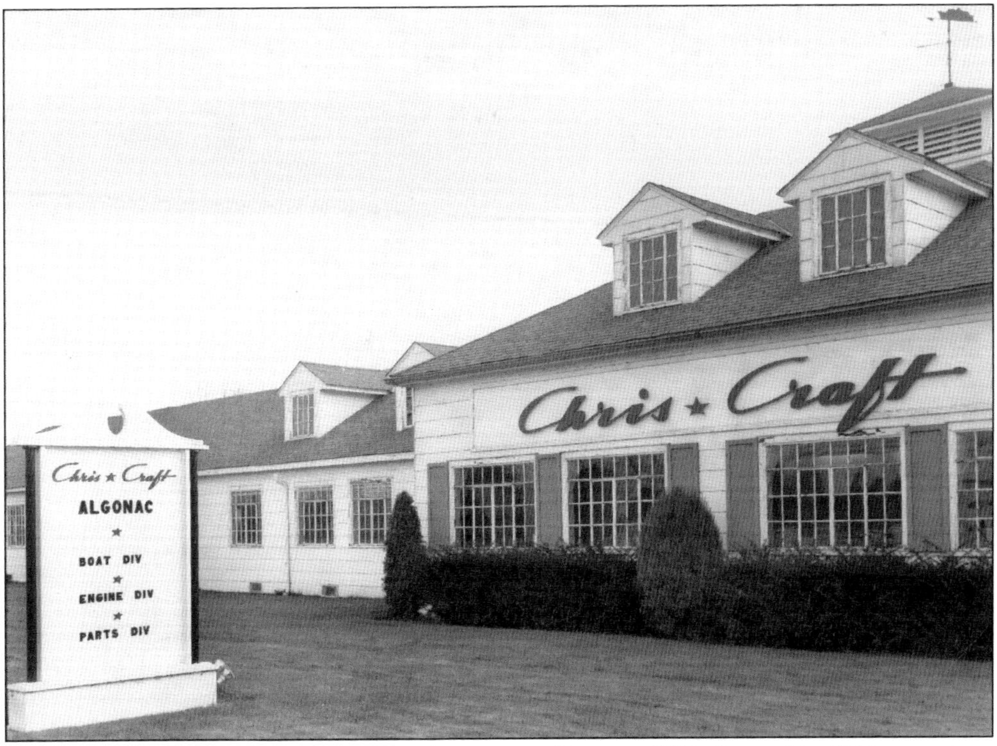

The national headquarters of Chris-Craft is pictured here in 1934. Formed in 1910 to produce runabouts, Chris-Craft started as the Smith-Ryan Boat Company.

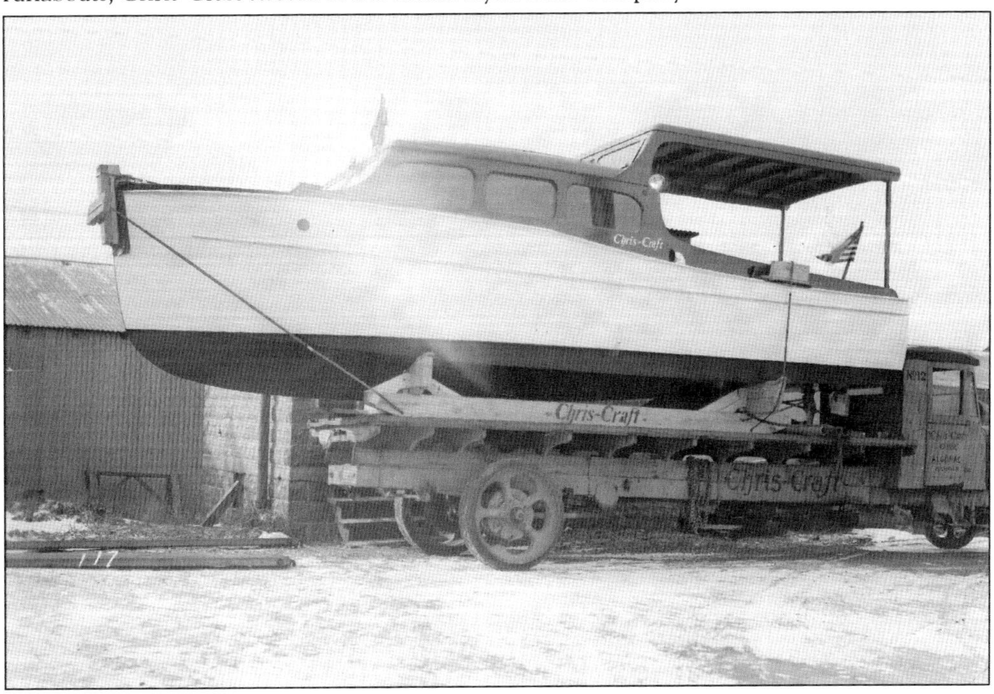

Chris-Craft used various means of transportation to delivery its boats. Pictured here is a Chris-Craft truck from the 1920s. Chris-Craft also owned its own 35-ton Plymouth locomotive.

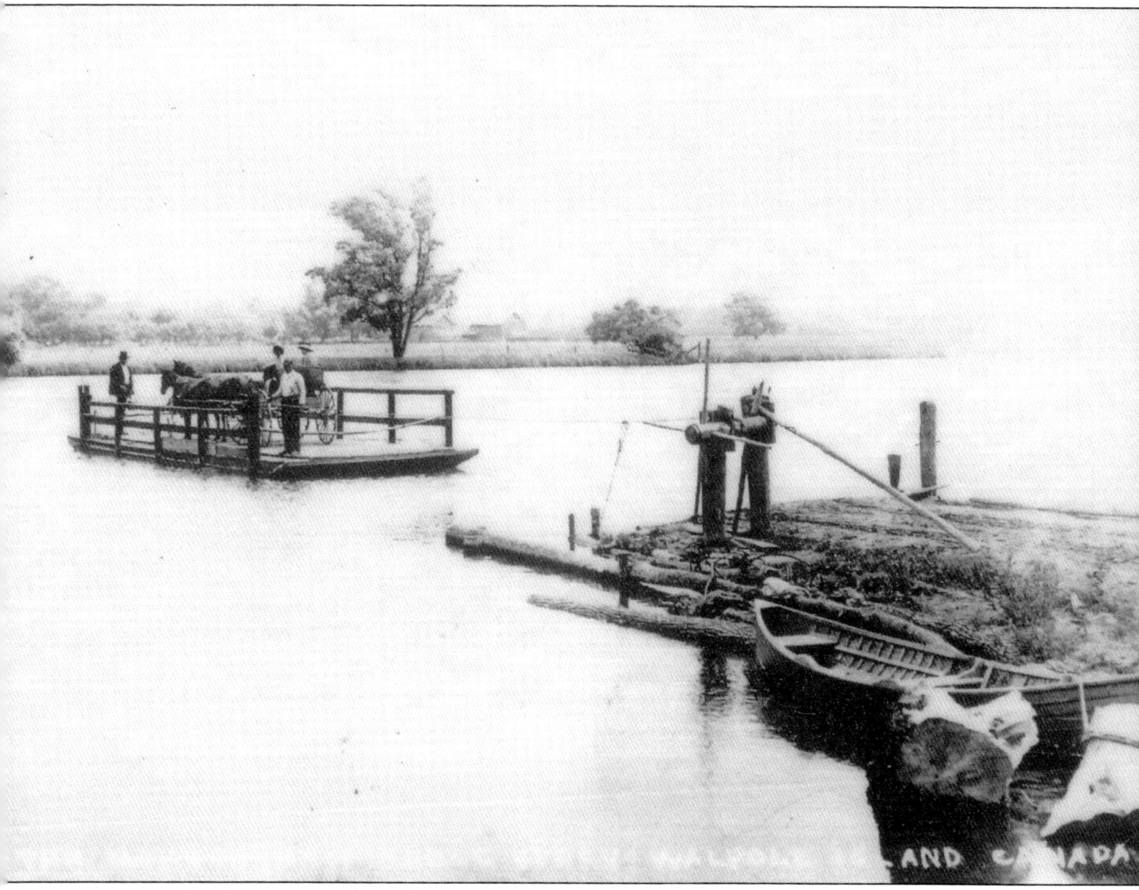

A wooden ferry is seen here leaving Sans Souci in the 1890s. The local area is interlaced with many waterways, including the St. Clair River and Lake St. Clair, as well as several channels, cuts, bays, canals, and streams. Because of this landscape, ferryboats were a necessary means of transportation. They were very primitive in the beginning; however, they were able to transport goods, passengers, and horse and carriages, as shown in this image.

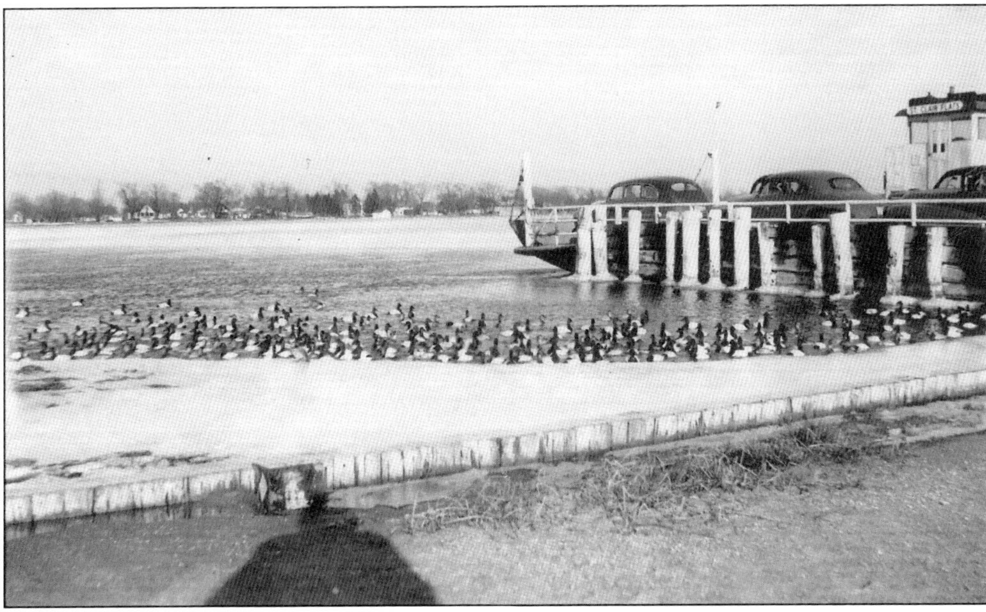
The Champion's Ferry landing is shown in this photograph from the 1930s. The *Harsens Island* was the name of the first ferry steel vessel purchased by the Champions, while the *St. Clair Flats* was the second. Once the ferries had cleared the water of ice, ducks and geese would gather by the shoreline.

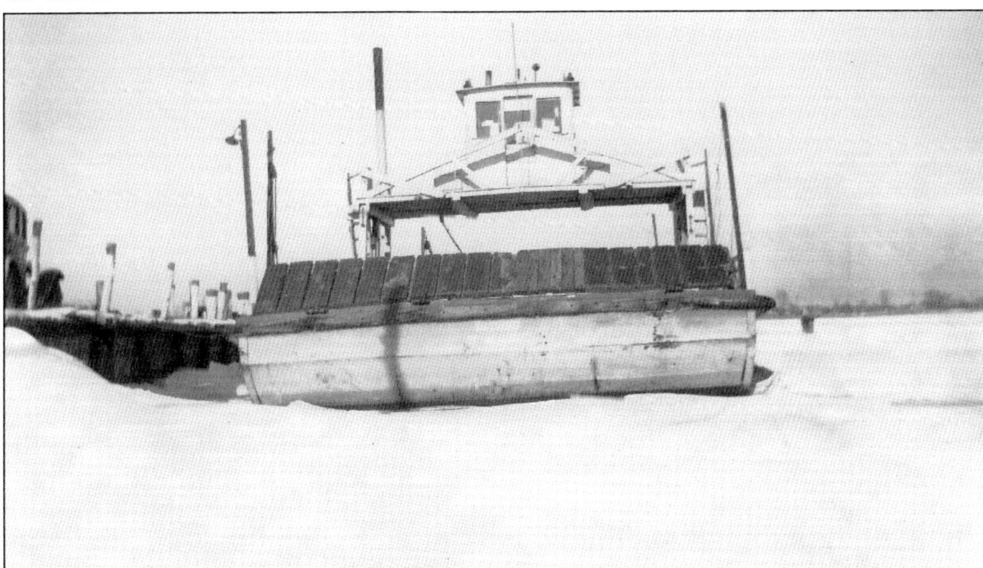
The *Chief Harsen* is stuck in the ice in this 1930s snapshot. Passenger ferries serviced various locations on the mainland, from which they carried people and goods to the islands of the area. The passenger launches had an inboard engine and varied in length from 25 to 35 feet. The covered engine was located in the center of the launch, with seating accommodations for the passengers arranged accordingly. When auto ferries came into being, they were towed by launches, operated by cables stretched across the waterway and then self-powered by gasoline and diesel engines. The auto ferries ranged in size from being able to carry only a couple of cars to a much larger 24-car ferry like the *Chief Harsen*.

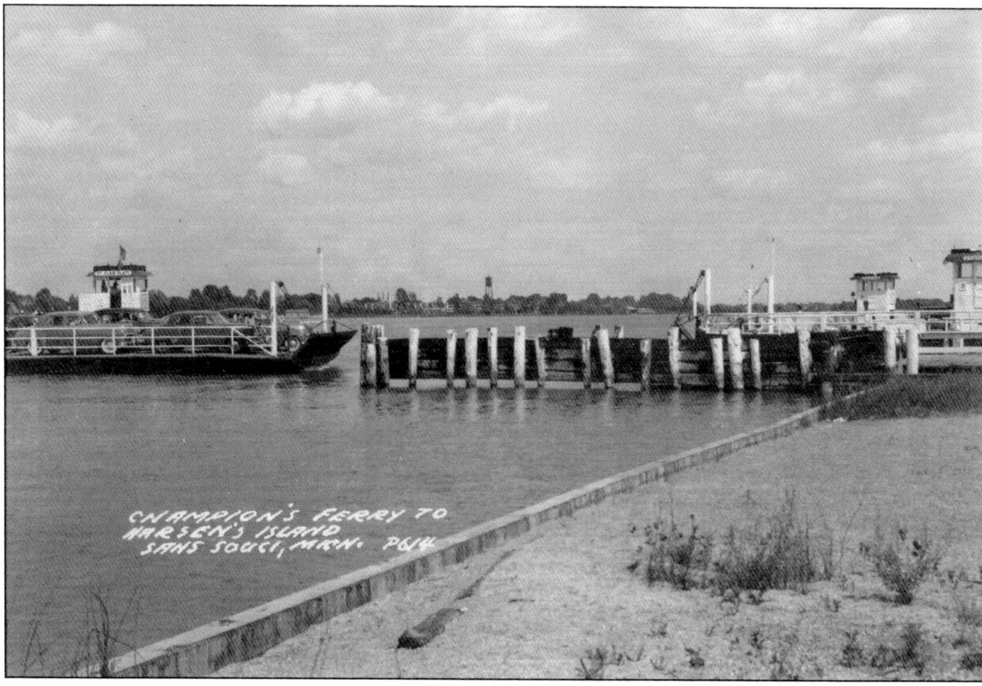

Art Champion began ferrying passengers in 1923, with service to both Harsens and Dickinson Islands. He operated three Chris-Craft vessels from his home on Dickinson Island to a pickup point across the North Channel at Pointe Tremble. This service continued until 1937 when he purchased his first auto ferry business from R.C. Witmiller and named it Champion's Auto Ferry.

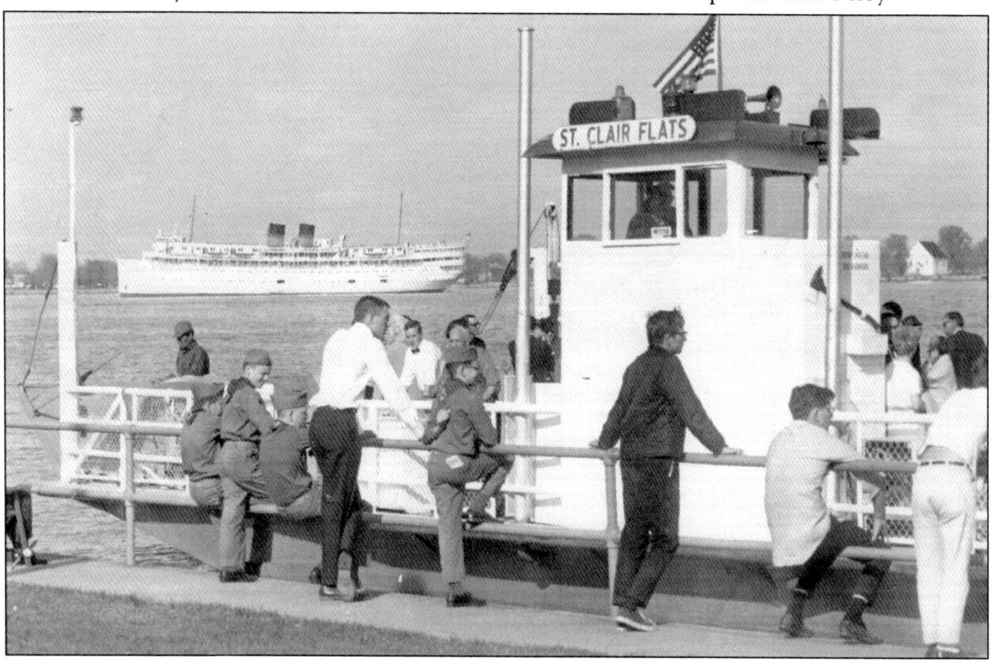

Champion's *St. Clair Flats* is pictured here with Boy Scouts in the 1950s. Built to handle the ever-increasing car traffic, the *St. Clair Flats* could hold up to 36 automobiles. The cruise ship SS *South America* is seen passing in the background.

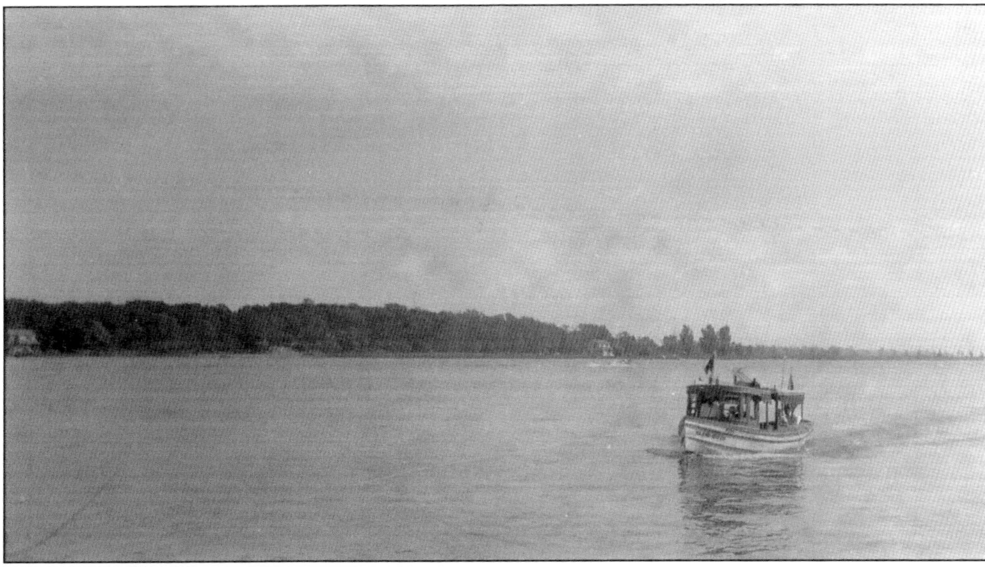

The *Island Queen* ferry is seen here in the 1920s. The oldest recorded information about a ferry service was the one operated by Chris Smith in 1902. He had two ferryboats: the *Eloise* and the *Charles S.* They were used for passenger service to the Flats and Tashmoo Park. In the 1920s and 1930s, numerous ferry companies competed for service because of a population increase in the area.

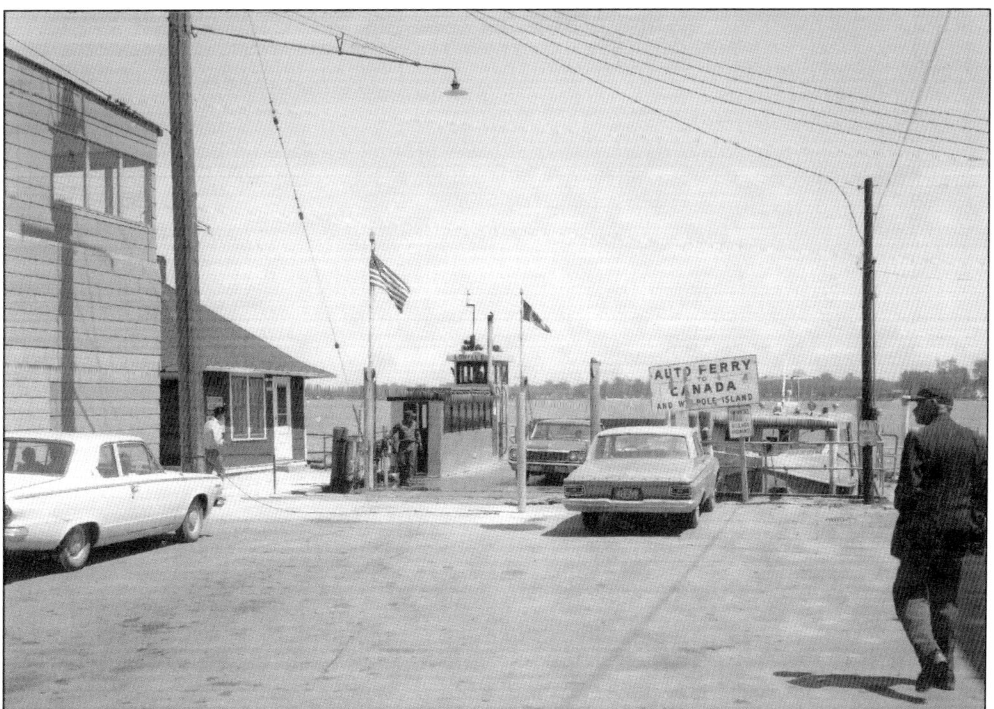

The *Lowell D.* car ferry is pictured here docked at the immigration office in Algonac. The ferry served residents of Walpole Island, who enjoy dual citizenship from both the United States and Canada. The island of Walpole itself is Canadian soil.

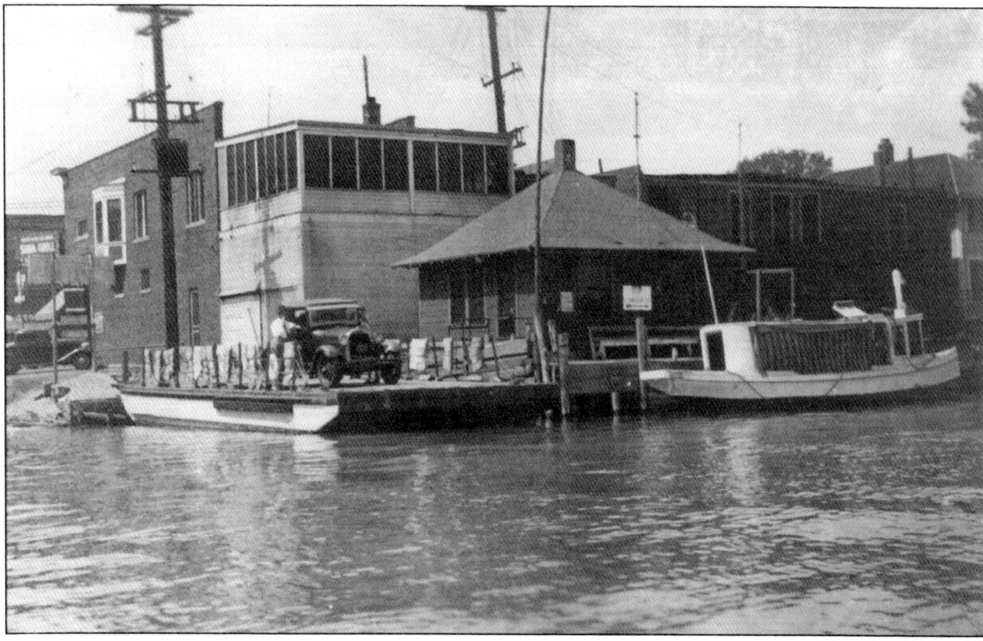

The Algonac immigration office is pictured here in the 1920s. Cars were brought in on barges that were towed behind passenger boats like the one seen at right in this image.

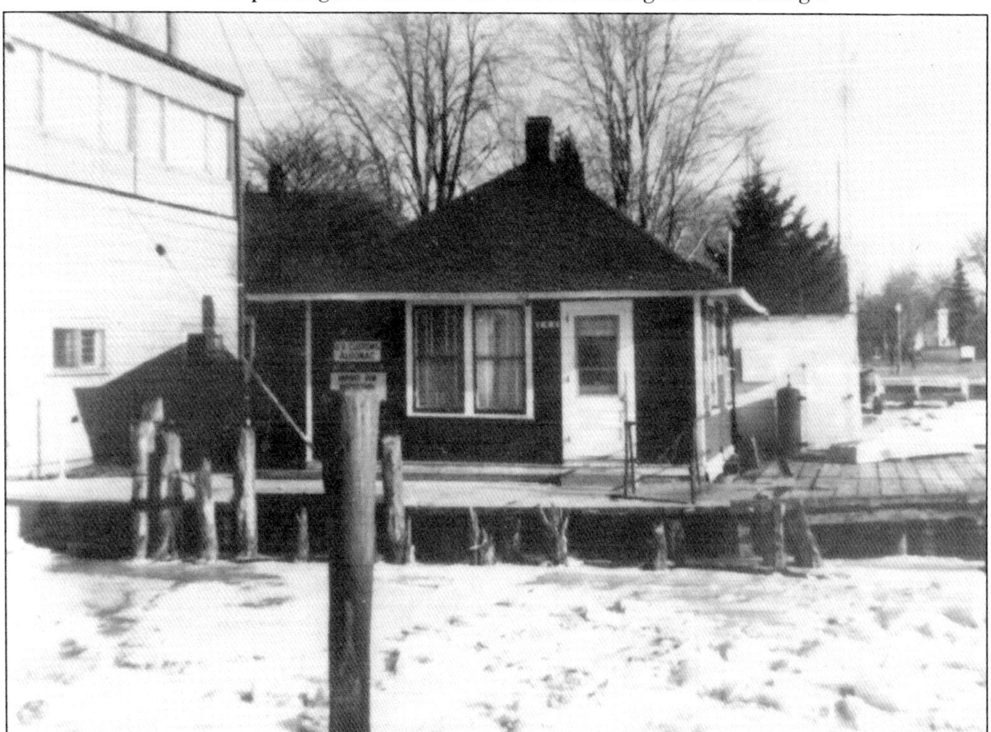

This is wintertime scene of the Algonac immigration office. During the winter, ferry service would come to a complete stop. All supplies were transported to the islands over the frozen St. Clair River at a great risk, as many people and cars fell through the ice.

A barge is pictured here arriving at the Walpole Island immigration office during the 1920s. Around 1900, James Williams and Ziba Brigham operated the first gasoline ferry across the river to Algonac. The next ferry was the *Della* launch, also operated by Williams. In 1919, Williams sold the ferry to an American, George Gilbert. In 1920, Edward Kiyoshk brought ownership back into Canadian hands.

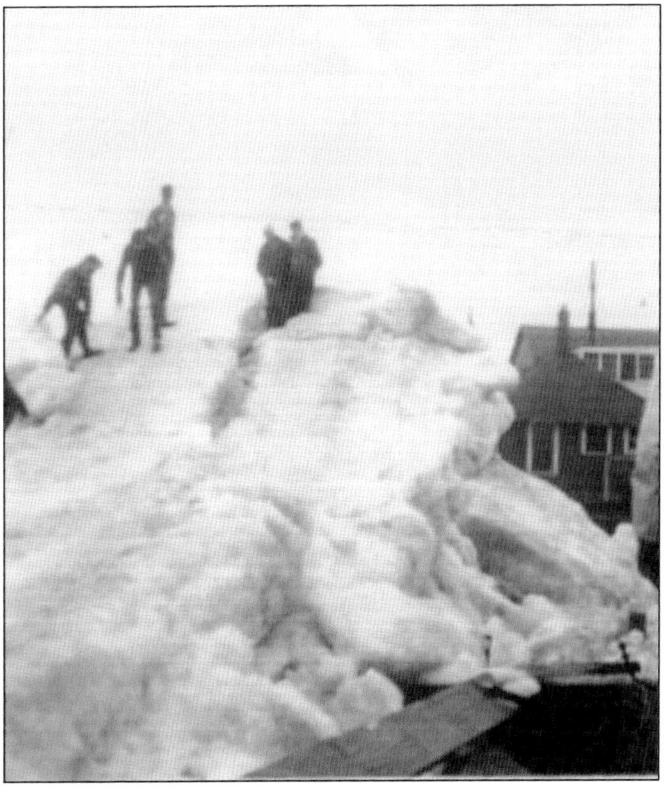

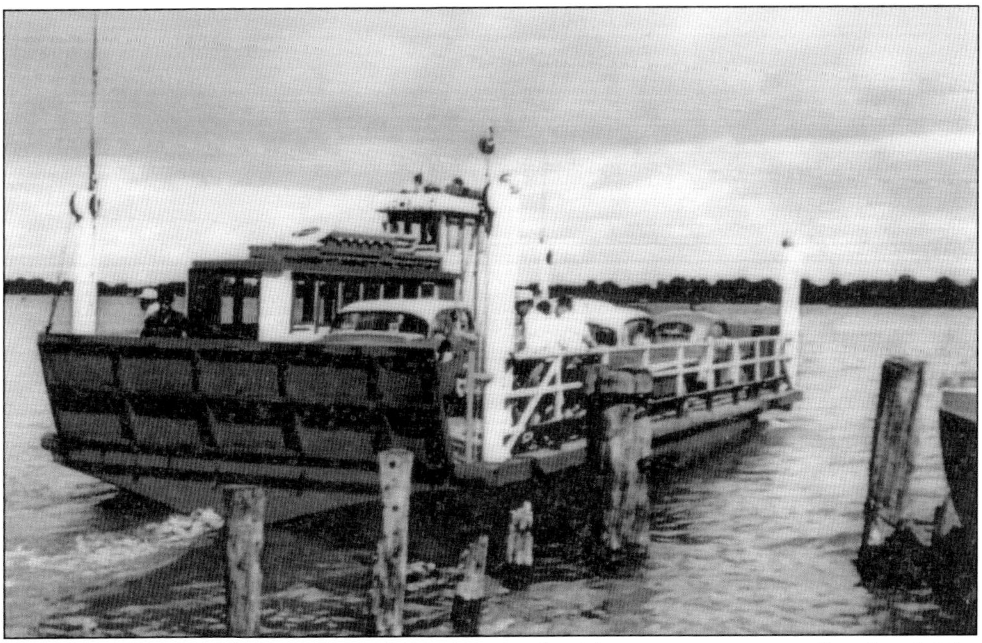

The *Lowell D.* of Chatham is pictured here leaving the Algonac immigration office, headed for Walpole Island. In 1825, there were only 25 Native Americans on the island, but a proclamation was issued declaring the island as an Indian reserve. By 1839, all white people living on the island had left.

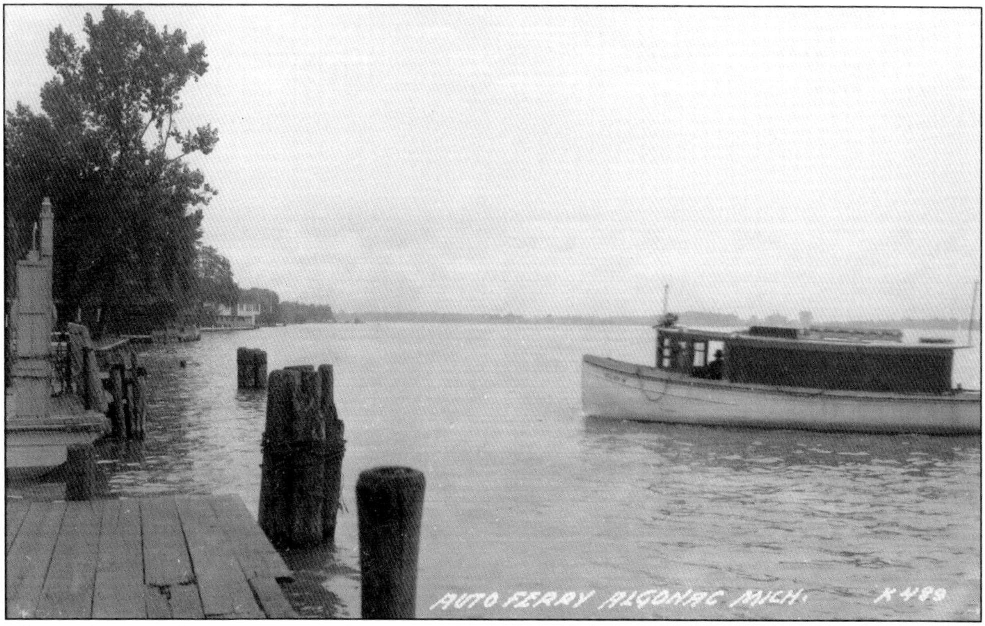

The earliest car ferries were wooden scows commonly referred to as barges. A launch would be fastened by cable to one side of the scow. In early years, a gangplank was fastened to only one end of the scow. The automobiles would pass over the gangplank onto the scow. With the scow secured and the gangplank in place, the cars would then be backed off the scow.

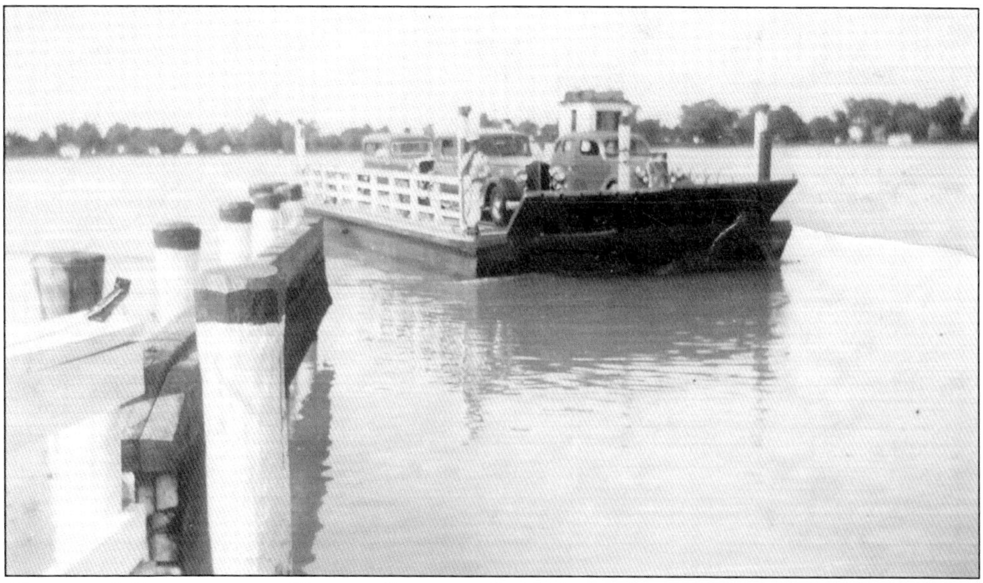

Champion's Ferry is pictured here pulling into the dock at Algonac during the summer of 1935. When Arthur Champion purchased the ferry business from Ralph Witmiller, the ferries were made of wood. Champion upgraded to steel ferries, enabling the service to run during winter months.

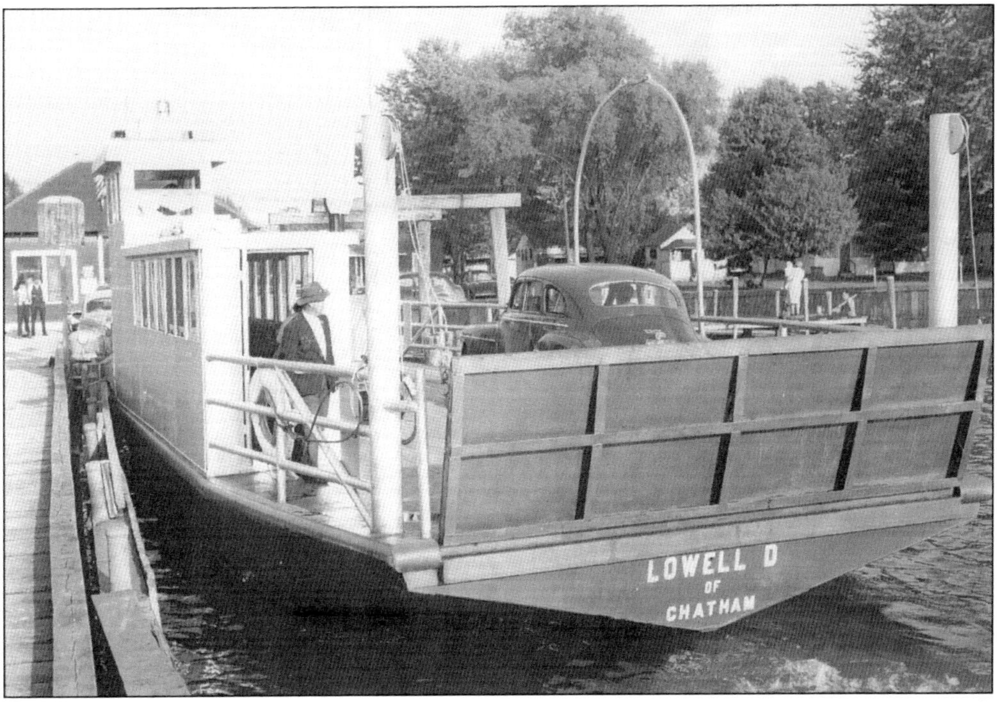

The *Lowell D.* ran between Algonac and Walpole Island and had a six-car capacity. In 1930, Frank Bray of Port Lambton, Ontario, bought the business and added two scows to carry cars. In 1939, Morgan Dalgety took over the ferry. He later replaced the wooden launches and scows with the *Lowell D.*, a diesel-powered steel ferry.

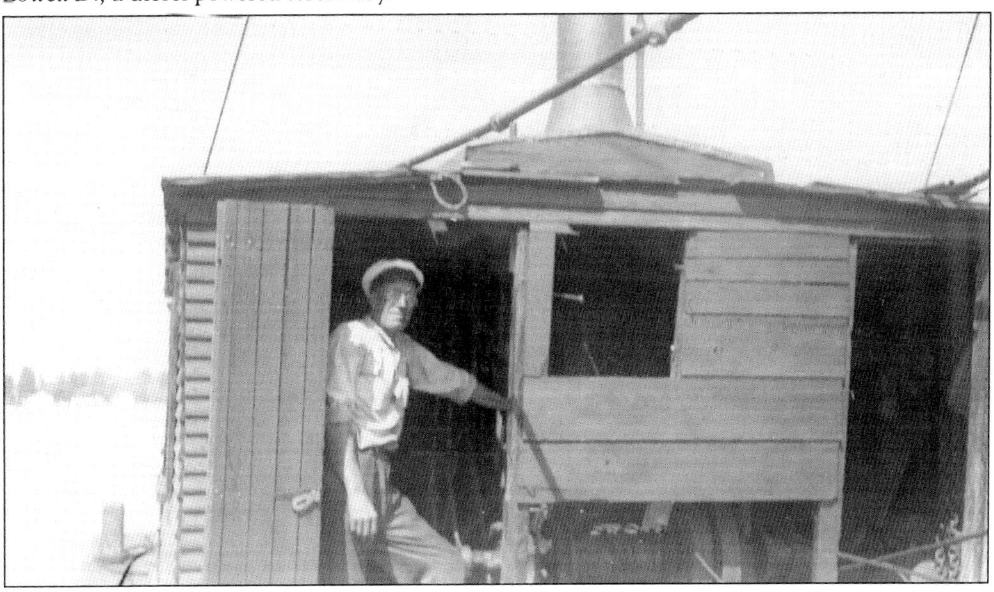

George Raymond is seen in the wheelhouse. In the 1920s, George and Stewart Raymond started an auto ferry service to the island known as Raymond's Ferry. It traveled between Pointe Du Chene and the Grande Pointe Cut. They had the first self-propelled auto ferry to the island. In 1929, the Raymonds had to move their ferry service from Pointe Du Chene because Garfield Wood was expanding his boat plant.

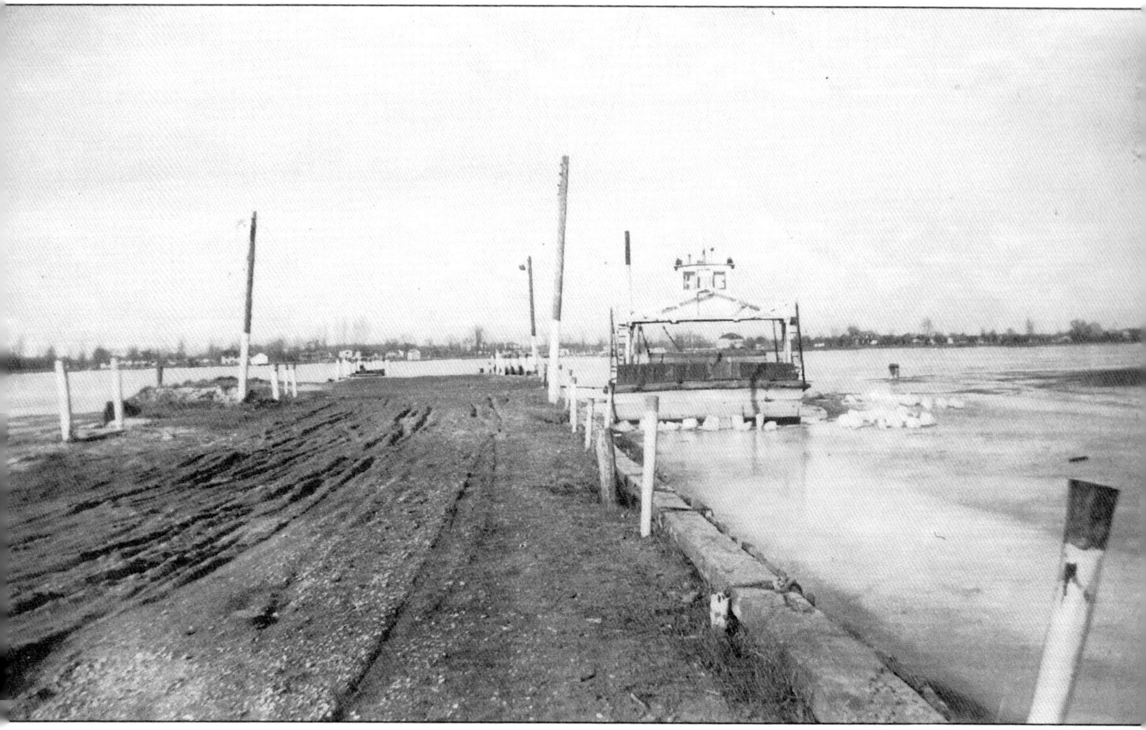

The *Chief Harsens*, owned by Raymond's Ferry, is pictured here in the 1930s. Scheduled crossings are not always enough to keep the course open during prolonged periods of frigid weather. At such times, some extra, unscheduled round-trips are necessary downstream from the regular crossing areas. This allows the large chunks of ice to flow away from the crossing route and minimizes the severity of any refreezing that occurs.

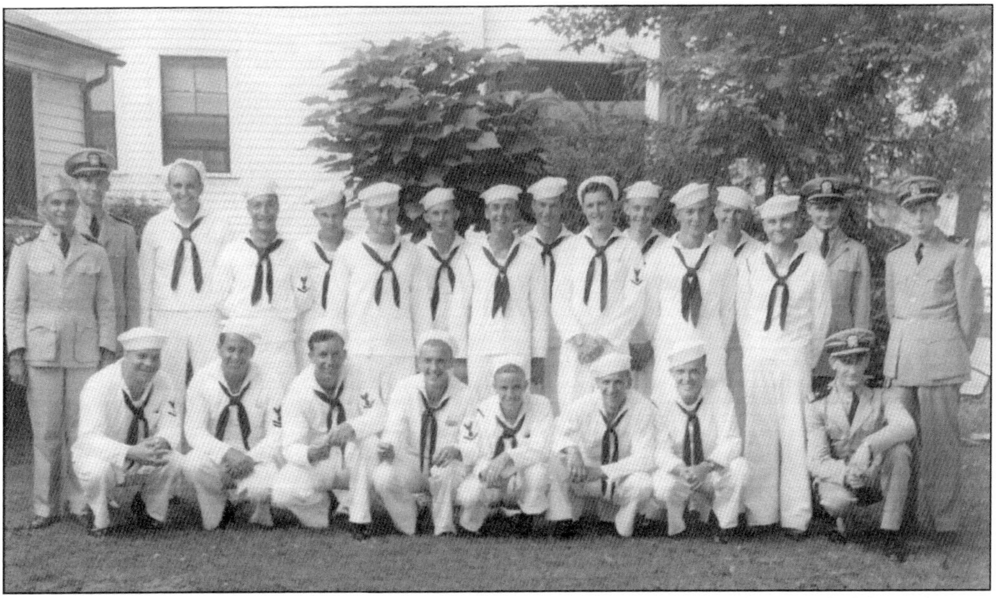

The compass compensating class is pictured here on July 14, 1943. The class was held in Algonac from July 1 through July 15, 1943. Gerald Mallon, plant manager of the Algonac Chris-Craft Plant, is standing at the far right.

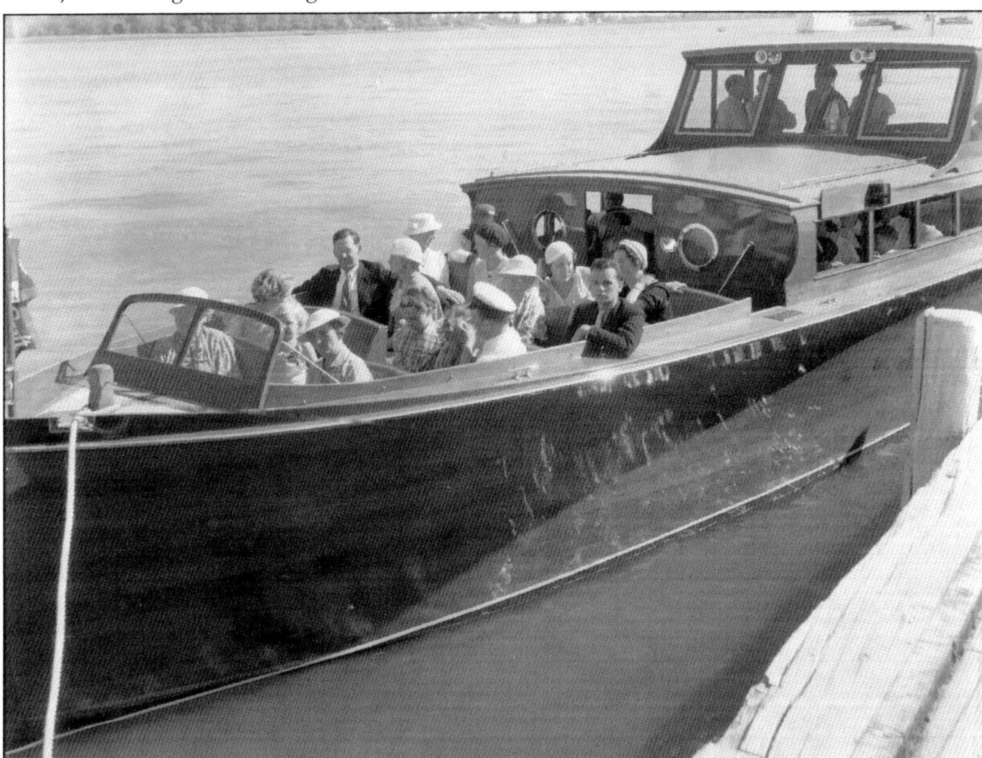

The *Florence K*, pictured here in 1943, was a 48-foot taxi for ferrying passengers to Mackinaw Island in Lake Michigan. The boat could accommodate up to 60 passengers in her open forward cockpit, central enclosed cabin, and open aft seating areas.

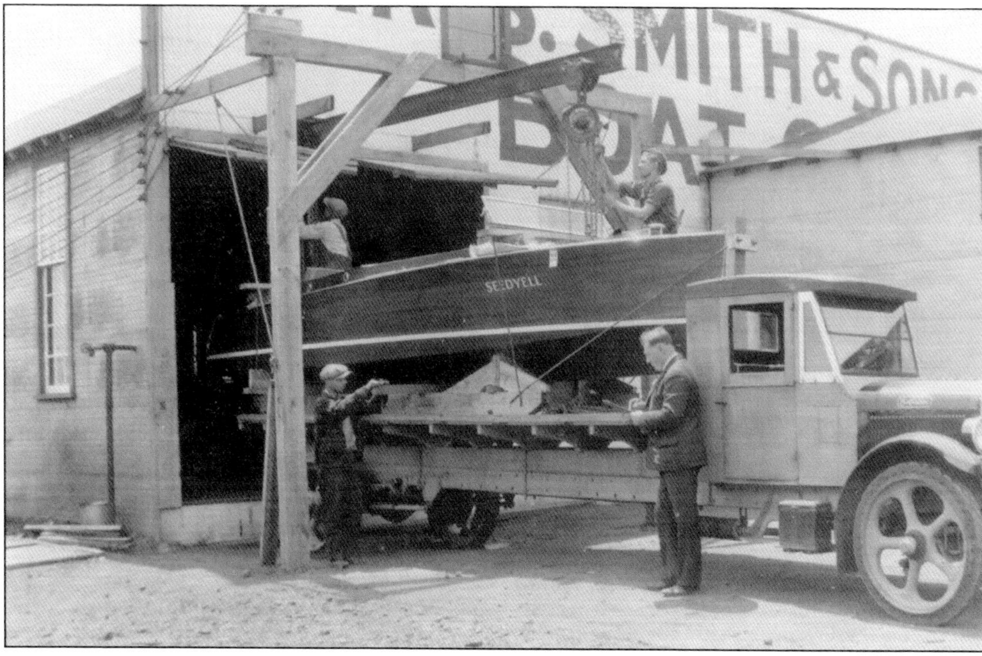

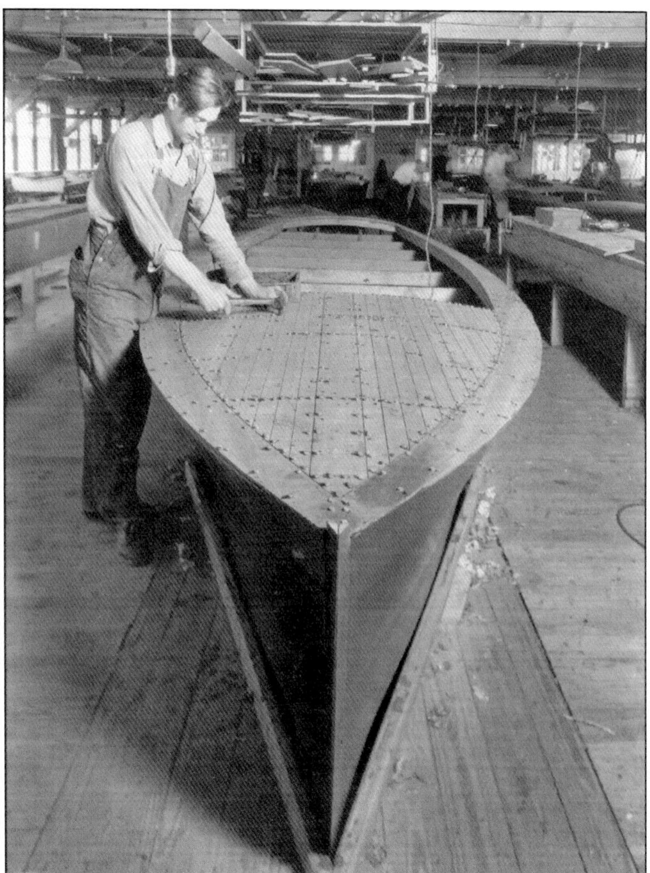

This photograph shows a Chris-Craft boat on a hoist over a truck parked outside the factory in 1929. Standing next to the truck cab is Bernard Smith, vice president in charge of manufacturing and production. Chris-Craft boats were so much in demand that, by 1929, the company was working six days a week to fill orders.

This photograph of a Chris-Craft worker from the 1920s illustrates the amount of Philippine mahogany bungs necessary to seal the holes left by bronze fastening screws.

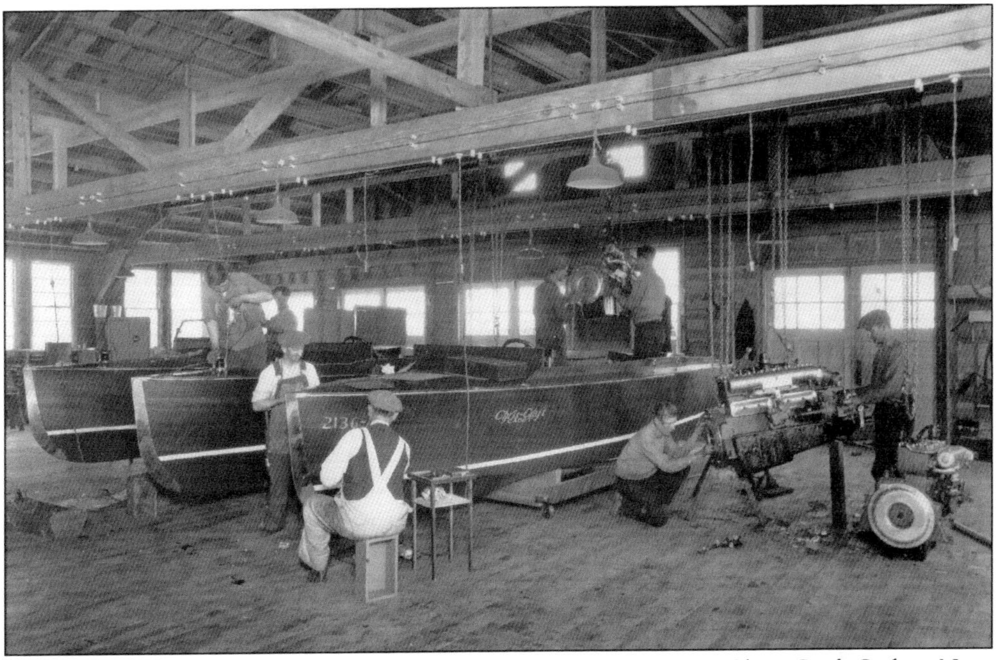

Workers are pictured here installing Chrysler Imperial engines into Chris-Craft Cadets. Note how the lettering specialist is applying the finishing touches.

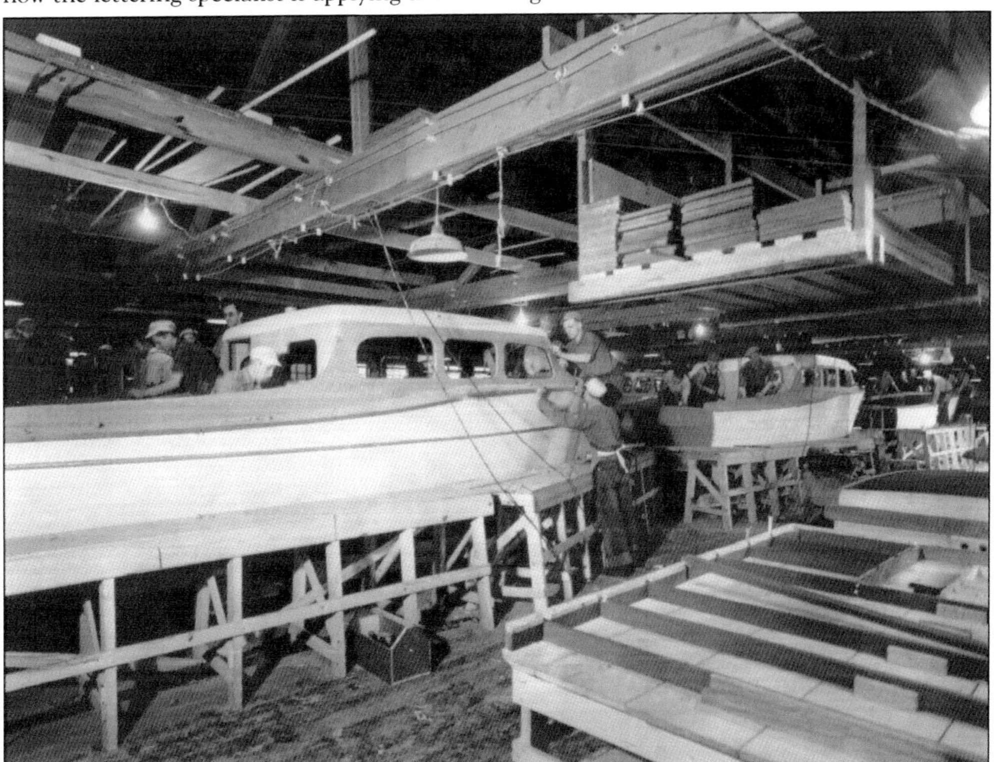

By 1952, Chris-Craft had produced its last military vessel, a 52-foot aircraft rescue boat, during the Korean War. In 1957, Chris-Craft moved its corporate offices to Pompano Beach, Florida.

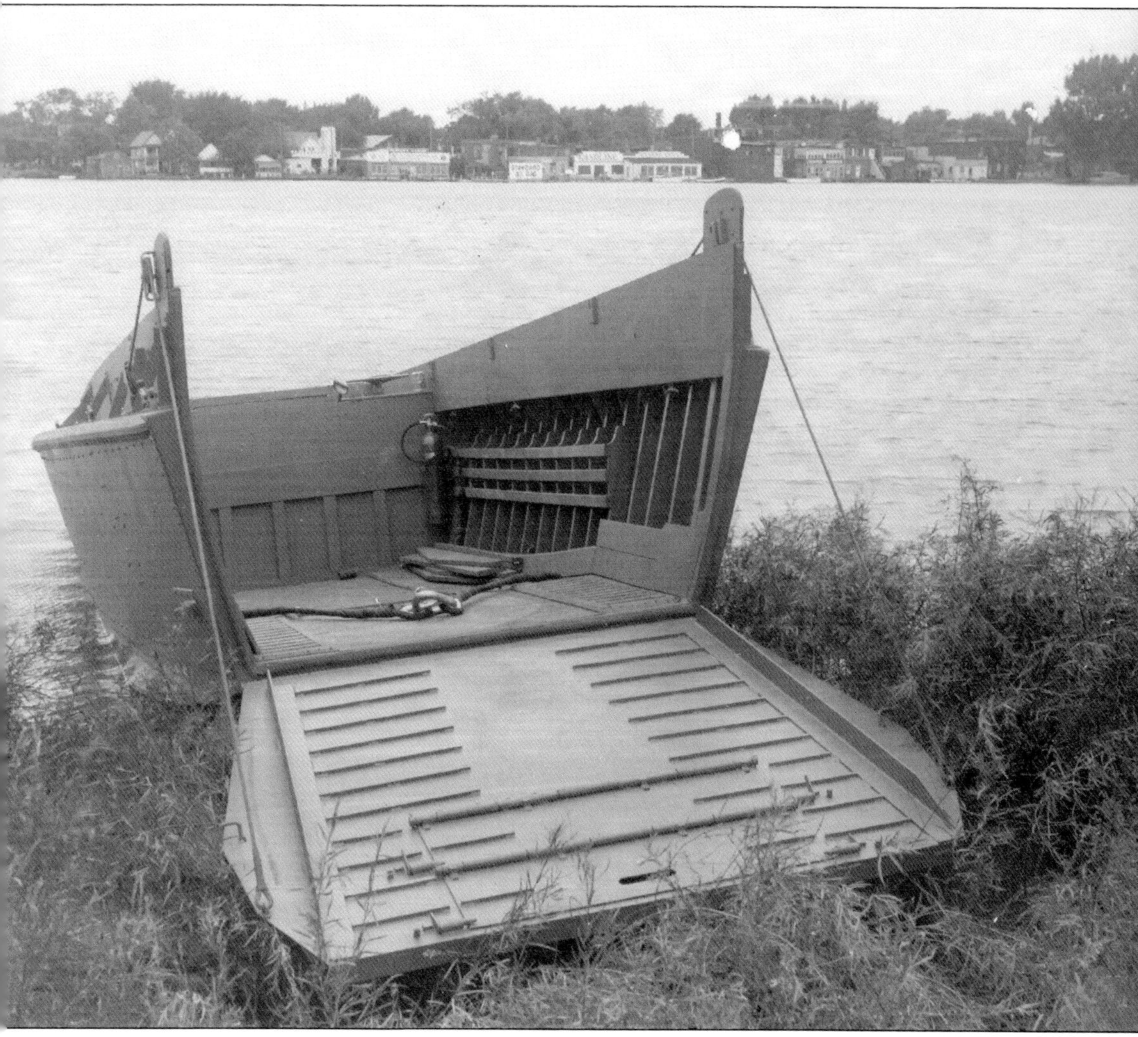

This LCVR (landing craft vehicle ramp) was tested by the Navy along the banks of the St. Clair River in Algonac. Powered by a 225-horsepower diesel engine from the Gray Marine Motor Company, this model could even transport the Army's smallest combat tank.

In a ceremony held on June 15, 1942, employees of all three Chris-Craft plants received the prestigious Navy "E" Award, which included a lapel pin. Receiving the highest civilian award for an American factory enabled the Algonac, Cadillac, and Holland plants to fly the "E" flag until victory was won. Owen Smith, vice president of sales, is standing to the right of the podium with his hands folded.

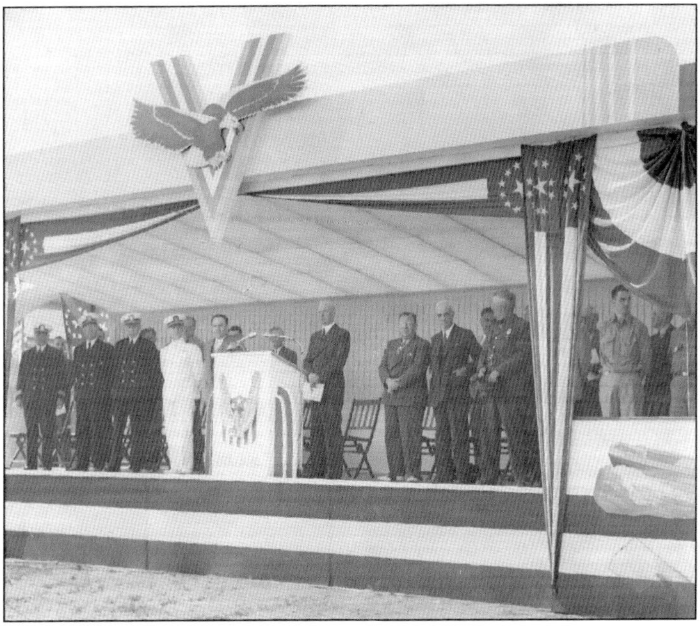

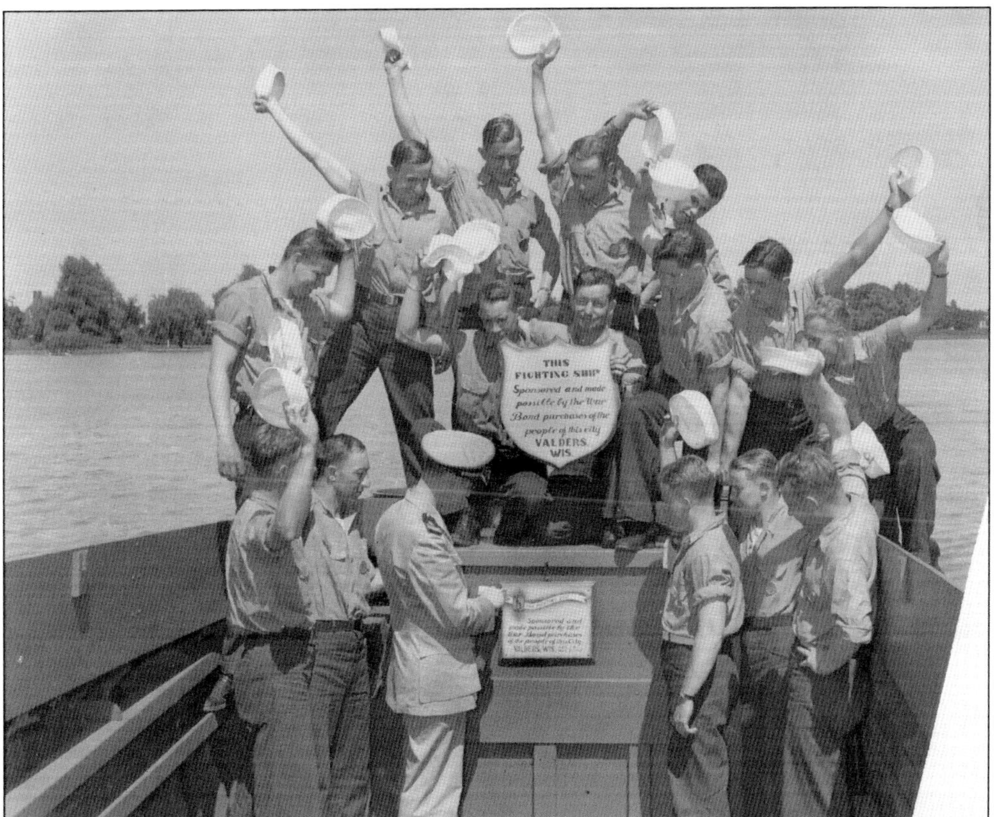

A Chris-Craft LCVR is shown here being used in a World War II bond promotion. The Chris-Craft LCVRs were the first landing craft to hit the beaches of Normandy, France, during the Allied invasion of Europe on June 6, 1944.

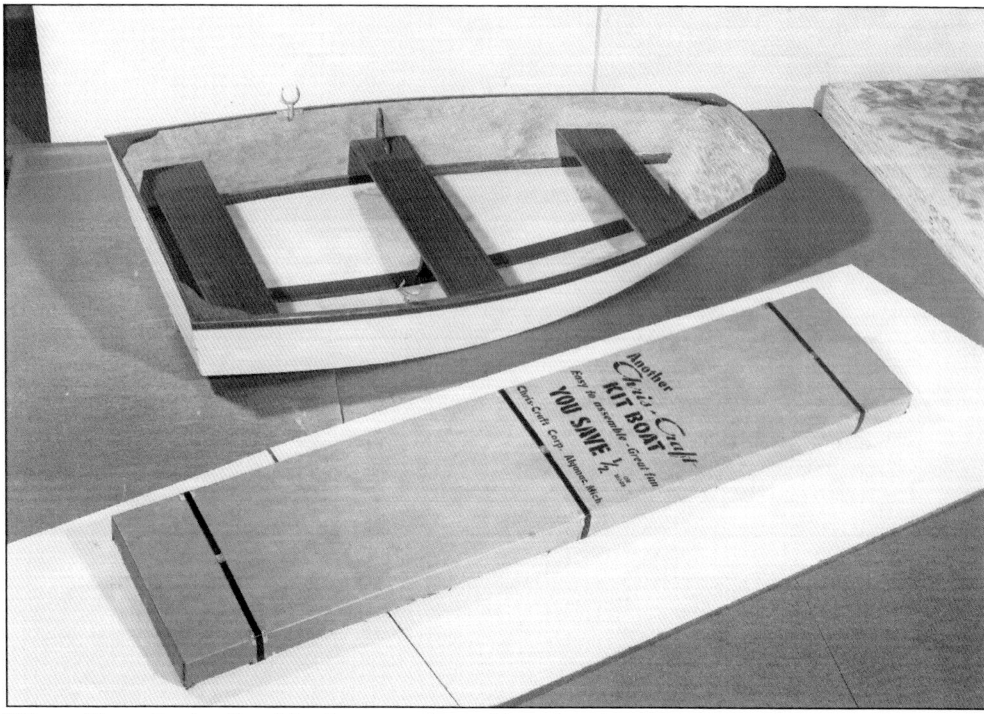

When Chris-Craft offered kit boats to the public, they became so popular that the Kit Boat Division was established in 1952. Pictured here is the eight-foot Pram kit, designed to be built in 8–10 hours and sold for $39.

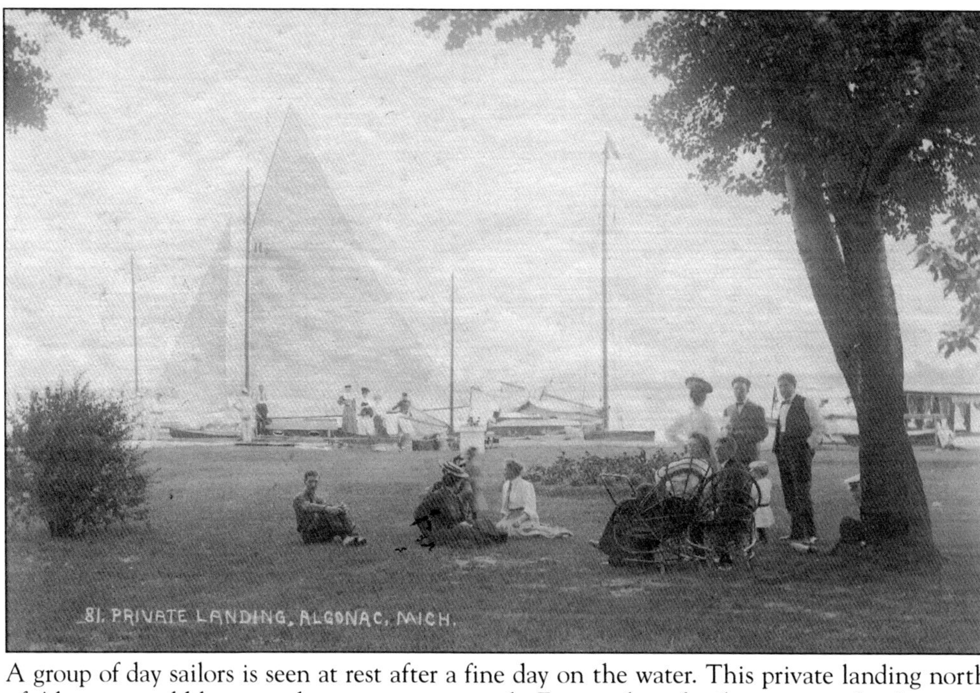

A group of day sailors is seen at rest after a fine day on the water. This private landing north of Algonac could be near the present state park. Even a day of sailing required a degree of formal dress.

Eight

People of Algonac

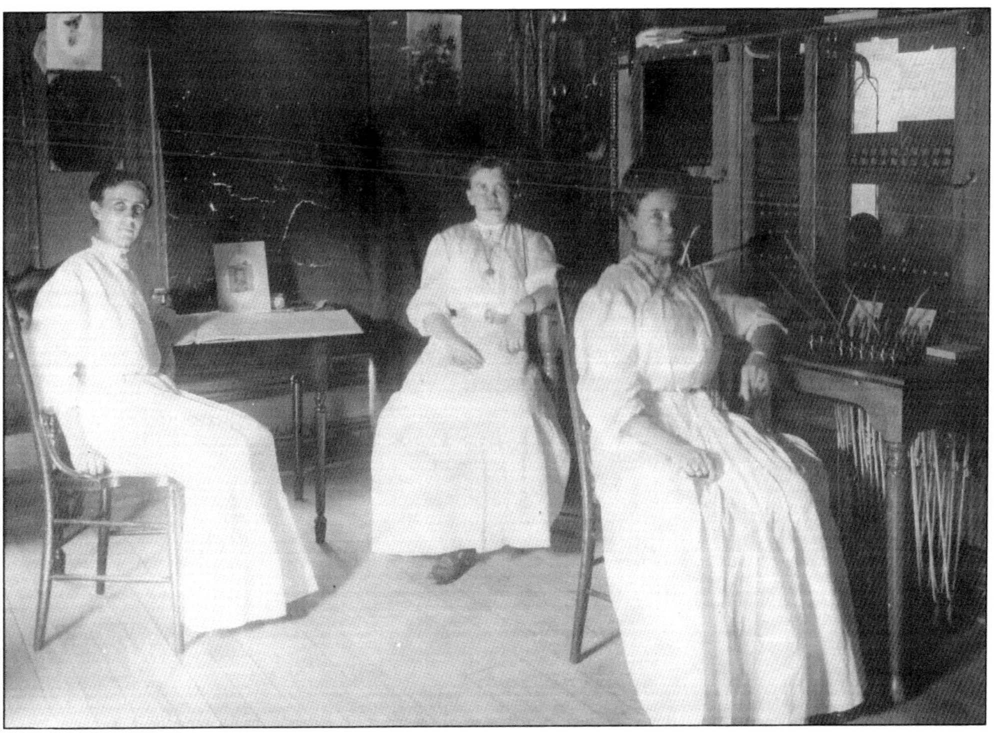

This photograph shows the telephone exchange above Ame's Barbershop in 1905. From left to right are Katy Lumley, Jessie Green, and Frances Cartwright. Although the exact date of Algonac's first telegraph office is uncertain, there was an advertisement in the *Courier* that read, "D. G. Jones – Postmaster Manager of Telegraph and Telephone Lines." In 1900, the State Telephone Company came to Algonac, and Chris Smith had the telephone exchange located behind the post office.

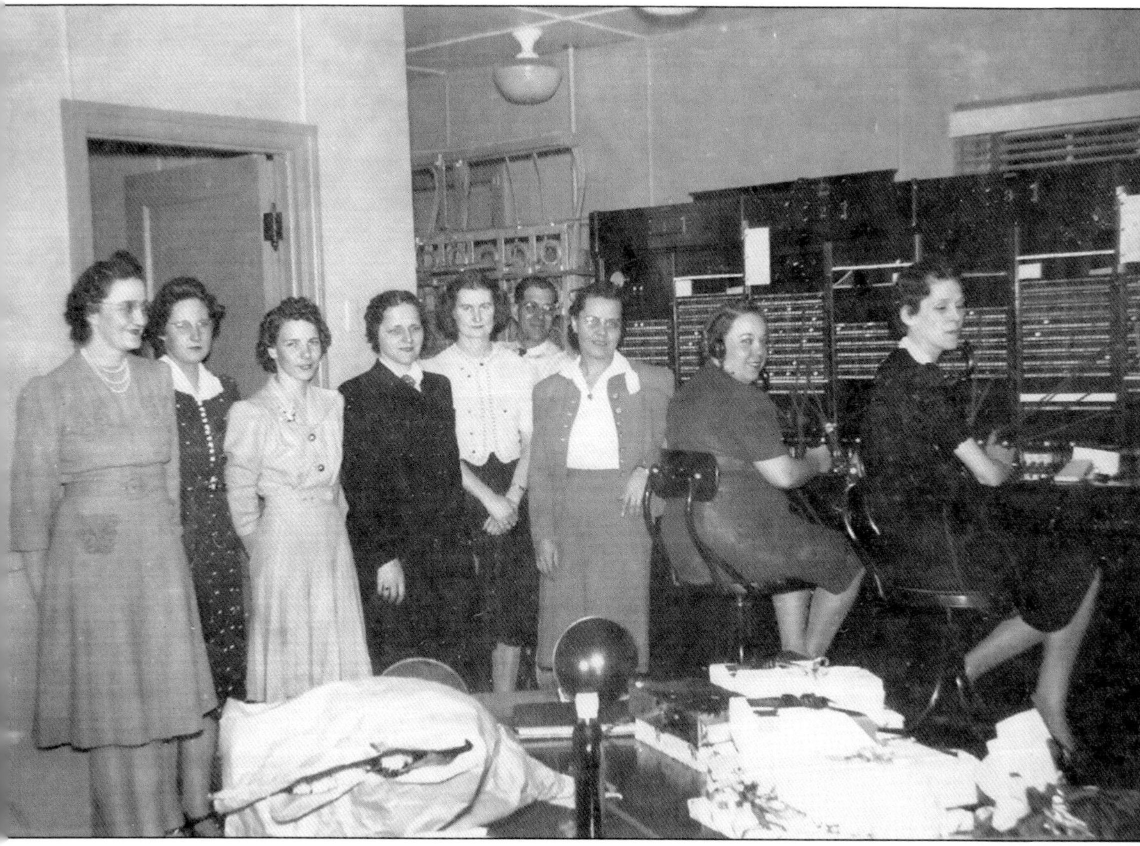

A group of telephone operators have gathered together for a Christmas party. Phone service packages included two- and four-party lines, or a private line was available for an extra fee. Numbers were four digits and a letter, such as 278J1.

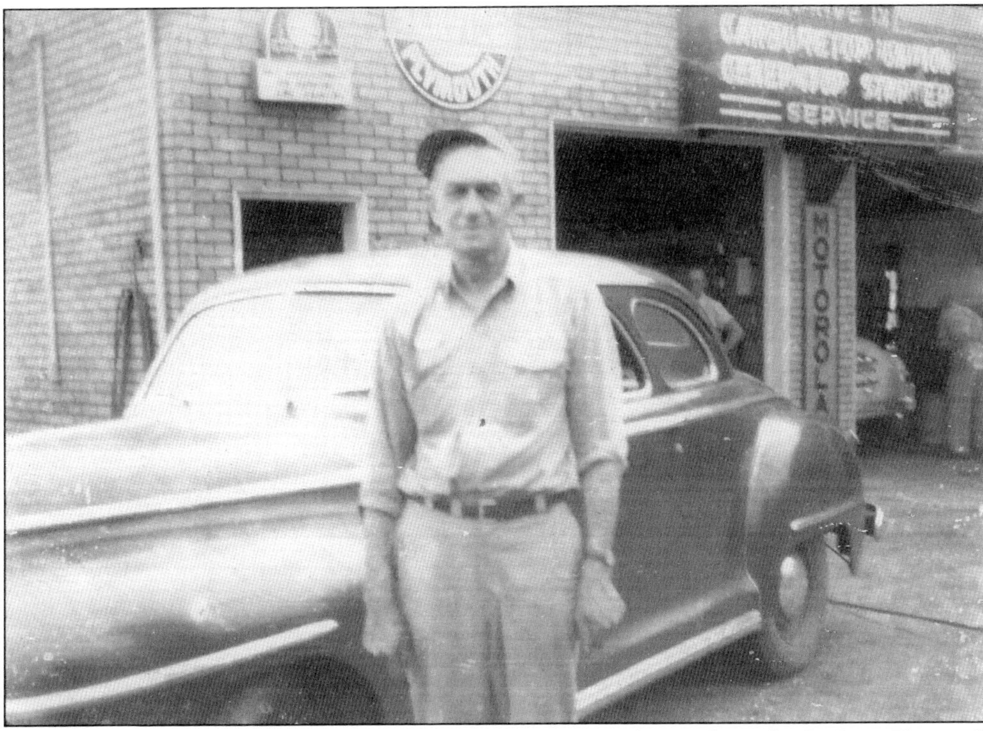

Stub Cartwright is pictured here standing next to a new Plymouth at the DeSoto Plymouth dealership. At small dealerships, the owner would often sell and service the cars.

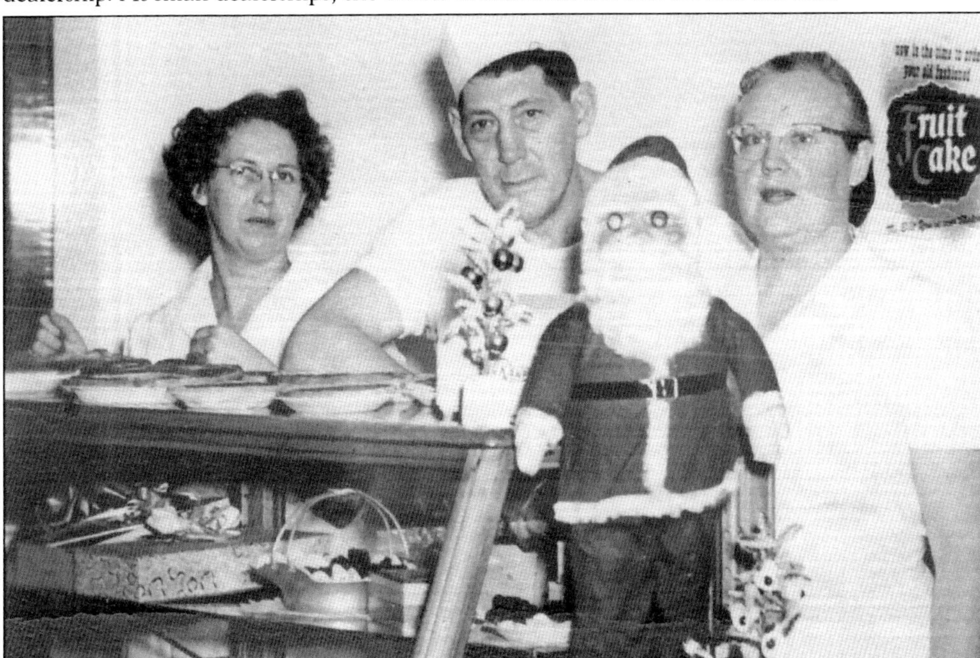

Algonac Bakery was located on the corner of Michigan and Summer Streets. The establishment boasted, "Pies as good as Mother's. Best Oatmeal Date in the world, just 5 cents each." The school traffic was brisk at lunch hour.

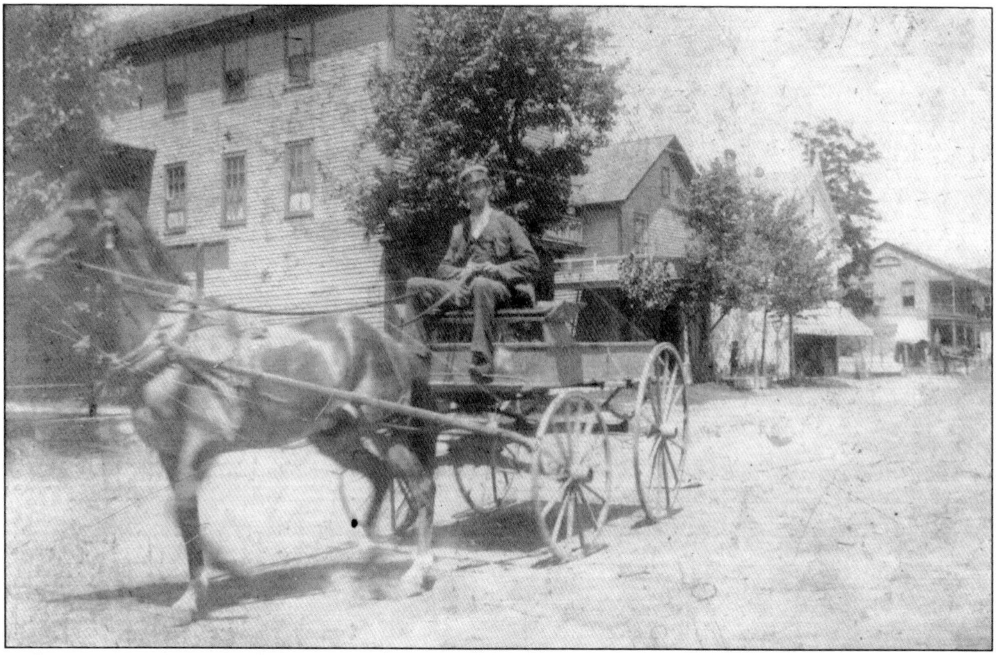

Gilbert Grocery operated a horse-drawn delivery wagon. Most merchants had delivery service in Algonac around the turn of the century. It was considered good business to provide a convenience to customers that would keep them shopping.

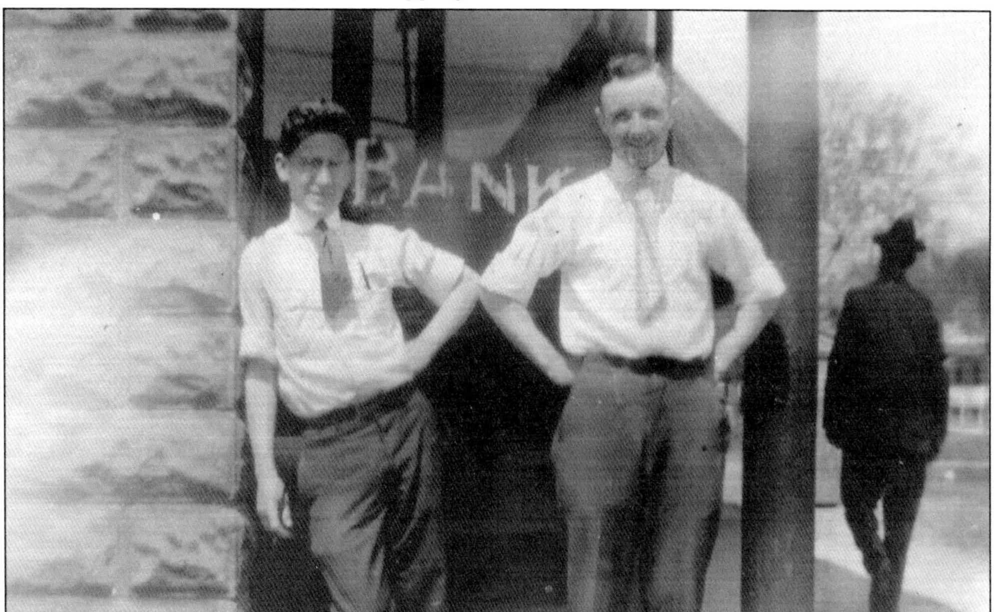

Standing in front of the Ward Carmon Bank are George Harvey (left) and Glen Young (right) in 1904. The bank was constructed on the northwest corner of Water and Fruit Streets in the same year. It was bought out by the Algonac Savings Bank in 1912. The building later became a drugstore successively owned by Gordon Guiness, William Newton, Arthur Miller, and Everett Watts. Dick Ames and Homer Nugent ran a meat market from the same location. The market was housed in the north portion of the Carmon Bank.

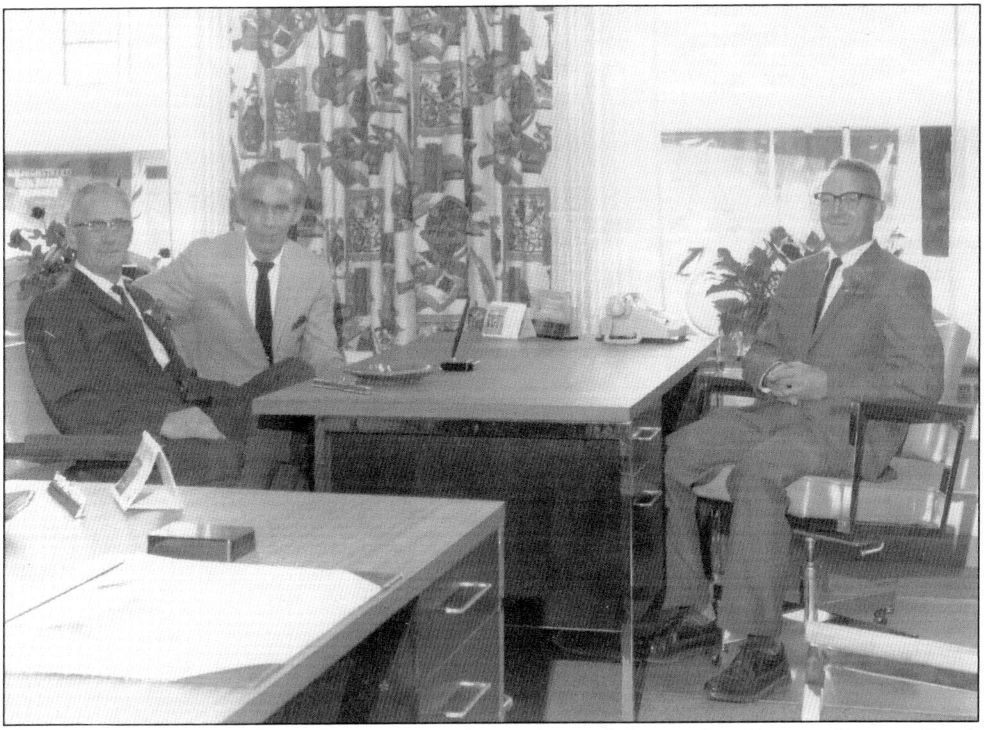

After the bowling alley and the Algonac Theater burned down, the Algonac Savings Bank acquired the property and built and addition on the north side of the bank.

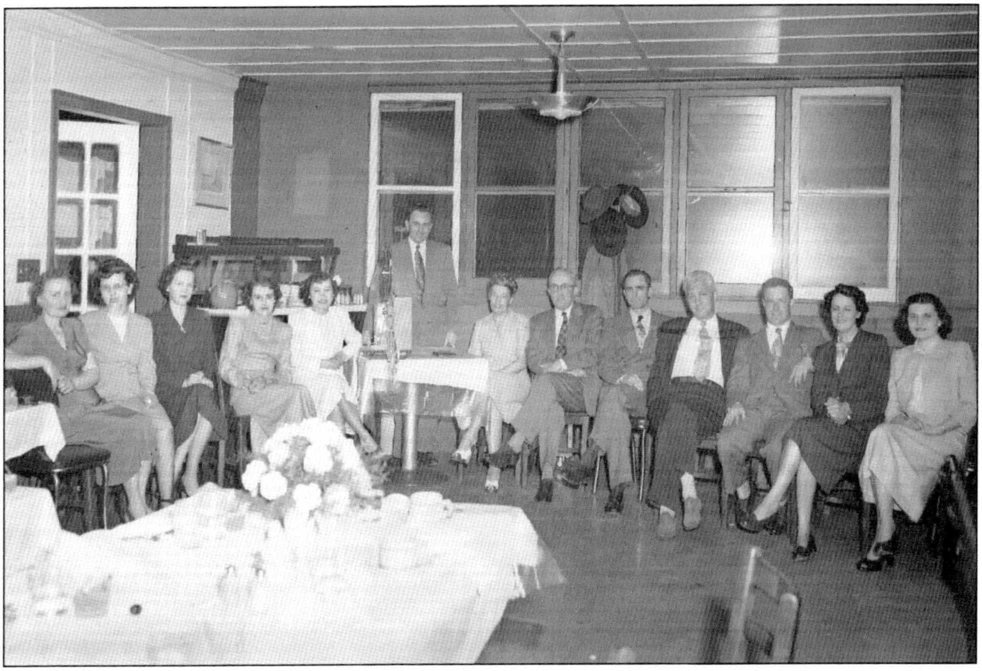

The staff of Algonac Savings Bank is pictured here attending an informational meeting at Marino Spaghetti House in Fair Haven. After Mario Spaghetti House closed, Algonac Savings Bank bought the property and built a branch office.

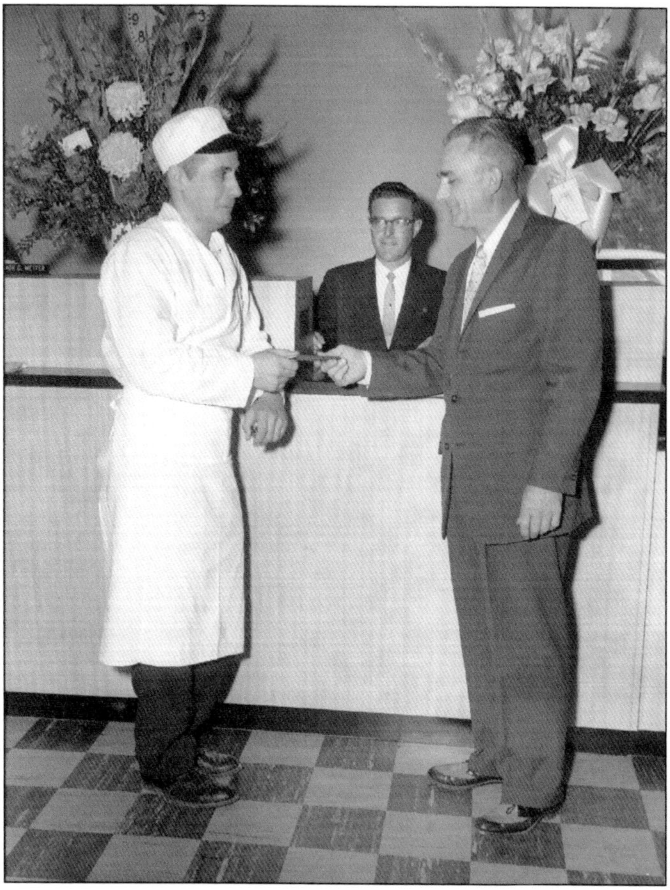

The Algonac Savings Bank's new branch in Fair Haven opened for business in 1959. The branch manager, Jack Ouimet, is pictured here behind the counter.

The Kimball House was built by Chester Kimball in 1866. In the summer, guests relaxed on swings and lawn chairs in the shade of huge willow trees or rocking chairs on the wide front porch. Patrons could buy a two-quart jar of beer for 10¢.

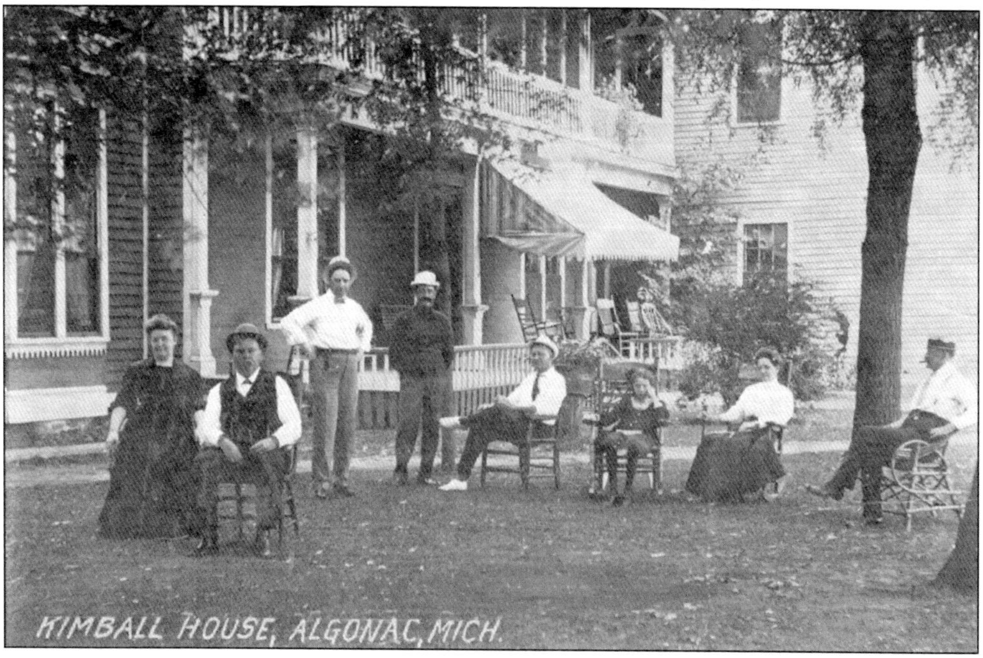

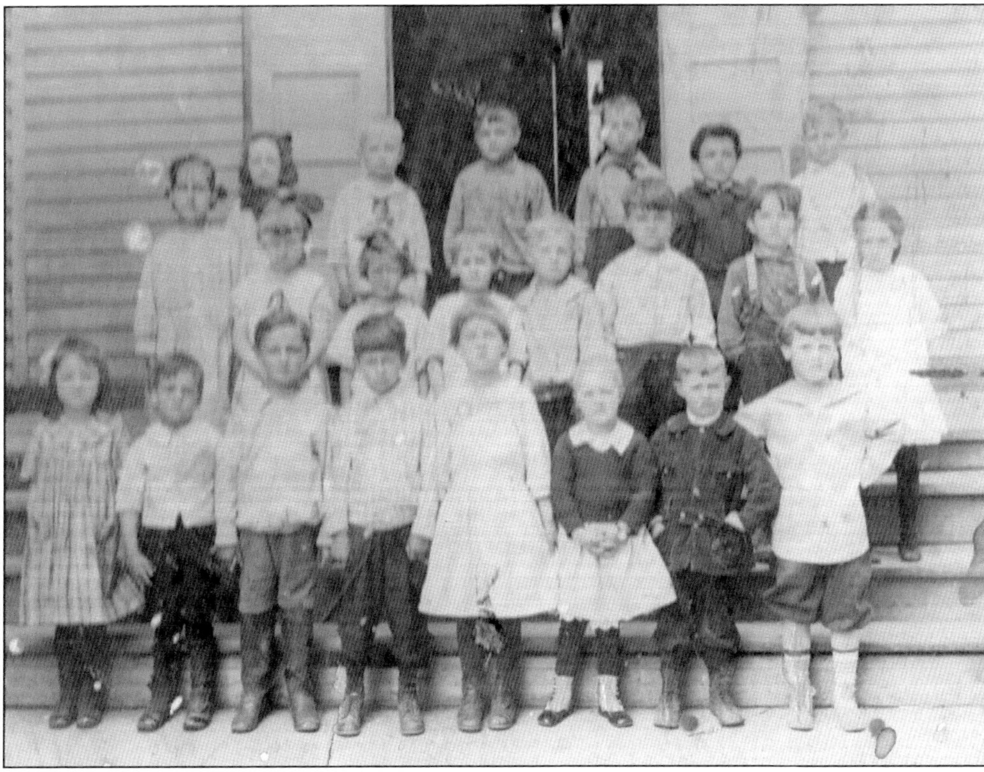

A group of students from the Algonac School is pictured here around the turn of the 20th century.

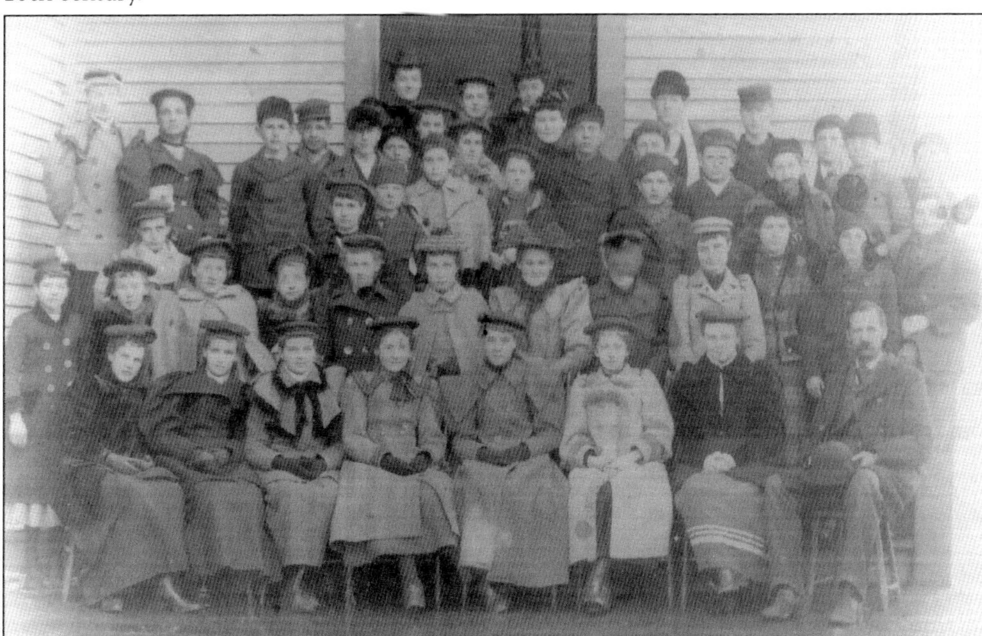

This photograph of Algonac School students was taken in 1897 with the graduates in the first row.

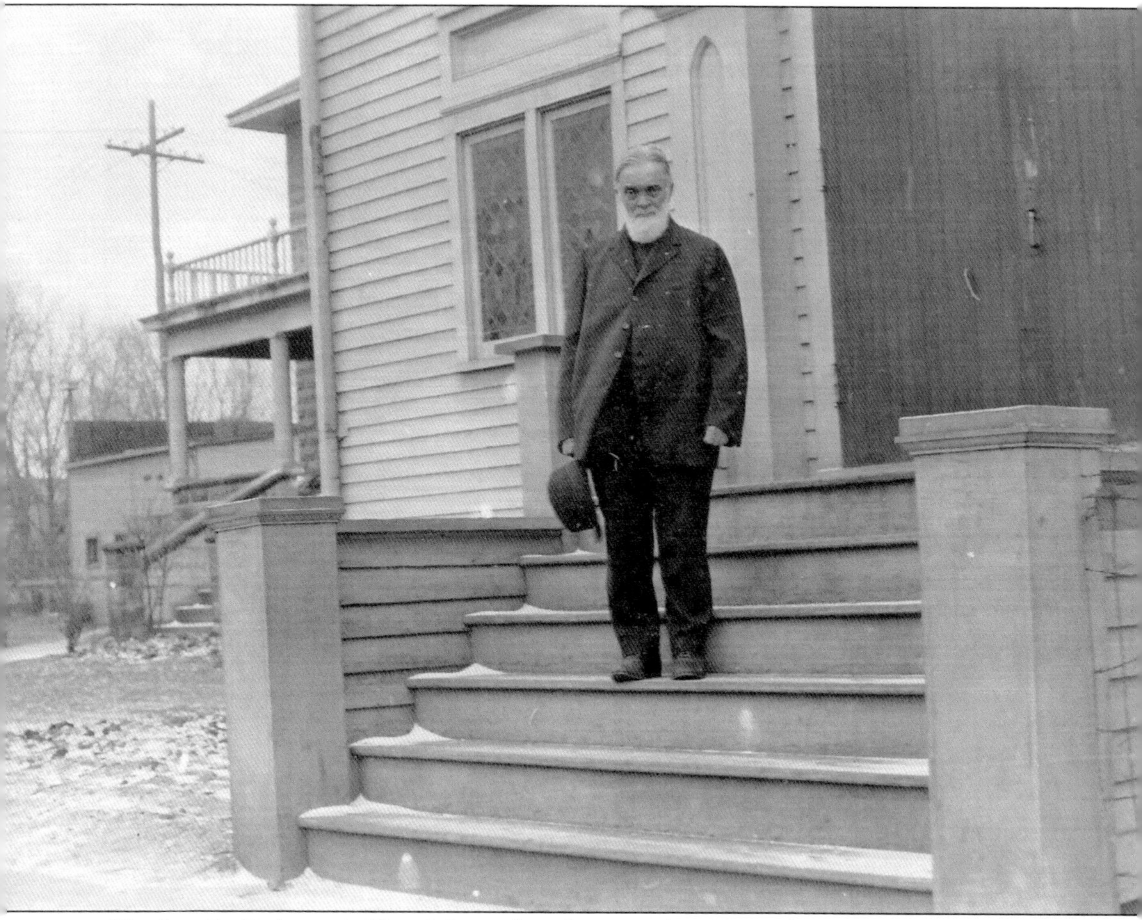

The first St. Catherine's Church burned to the ground on November 30, 1895. At this time, Fr. Benoit Gery (pictured here) immediately began building a church on the southeast corner of Fruit Street and St. Clair Boulevard.

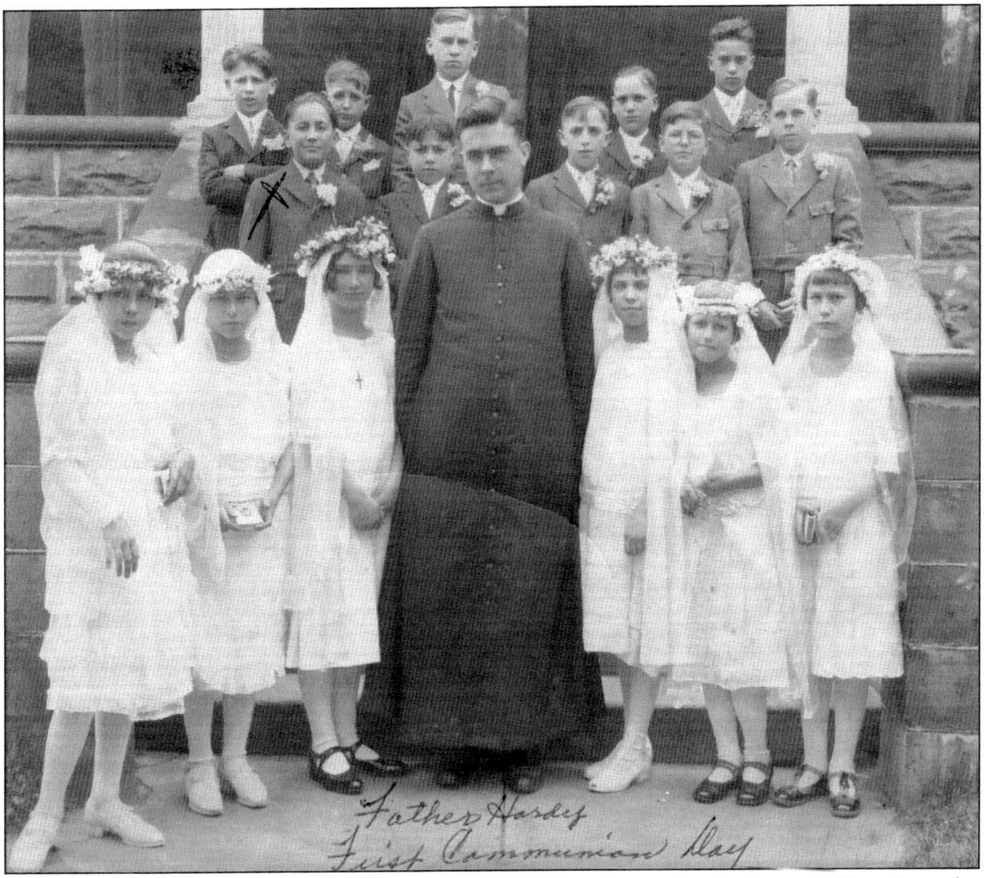

Father Hardy is pictured here with his First Communion class at St. Catherine's Church in the 1930s. In November 1934, he was succeeded by John C. Sullivan, who remained pastor until 1942, when he was succeeded by Fr. James J. O'Mara, who retired in 1965.

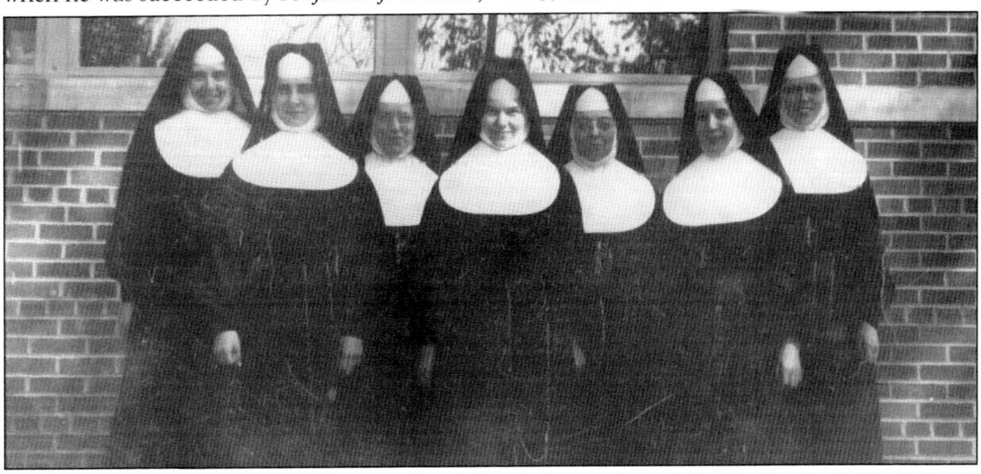

Seven Nuns arrive at the newly completed St. Catherine's and St. Marks Catholic School, pictured here in 1951. From left to right are Sister Agnes Marie, Sister Dauidia, Sister Josetta, Sister June Rose, Sister Angeline, Sister Dilecta, and Sister Thereesina. They would be staying in the convent attached to the school.

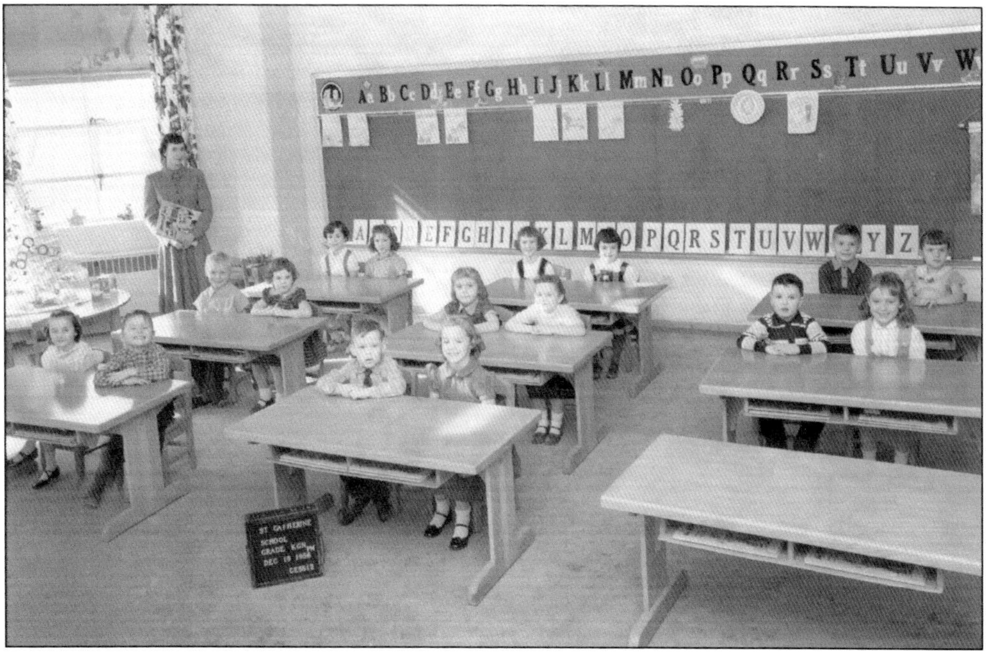

Betty McKay taught the kindergarten class of 1956 at St. Catherine's and St. Mark's School. Note the Christmas tree in the corner.

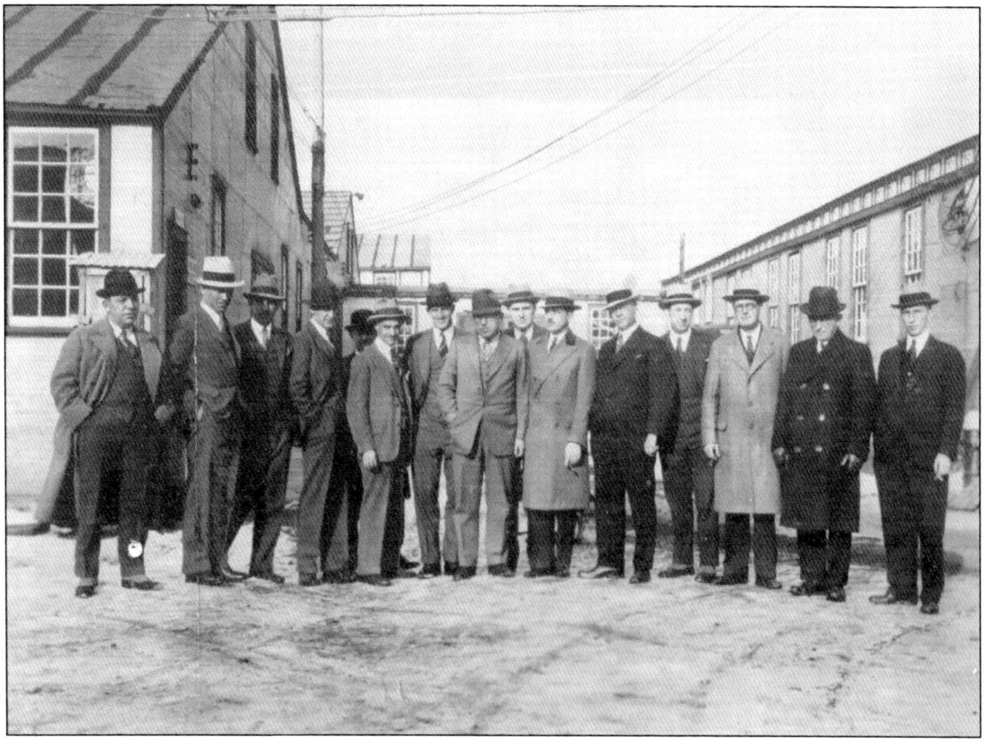

Chris-Craft upper management poses for a photograph at their Holland plant in the 1930s. The company had been wanting to build new plants in other cities because of the near saturation of production and workforces in Algonac.

Christopher Columbus Smith, one of six children, was born on May 20, 1861. He was an avid hunter and fisherman, leading him to design and build duck boats. His love of the water kept him busy building bigger and faster boats by installing gasoline motors. Later in life, he teamed up with Garfield Wood and built racing boats.

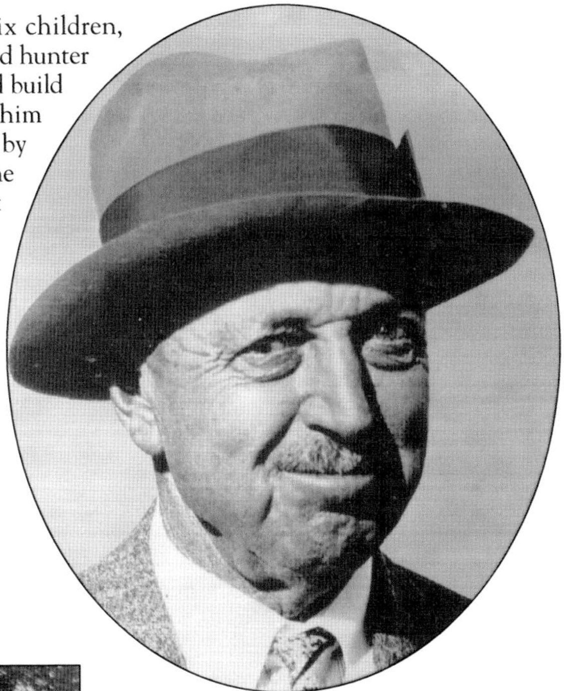

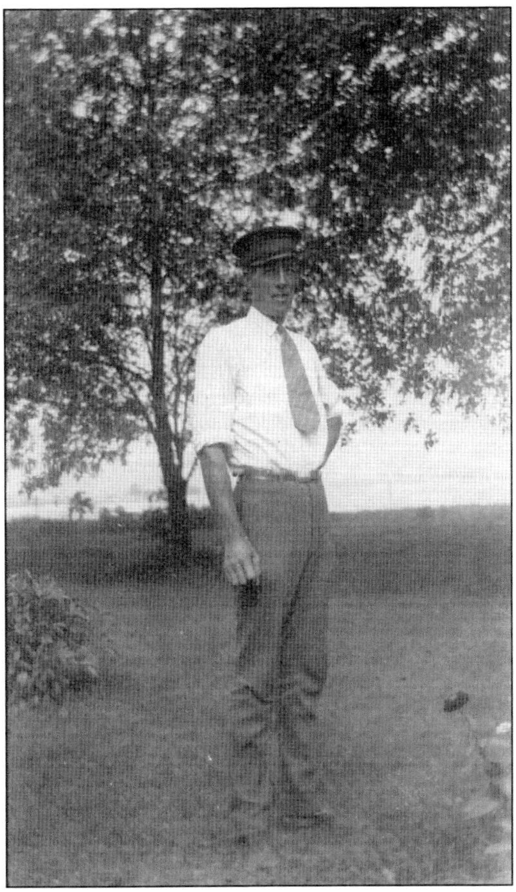

Stewart Raymond is pictured here in the 1930s. In 1930, he and his father, George, bought the Tashmoo Park Auto Ferry from R.C. Witmiller. They provided service to the Island Stop dock. The fare was 75¢ one way. Their ferries were the *Chief Harsen*, a 24-car ferry; the *Raymond*, a 12-car ferry; and the *Junior*, a 6-car ferry. The Raymonds operated their service until 1942.

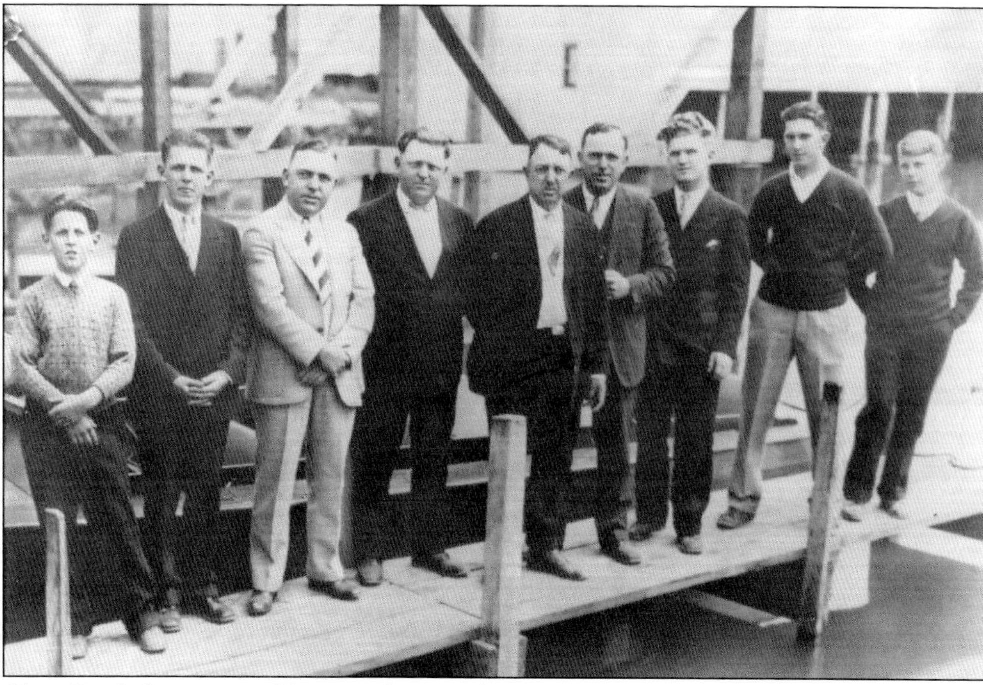

Chris Smith, his sons, and his grandsons took time out on the dock at the plant for a family photograph. All the adult sons were employees of the company.

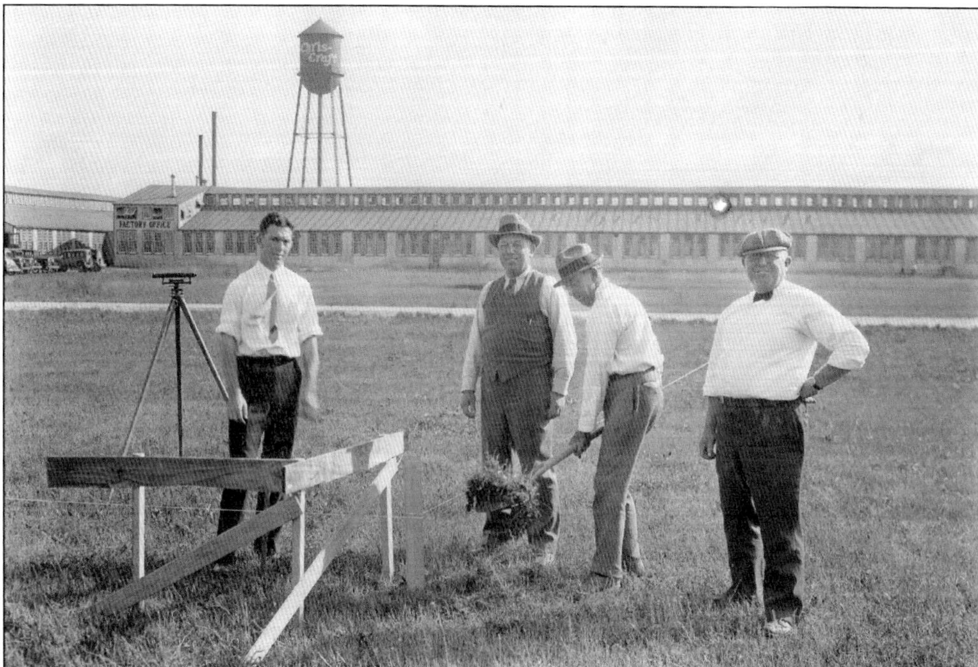

Chris Smith, chairman of the board, is pictured here holding the shovel, breaking ground for the new office building at the Algonac plant in 1934. From left to right are Harsen Smith, assistant to the president; Jay W. Smith, president; and Bernard Smith, vice president in charge of manufacturing.

Augustus Harsen was the great-grandson of Jacob Harsen, a first settler of Harsens Island. He took over operation of the Kimball House from William Lankin. The Kimball House was torn down and replaced by the Algonquin Hotel in 1913.

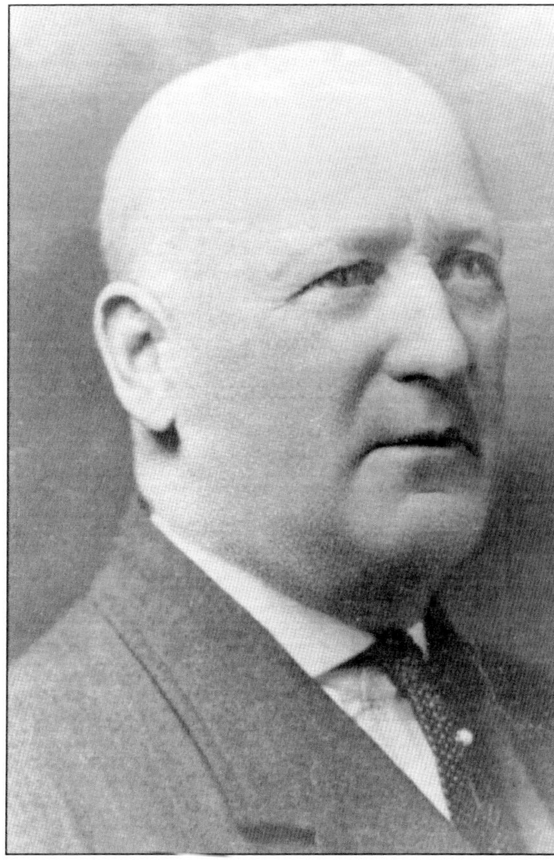

Pictured in the 1910s, these band members played at dances for Camp Algonac on Russell Island, as well as others throughout the area.

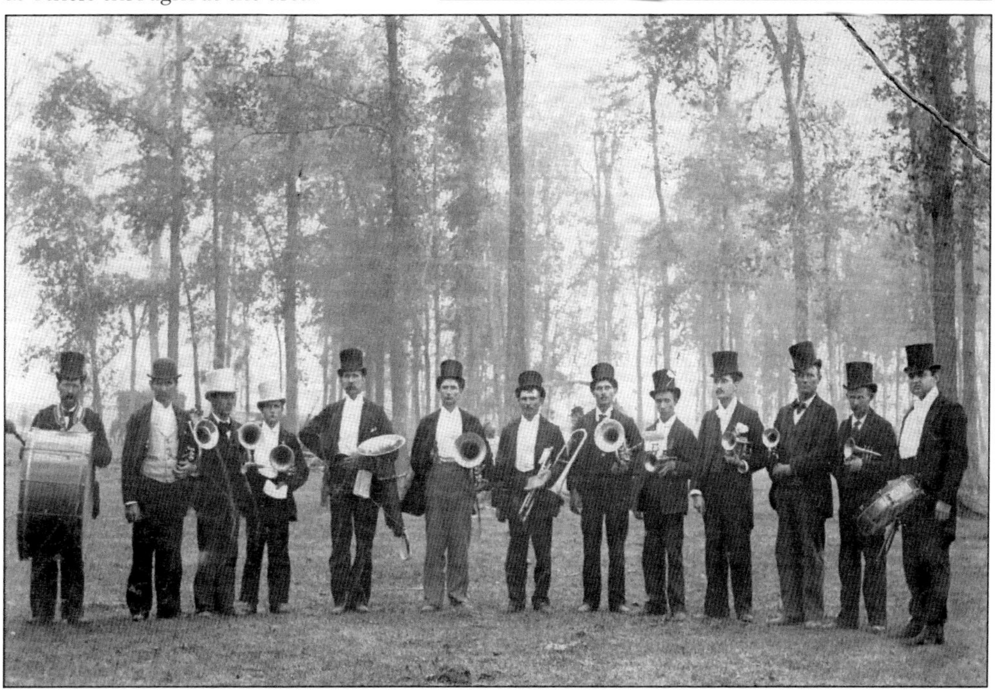

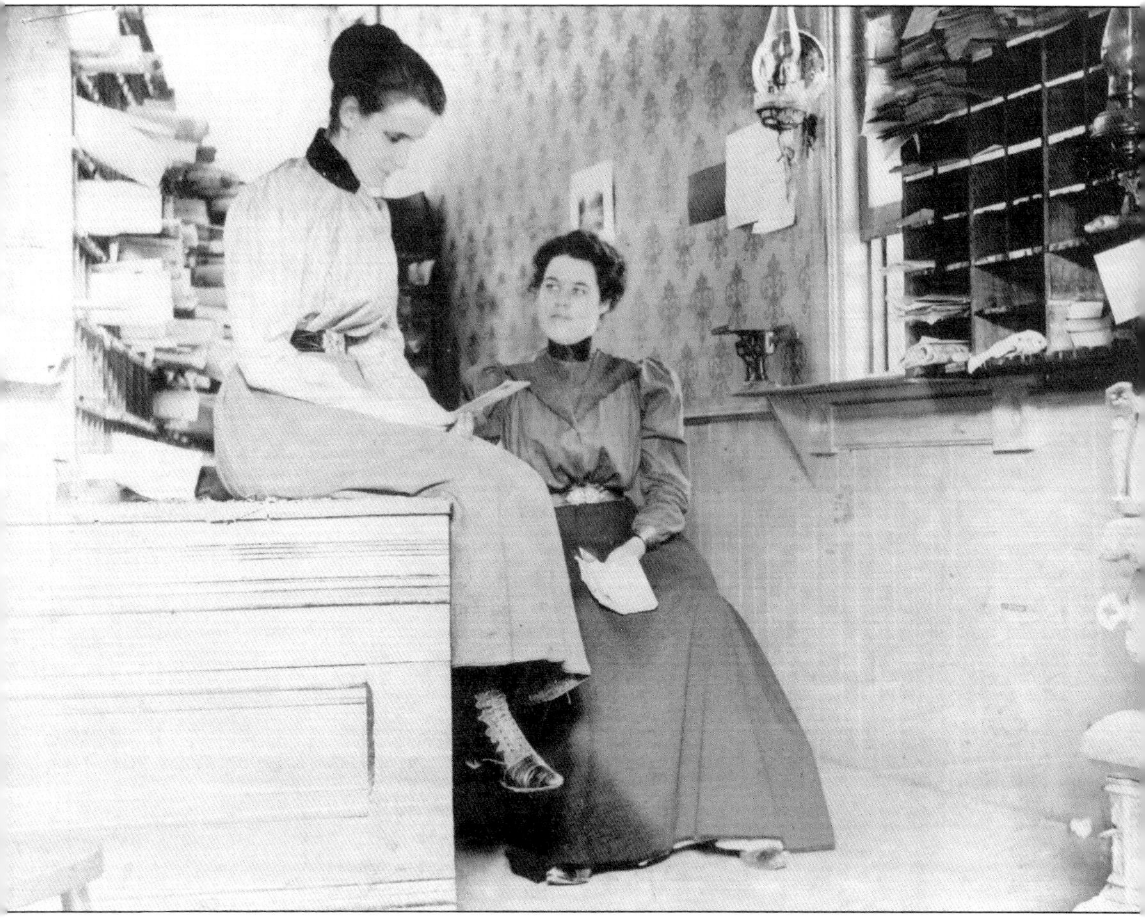

Pictured here are postal workers Nellie Nugent (left) and Jessie Currie (right) in the 1890s. Rural mail carriers made deliveries on horseback or by horse and buggy. The carriers were responsible for their own horses, which were usually kept at their homes.

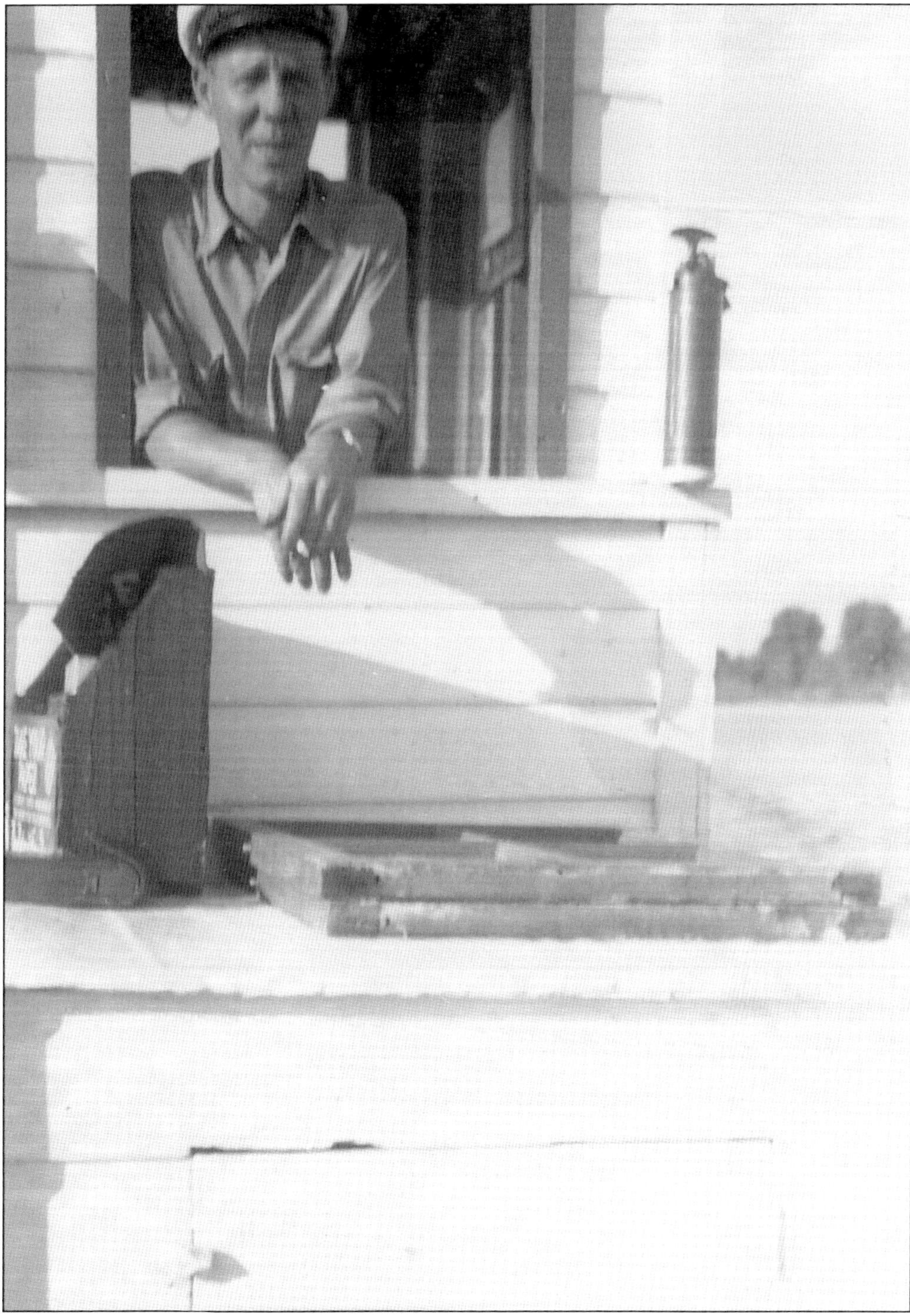

Pictured here is George Raymond. He and his son Stewart were partners operating a ferry service from Pointe Du Chene to Grand Pointe Cut on Harsens Island. They moved their landings to the foot of Island Drive on the mainland and the Beardslee property on Harsens Island.